CHANGE
IS LIKE A
SLINKY®

CHANGE
IS LIKE A
SLINKY®

30 Strategies for Promoting and Surviving
Change in Your Organization

Hans Finzel

NORTHFIELD PUBLISHING
CHICAGO

Scripture taken from the *Holy Bible, New International Version*®. NIV®.
Copyright © 1973, 1978, 1984 by International Bible Society. Used by
permission of Zondervan Publishing House. All rights reserved.

Library of Congress Cataloging-in-Publication Data

Finzel, Hans.
    Change is like a slinky: 30 strategies for promoting and surviving
change in your organization/by Hans Finzel.
        p.cm.
    ISBN 1-881273-68-7
    1. Organizational change. I. Title

HD58.8. F525 2004
658.4'.06—dc22

                                                           2003016322

                            1 3 5 7 9 10 8 6 4 2

                Printed in the United States of America

to all those dreamers,
pioneers, and change agents
who are in the battle
to improve their workplace
and to make a difference

CONTENTS

FOREWORD

Can you remember back to the days when change was considered optional? When it was part of a laundry list of potential options for an organization and its leaders? I can—in the same way I remember black-and-white televisions and Cadillacs with fins. Today, change is a law of organizational life. It's the relentless stalker of a leader's every waking second. We live in a world where the pace of change increases not only incrementally but exponentially. By the time we adapt to a new paradigm, it seems another one has appeared in its place.

As heartless as it may sound, adapting to and mastering change is not a choice. In fact, today's motto for leadership is "change or perish." The last time I remember change being written about as an option was in the career obituary of a leader who had just been unceremoniously fired. Anyone in modern leadership knows that a significant part of his or her responsibility will be to act as a change agent within his or her corporate culture. In a time when changes come so fast and from so many unexpected angles, it is no longer a luxury but an imperative. Neither size, previous success, tradition, nor a once-loyal customer base can protect an organization from apathy toward change.

The corporate hulks littering today's corporate landscape bear stark testimony to that sad truth.

Still, even though change is a must in today's organizations, the "how-tos" can often prove a problem. Many people lunge into change with no idea of its rules, its guiding principles, its nuances—or its dangers. Quite often disaster is the result. The only thing worse than ignoring change is leaping into it willy-nilly.

That's why you need a master helmsman like Hans Finzel to guide you through the treacherous shoals of change in the twenty-first century. Hans has done a great job of putting together a practical guide to navigate these ever-changing challenges. It is one thing to spout theory, but it's quite another to speak from years of practical experience. Hans Finzel has a long and successful history of effectively bringing about organizational change. His principles are taken from real life—and while they are definitely down-to-earth, they are also grounded in the crucible of reality.

Those of us who have been asked to lead organizations face submerged icebergs and jagged shorelines that can bring peril to us all. How do we get from point A to point B? What are the dangers? What are the laws we should follow? How do we navigate the leadership of change successfully and hopefully come out all the better for it in the end? You'll find the answers in this modern classic.

But this book is aimed at far more than leaders. You may be a leader-in-waiting, seeking to educate yourself on the secrets successful executives put into action. Or better yet, you may simply be a dedicated member of an organization who wants to become a change agent "right where you live." In either case, congratulations. Without support from forward-thinking people like you, the average change-minded leader never stands a chance.

Regardless of your role in your organization, you probably sense the need for change in your group. It's hard to spend any time in an organization and not discern where the gaps lie. And you know that the journey of change can be a treacherous one. The risks can even seem to overwhelm the possible rewards at times. Don't worry, but pay close attention to the points contained in this book. The pages that follow can become your navigational map. You might view the six major phases in the cycles of change in this book as six lighthouses along your journey. And view Hans Finzel as your sage voice of reason and experience.

Finzel's instruction is worth listening to, as we all desire a better future for the organizations we lead. I could not recommend the book more highly for anyone involved in trying to steer an organization successfully through the journey of change. You *can* be a successful change agent, regardless of where you land on the organizational chart. From any place within your group, you can make change work if armed with these practical guidelines.

As you move along in the journey of change, make this book an essential part of your leadership library. And let Hans Finzel be your lighthouse keeper through the circuitous route to positive, constructive, well-tolerated change. Ignore him at your peril.

JOHN MAXWELL
FOUNDER, THE INJOY GROUP

ACKNOWLEDGMENTS

During the course of writing this book, I called on a number of people for reality therapy. It seemed to me that if I tried out my material as live ammunition on people in the trenches of organizational change, I might have a more useful tool to give my readers. I asked a group of friends and colleagues whom I highly respect to go through the rough draft of this book. I asked them specifically to tell me, "What does not make sense, what does not work, where are the potholes, and where does the material just flat out stink?" I asked them to be brutal. Regrettably perhaps, they were! They also offered additional insights that I have incorporated. They have made the tool in your hands much more practical and useful.

I owe a special thanks to these folks who were readers of some of the original material: Dan Claussen, Bobby Clinton, Peter Iliyn, Joel MacDonald, John Nordlander, Bob Norris, Jim O'Neill, Peter Pendell, and Dave Schroeder.

There were three people who helped me a great deal with wordsmithing, organization, structure, and style on most of the book: Armin Sommer, Bob Vouga, and Joyce McCollum.

An exceptional recognition goes to Mark Olsen of Cascade, Colorado, who was a huge help in the creative writing phase of this entire project. I want to single out a big thank-you to my longtime friend Craig Weaver (Cypress, California), the engine parts wizard from Los Angeles. He helped me with many of the practical "Takeaways" at the end of each chapter. Craig has made a career of changing things in the automotive supply industry. I appreciate his excellent, down-to-earth help.

A special thanks goes to James Industries of Plymouth, Michigan, and its Chief Operating Officer and Executive Vice President Doug Ferner for permission to use the Slinky name and the phrase "Change is like a Slinky" in this book. Slinky is registered and a trademark of POOF Products, a division of James Industries, and is used with permission of POOF Products and James Industries.

Finally, a huge thanks goes to my wife, Donna, who puts up with me during the labor pains of birthing books. At times it becomes an annoying "great obsession" that consumes me—but she is always here to support me.

CHANGE IS...

Change is about the future.

Change is about getting comfortable with the uncomfortable.

Change is about how to make great things happen in your organization.

Change happens over and over again in a never-ending, cycling spin.

CHANGE'S SIX PHASES

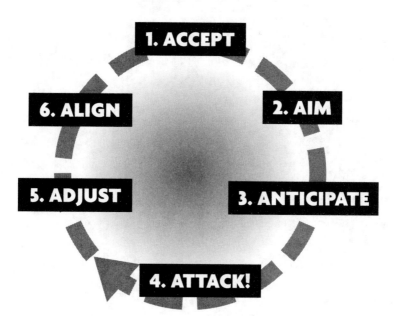

INTRODUCTION
Change Is a
Runaway Slinky

I love toys. Even though I am no longer a kid (my wife Donna would argue with me on that point), I still love toys. I earnestly believe, with the ferocity of a true believer, that the acid test of a truly great, endearing toy is this: Do your own children play with it today? And the second test: Does it run without batteries to provide maximum fun?

Any toy that doesn't pass those requirements is second-tier.

The Slinky® spring toy was one of my all-time favorites as a child. Needless to say, the Slinky sails through each of the above-mentioned criteria. As a kid I owned an original Slinky, the one made out of dark blue metal. (In the 1960s, Slinky changed to its classic silver metal version that endures today.) Lately, I have seen them in neon-colored plastic, which, in my view, fails to capture that true Slinky spirit.

Change is a lot like a Slinky. I know it sounds somewhat silly, but give me a minute. A Slinky can be a lot of fun, but it is also completely unpredictable.

The other day I bought a brand new Slinky just to remind myself how cool this toy still is. I discovered that it now comes in so many variations that I bought four: Neon orange plastic, the original steel in large and small, and a cool green plastic version with a yellow racing stripe! Standing in the checkout line, holding nothing but those colorful, unmistakable boxes, I felt vaguely self-conscious, like some guy indulging his midlife crisis. I could almost hear the people thinking to themselves, "Come on, man. Can't you afford a Corvette?" The four cost me only eight dollars and change.

I brought the Slinkys home and peeled forty years off my calendar.

With a Slinky, the first order of business is to remove it from its box and start playing with it. (After all, what good is a Slinky in a box?) I revisited the maneuver I always loved making with my Slinky: holding one end in each hand and making it gyrate back and forth as I move my opposing hands up and down. The thing is so shiny, wiggly; it makes this cool sound as it swishes back and forth between my hands. In case you get stumped, the box gives you these instructions: "juggle it, flip it, jiggle it."

Although you can do all kinds of fun things with these toys, I really think their highest purpose, their ultimate use, is to be sent cascading down a stairway. Once in their downward walk, Slinkys become autonomous—freely functioning, self-thinking beings. Once you start them down that road, you never know what's going to happen or where they are going to end up. And they rarely end up where you sent them. That, plus some of the following reasons, is why change is so much like a runaway Slinky.

WHY CHANGE IS LIKE A SLINKY

1. You have to take it out of the box to have fun with it.
2. It comes in many styles and colors.
3. Somebody has to launch it on its way.
4. The course it takes once it begins is entirely unpredictable.
5. It routinely gets stuck halfway down the stairs, and has to be relaunched. Repeat as necessary.
6. It is messy, noisy, and chaotic.
7. Before it is launched, it has stored potential energy—when launched, that energy force becomes kinetic energy.
8. You really don't control it once it begins its journey.
9. It rarely lands where you predict.

The more I have considered the Slinky and observed its characteristics, the more parallels I see between its properties and the process of change. Consider just a few. A Slinky is one long continuous wire that loops around as it forms a long cylindrical tube. It is a two-inch stack of ninety-eight coils. Change is like that as well; it loops around and continually regenerates itself as an ever-spiraling process. As I have studied change, I have found six parts to this loop of change, which continually cycle through organizations. We might call them steps or phases, but they are more like forever repeating cycles.

Change happens constantly. Leaders initiate it, but others cause it to happen just as often. The effective leader is the person who harnesses, then processes change for the good of the organization. Thus each chapter concludes with "Takeaways," applications and projects that begin, modify, or evaluate the change process. You will benefit greatly by taking the time to work through these projects. Get a spiral notebook, write "Change Strategies" on the cover, and let it become your application book as you apply the principles of this book to your workplace.

Just like Slinky's endless metal loop, change goes in cycles. These cycles are like cyclones swirling throughout our organizations. Some are tiny, like the dirt devils we watched with fascination in a parking lot as young children—dirt and debris circling up and down and around, tracing an unpredictable path. Others are larger and can do more damage. One is fizzling out as the next is gaining steam. Like waves crashing on the beach, they just keep coming and cannot be controlled. Maybe this is why I also love watching the ocean. Something about waves and campfires . . . they are fun to stare at because no two waves or flames are ever alike.

After you've read this book, I hope you'll see change with those kind of appreciative eyes—free of fear, resistance, or resentment. Even the sort of change you didn't ask for or initiate can turn into an opportunity you'll know how to seize. Change will become part of your personal arsenal of workplace tools—something you can embrace and even lead, rather than resent or fear.

Since change is not only a constant but a powerful force you'll encounter throughout your career, why not master it and turn it in your favor? After all, in today's working climate, it seems that only the flexible and adaptable will survive. Enjoy it, have fun with it.

The Little Word With a Big Punch

This is a book about *change* . . . because change is a fact of modern and postmodern life. It can hurt us or help us. We can react to it as fast as it comes our way, or be leaders in the cycles of change. Consider what you hold in your hands a survival kit: *A handbook of proven strategies for promoting and surviving change in your organization.*

We probably all know the meaning of the word *change*, but here is a refresher course on the depths of this little word that wreaks havoc in our lives. According to the dictionary, change means, literally, "to exchange"—as in one thing for another. That is just what we do. The old is given up and the new arrives whether we like it or not.

Change could be defined in these ways:
- "To make different."
- "To make radically different."
- "To transform."
- "To give a different position, course or direction."
- "To make a shift."
- "To undergo modification."
- "To pass from one phase to another."
- "To undergo transformation, transition, or substitution."

Change . . . has many applications in our daily lives

Consider the many ways changes can and should affect you and me:
- Change is about courage.
- Change is about hope.

- Change is about taking risks.
- Change is about having fun.
- Change is about having a cause.
- Change is about survival.
- Change is about the future.
- Change is about getting comfortable with the uncomfortable.
- Change is about how to make great things happen in your organization.
- Change happens over and over again in a never-ending, cycling spin.

PHASE ONE
Accept the Need for Change

1. ACCEPT

The future is not what it used to be. More and more people are agreeing, "If we don't change we will die!"

We have to accept that where we are today is not where we need to be for the future. A map for a plan for change begins with "reality therapy"—taking stock of the present to prepare for the future. That's where organizational change begins. We must be willing to lay everything on the drawing board as we face the future.

Wherever you find yourself in your organization—on the bottom, somewhere in middle management, or at the top—there is always room for more dreamers, because dreamers think about the future and the "what-ifs." Dreams drive change. Without a hope for a better future, there is no need to change. In fact, those who resist change are the ones who are in love with the status quo. They thrive on the past more than they envision the future.

When a leader gets right down to being a change agent, it all begins with dreams. Leaders have to accept that change strategy is a fundamental building block to figure out where we would like to be. If we always do what we always did—we'll always get what we always got. If that is good enough for you, you're done with this book. If not . . . read on!

1
Keep Your Coils Light

I think and think for months and years. Ninety-nine times, the conclusion is false. The hundredth time, I am right.

Albert Einstein

Go ahead. Pick up a Slinky. No, not the newfangled plastic models. I'm talking about the good ol' metal kind, circa 1964. If you don't have one handy, then go ahead— you have my permission—put down the book (you just started chapter 1, so it won't be hard to find your place) and buy one.

And no, I'm not getting kickbacks from the makers of Slinky. Nor am I an employee, or even a shareholder. (Although, now that I think of it . . . maybe I'll take a break of my own, and call my stockbroker.)

OK, got one? Now set the toy to its highest level. You

know what I'm talking about: top of the stairs. Then do the deed. Tip it over. Watch it. Laugh. Now go chase it to the random location where it came to a stop.

Isn't this cool? Don't you feel a couple of years younger?

Probably the most delightful, childhood-restoring moment is that split second when the pile of coils tips over just far enough to lose its balance and fall tumbling onto the next step. Teetering over the precipice, as it were.

Wouldn't you agree that this is the most awesome part?

See? It's a matter of weight shifting, causing motion. If some section of those beloved metal coils were even a third again heavier, the process would not happen. If they were somehow encrusted with grime or rust or a coat of lead paint, the illusion of perpetual motion that makes us love the Slinky simply would not take place.

My point? First of all, you have to *keep your coils light.* If your Slinky is too heavy it will go nowhere. Or to mix another metaphor, learn to be light on your feet. Learn to dance. Move quickly, responsively, without the delay heaviness imparts. Be nimble.

To paraphrase songwriter Paul Simon, *"Hop on the bus, Gus."*

The future belongs to those who can adapt rapidly. You've heard it before: The information explosion has simply resulted in too much data coming too fast for folks with slow reaction times. Today that weekday edition of the *New York Times* lying on the sidewalk contains more data than the average seventeenth-century human digested in a whole lifetime.

Whoa! What happened in all that time? Did we grow an extra brain?

Don't laugh, my friend. Because the same amount of change projected ahead into our future won't take four hundred years. It'll take twenty-five. Which means by the time your son or daughter picks up your dog-eared copy of this book twenty-five years from now, he or she will have the same vantage point you have right now over that hapless inhabitant of the 1600s.

Remember those poor souls in the old Westerns who didn't recognize the gunfighter, rubbed him the wrong way, and wound up dancing a lead-inspired jig out in the dust beside the horse troughs?

STAY LIGHT ON YOUR COILS.

Think of yourself as that person. Dancing—perpetually. Only the bullets never run out, and the one doing the shooting isn't a person, but a force of nature—think of the Terminator crossed with the Sundance Kid. In your case, the shooter is *change*. Life. The twenty-first-century marketplace. You don't have time to beg for a pause.

Hugely successful and always profitable Southwest Airlines prides itself on three company characteristics: *nimble*, *quick*, and *opportunistic*. How did Southwest Airlines get that way, and how does it keep it up? Whenever possible, Southwest flies in the face of bureaucracy—it stays lean, thinks small, keeps it simple . . . and more. As the big boys in the airline industry are fighting for their very survival, lean, mean Southwest flies on. They stay very light on their coils.

One way I've tried to prepare my four children for life is to teach them that fast-and-done is better than thorough-and-never-turned-in. Ninety-eight percent of success today is showing up on time with something to show for yourself. To the speedy and fast adapters belong the spoils of our modern world. We don't have time to be as thorough as we did in the slow-moving world of the twentieth century. A friend of mine likes to tell me, "We can't wait for all the lights to turn green before we leave the house."

The longer it takes to make a decision, the less likely it will be a good one. We have to learn in today's climate to turn on a dime. Organizations trying to respond to outside forces successfully have to be rapid-action strike forces. They need employees who can corner quickly. Who can deploy faster than the troops of Desert Storm? Who can adapt to a new environment faster than a chameleon on espresso? Jim Crowe of Level 3 Communications is known to live by this mantra, "Take risks, learn quickly from your mistakes, and above all . . . do not stand still."

A Sense of Urgency

Who has time for a slow adjustment process? By the time some people adjust to the new, it has become the old that no longer works. Today's successful groups don't have time for individuals to gear down while people decide whether they will get on board or not. Change has to be on-the-fly, like the difference between old-time Jeeps—which required you to stop the car, get out, and turn a large knob in order to shift in or out of four-wheel drive—and the new, push-a-button-and-it's-done models. As much as I love vintage Jeeps, the problem with the old models was that if you found yourself on the kind of perilous mountainside that required an immediate shift change, then you were literally in the scariest place on earth to stop your momentum, slam on your emergency brake, and climb out into the elements.

Nice and neat are out. Operate with a strong sense of urgency. Accelerate even if it means your product or program has rough edges. You have to be light on your feet to be a good agent of change.

It's been said that revolutions throw people into three different roles or modes of performance: those who *lead* the revolution, those who *follow it*, and those who *sleep* through it. "These days," says Karl Albrecht in his book *The Northbound Train*, "the sleepers are in real trouble. What you don't know can kill you." We cannot be asleep at the wheel of our organization in times like these.

Are you out of breath yet? Tired of running up and down the stairs chasing Slinky? Ready to hop off the speeding train of the twenty-first century? This book is about the change crisis. You've heard it said before, probably, but it bears repeating:

CHANGE ITSELF IS CHANGING.

At a recent World Economic Forum, Microsoft founder and chairman Bill Gates declared, "The first ten years of this twenty-first century will be the digital decade." To illustrate the point, look at these numbers: It took forty years for radio to gain fifty million domestic listeners in the United States. Then it took only thirteen years for television and cable TV to gain fifty million viewers. And the Internet? It took only four years to gain fifty million domestic users.

With the advent of hand-held computers (known as personal digital assistants, or PDAs) and wireless phones, Internet usage worldwide will exceed 1.1 billion in 2005. That means one of every six residents of planet earth will be using the Internet in 2005.[1] And look at the explosion of cell phone usage. Today there are already one billion mobile phone users worldwide. China is adding five million new cell users per month! By 2003 there were more non-PC devices (cellular phones and PDAs) than PCs hooked up to the Internet.[2] It won't be long before most cars are hooked up to the Internet. Are there other revolutions around the corner as foundation-shaking as the Internet Revolution?

Sure there are. Probably a dozen.

Name an age-old problem you hardly even imagined would be turned on its ear. I can name an upcoming technology with a strong chance of solving it within the next twenty years. And then the new solution will create three more problems (*challenges*, remember; or better yet, *opportunities*) we never dreamed of. Some of those age-old problems needing solutions?

- Finite reserves of fossil fuel
- World hunger
- Topsoil depletion and dwindling agriculture
- Water shortages
- Air pollution
- Environmental toxins
- Disease
- Terrorism
- Poverty, or the relative scarcity of material goods

- Overcrowding
- Inner-city squalor
- And a hundred others

You name it, and if your organization is founded upon solving the last millennium's paradigms, you're in trouble. I'm not telling you to abandon your mission, but rather to work very, very hard at keeping your coils light. Get ready to adapt to changes of a magnitude that will make your head spin.

My second point about keeping your coils light is probably the more difficult and subtle one. After all, anyone can talk about staying light on your feet and nimble. But how do you *do it?* How does one remove the debris weighing him or her down once it's accumulated? Most of us aren't a Slinky right out of the box, shiny and pristine. Most of us have been tossed around houses and play boxes and built up quite a coating of heavy residue in the process.

Let's take the rapid deployment force mentioned earlier. As someone who lives not forty miles from one of the biggest air force bases in the West, I know what an incredible mobile force the armed forces has built up in order to achieve that quick response capability. I've seen it on the rails just in the last few months as car after car of armored personnel carriers and tanks and Humvees have hurtled past on their way to distribution centers. The military infrastructure has taken new generations of transport ships and cargo planes, as well as a complete reorganization of yesterday's base and command structure. The old way of organizing a military installation has been turned on its head in the last few years.

And all for the purpose of being able to mobilize people and material to whisk them across the planet in a matter of a few weeks—working toward a matter of days.

That's fine, you say. But I'm not in the U.S. Air Force. Nor am I even the equivalent of a general in my organization.

Leaving Behind Resistance . . . and Nostalgia

You may not have the authority or the ability to shift huge amounts of machinery in order to stay light on your coils. But you can do it in your head—and that may be far more important. You can work hard at keeping your mental functions free of barnacles, clean of cobwebs, and devoid of inertia and resistance.

One of the most potent and challenging examples of this is to rid your mind—your workaday business mind, at least—of nostalgia, of emotional attachment to "The Way Things Were."

Now, please don't get the wrong idea. Privately, I'm capable of enormous amounts of nostalgia. And that's entirely appropriate. But I force myself to keep that out of my working-world life.

A colleague recently told me about a famous old downtown department store. It had stood for over a century in its own rambling fortress of a Victorian building. The family name for which it was called was still traced in brick along its front facade. Just a few years ago people still spoke of it in reverent tones: its dusty, wood-paneled counters, its floors filled with sleepy, arcane merchandise, the antique elevator with its elderly operator who asked you for your floor, and the pneumatic tubes that whisked money away to a hidden cashier for your change.

It was a place you brought your kids for a deep whiff of yesteryear.

But invariably, you walked out without buying anything. Recently, the store went bankrupt. (How could it not, when huge monoliths like K-Mart couldn't even keep up?) Its vast building was unceremoniously converted into modern, *tres chic* office space. An Internet firm's suite now occupies the building's expensively refurbished third floor. My colleague attended the office opening. Rather than thinking "how sad," or "what an outrage," he found himself thinking, "What a great use for the old lady!"

Nostalgia doesn't outlast change. It never can. It belongs in your family life, but not in business.

I'll say it again. Change is a juggernaut. But if you allow yourself to be weighed down by a meritless attachment to yesteryear, you won't stand a chance.

What's the Point? Keep your coils light. To survive in any organization today requires a willingness to be flexible. Accept the need for change. We have to stay light on our feet, ready to dance and move at a moment's notice. Slow and heavy are out. Lightness and nimbleness are the keys to developing the rapid response time that is so essential to survival in today's change-laden environment. People in your group who push the change envelope should be rewarded for taking you to the future, not punished as rebels to the status quo.

TAKEAWAYS

1. What forms of mental and physical residue are holding your organization back from being light on its feet?

2. What things do you do now because it is the way you have always done them? What things do you do because it has been company policy as long as you can remember? Ask yourself, "Why/when did it start?" Remember that today's problems are yesterdays solutions. Ask yourself, "Does it make sense today?"

3. Would you get rid of that way of doing things today if you could? List the barriers to changing the way of doing things if you answered yes.

4. How many permission slips have to be signed in your organization before you can start to change anything? Can that approval process be simplified and streamlined? Can a few be empowered to make change decisions?

5. What mental tactics and strategies can you employ to build responsiveness into your own personal arsenal—and then that of your organization?

6. How are your coworkers treated when they report needs for change in systems, products, or services? Is it safe for them to bring a bad report to management? The first rule of successful change is to stare reality square in the face and admit your problems. Don't shoot the messengers.

2
Resistance Is Futile

**For any student of history,
change is a law of life.**

Henry Kissinger

I don't mean to sound like the Borg, the implacable robotic foe of the *Star Trek: The Next Generation* television series. But in this context, resistance is truly futile. The Borg is an opponent that you cannot resist. You cannot win. You must submit. Nor can you resist "the change Borg."

However, "the change Borg" is a neutral force, one just as capable of bringing success and freedom as slavery. It all depends on us.

There's no reason to resist in knee-jerk fashion the changes that are coming your way. In fact, just as in electricity, resistance to necessary change is something to be eliminated as forcefully as possible. You probably got the point already: It is futile in our world of change. To fight the inevitable is a dead-end street. The best future career opportunities wait for those who can align themselves as quickly as possible with the new and better order of things. Show a capacity to change quickly and produce results in new paradigms and people will love you!

You have to allow the Slinky to come out of the box. Don't try to tape the box shut and hope that it stays put. It was born to slink! Today's successful groups must not only embrace change but build it into the DNA.

Successful organizations and groups are looking to the future. They are making the right changes to embrace change—instead of running from it. They do so largely by organizing themselves for rapid response, and staffing themselves with forward-thinking people. Think backward, and you'll limit your employment prospects immeasurably.

Henry Kissinger observed, "For any student of history, change is a law of life. Any attempt to contain it guarantees an explosion down the road; the more rigid the adherence to the status quo, the more violent the ultimate outcome will be."

> IN TODAY'S ORGANIZATIONS, CHANGE IS NOT A RESPONSE TO A CHALLENGE. IT *IS* THE CHALLENGE.

Change is mandatory for any group that wants to make a mark today. Because if something works today, it is already half obsolete. In fact, the problems you face today in your organization are yesterday's solutions. But the time gap is shrinking. Maybe a hundred years ago, major structural changes were appropriate for each generation. I have read old management books that taught the need for making new organizational structures perhaps once a decade. Now the time is compacted to perhaps every two or three years. Some are advocating every eighteen months!

New employees are willing to flex and start from scratch without previous bias and history, so why not you? Here's a vital exercise: Pretend you are new to the group even if you have been around forever. Have the mindset of a paradigm pioneer, not a nostalgic. Today's dynamic organizations thrive on people who adapt fast—not those who resist change and unplug themselves emotionally when change is rolled out.

Why Change? To Better the Status Quo

My own personal passion about change has to do with being unwilling to accept the status quo. I have the kind of personality that always wants to see things improved and done better. We can always make the world a better place. We can always improve our organizations. There is always something we can do better—whether it's a product we develop, or a service we provide. I love continuous improvement. The Japanese have a term for it: *kaizen*. It means tiny little improvements are all we want, but we want them each and every day! In a later chapter, however, we will learn the downside of moving too slowly (chapter 19, "Think Leaps, Not Tweaks").

People who settle for mediocrity and the status quo

39

irritate me. In the movie *Almost Famous*, one character drives this point home: "You will meet a lot of people who will try to get you to join them on the long road to the middle." I've met plenty of such people along my journey, and they try my patience to its limits. The middle bores me. And I find it unacceptable in my constant quest toward excellence.

In their book *Visionary Leadership*, Warren Bennis and Burt Nanus talk about leaders as change agents: "Visionary leaders disrupt the status quo, challenge the Gospel, and disequilibriate the system in the interest of affecting change that ultimately benefits us all."

Note the final clause of that sentence: ". . . that ultimately benefits us all." I'm not talking about forcing change simply to justify my own existence, to force out adversaries, or even change simply for its own sake. The change brought about by a good and visionary leader is the kind that is necessary and benefits the entire organization—not just his or her own career prospects.

Theodore Roosevelt also was obsessed with a passion to fight mediocrity. On April 10, 1899, he told the Hamilton Club in Chicago, "Far better it is to dare mighty things, to win glorious triumphs, even though checkered by failure, than to take rank with those poor spirits who neither enjoy much nor suffer much, because they live in the gray twilight that knows not victory nor defeat." If there is one place I don't want to live, it's in the gray twilight!

I serve on the board of trustees of a small university with a very successful businessman who owns dozens of Burger King franchises in Georgia. I like serving on the board with him because he is one of those no-holds-barred, tell-it-like-it-is, straight shooters. Recently, he had this to say about why companies go out of business. He cited four basic reasons:

1. An unmotivated workforce
2. Being out of touch with the marketplace
3. Not pushing innovation
4. Losing sight of the bottom line—profit, loss, and accountability

Notice how at least two of the four points have to do with change. Change isn't window dressing. It's about whether you survive or not.

Why Change? A Few Other Good Reasons

Of course, just to fight the status quo is not enough reason for some people to get on the bandwagon of change. Many reasons drive people and groups to embark on the journey. Here are a score plus one that I have discovered during my years of watching people work in organizations that try to make a difference in the world:

1. *Globalization of the marketplace.* How has the world moved to your doorstep? With the advent of the Internet, E-mail, and ease of global shipping, your competition is only eight seconds away. Anyone from anywhere can compete with what you have to offer.
2. *The changing nature of our constituencies.* Have the people whom you serve changed dramatically in recent years? These are the people who are the end

users of your organization's purpose for existence. If you don't offer them what they want on their terms, they are going elsewhere. This is similar to what the apostle and evangelist Paul meant when he explained in the New Testament that he would "become all things to all men" to reach them.[1]

3. *The changing nature of our customers.* This is similar to the point above. Are you scratching people where they itch? Whether you are in a business that provides goods or services, or in the nonprofit sector, the people who use our services or products are changing dramatically today.

4. *The changing nature of our work force.* How has the changing of the generations affected how you do your work? The arrival of Generation X and now the Millennial Generation[2] into our mainstream work force makes new demands on managers of workers and volunteers.

5. *The powerful new role of women in marketplace leadership.* Women of influence are bringing dramatic and needed changes to the former men's clubs of corporate and private America.

6. *Demographics.* Your community and social surroundings have changed dramatically—have you changed with them? Neighborhoods grow and die.

7. *Changing markets.* Aside from the globalization issues, the very nature of doing your kind of work has changed in our culture, and you must make the necessary adjustments just to survive.

8. *Lack of organizational vision.* Are you suffering from organizational anemia? When organizations

lack passion for the future or seem to be chronically drifting, they may recognize the need for change.

9. *Organizational ineffectiveness.* Are you no longer effective in what you are in service to accomplish? When organizations are attracting fewer and fewer people or flat-out failing, they should recognize the need for change.

10. *The graying of your group.* Are most of your people gray heads? If you are a senior center, that's great. But if you are trying to meet the mainstream of our culture you are in trouble, because a new generation has arrived!

11. *Changing cultural values.* Many are talking today about the mega-shift from modern to postmodern thinking in our culture. This changes the rules about many things that have been constants in our world.

12. *Patterns of repeated failure.* Leaders are seeing one failure after another in their programs. At times people just are not following where the managers are leading.

13. *Lack of clear goals and objectives.* Everyone has a different version of where the company should be going and what its priorities should be.

14. *Chronic plateau.* Nothing much exciting is happening in your group—just more of the same as last year.

15. *Decline in impact.* The organization seems to have lost its punch. Along with internal failure and drift, there is an obvious lack of visible, viable results.

16. *High attrition levels.* When people are leaving the organization in large numbers, change may be in order. Are you not growing? Are people no longer attracted to your group?

17. *Confusion about lines of responsibility/authority.* Organizational chaos has appeared in the group. No one seems to know who is actually responsible for what, so there is considerable wasted effort, confusion, and poor use of resources.

18. *Low morale.* When people are discouraged about being members of the staff, changes often are needed. The company should be a fun, challenging place to be. One sign of low morale is when the faithful insiders hang on out of sheer loyalty instead of heartfelt passion.

19. *Ongoing financial failure.* How is your bottom line? Change occurs at some companies when they finish every year in the red or they are not growing their revenue.

20. *The stirrings of God to do a new thing.* Is God asking you to change? If you are a spiritual person, then serious prayer often brings a stirring of God to start fresh and do a new thing in your ministry.[3] Ignore it and perish. And, leaders beware—sometimes the stirrings begin at the bottom of the organizational chart!

21. *A growing sense of urgency.* Is there a restlessness with the status quo? At times you may develop a sense of urgency to rekindle your first love and foremost priorities and do a new thing. Heed it!

Exhausted yet? No doubt, you can think of other reasons that stir us to change how we do what we do, but this list is a step up the mountain of challenge lying before us.

And if you are a leader, then you have to be the one most concerned about doing something. Followers may see the problems, but they will usually wait for leaders to take the risks to bring about the change process. In my experience, followers rarely have the 20/20 vision that leaders have about the looming problems that are just over the horizon of the group.

If you are midmanagement in an organization that needs radical change, start working on your leaders. Perhaps the place to begin is to help them see some of the issues mentioned above. But be kind and diplomatic, because many leaders become defensive. Regardless of how your group got there and what its growth needs are, you can be a pioneer of the change process. In effect, you will be demonstrating leadership yourself!

A word of reality about leaders and the change process. Sooner or later leaders have to buy into the process or the leaders have to be changed. Because without leadership buy-in, it will not happen. Perhaps it is time for you to step up as a leader in the campaign of change in your organization.

> Leaders are pioneers. They are people who venture into unexplored territory. They guide us to new and often unfamiliar destinations. People who take the lead are the foot soldiers in the campaigns for change. . . . The unique reason for having leaders—their differentiating function—is to move us forward. Leaders get us going someplace.[4]

What's the Point? If we don't change, we will probably go out of business at worst or be totally irrelevant at best. It is futile to dig in our heels and resist the inevitable changes that the forces in our external environment are thrusting upon us. There are many reasons to change. Improving the status quo is one of the chief reasons.

TAKEAWAYS

1. Go through the list of reasons for change in this chapter and ask yourself, "Are we experiencing any of these?" Describe them.

2. Build your rationale list for why you as a group really need some changes.

3. Make a list of the things that you have already seen in your organization that need changing. What are you hearing? What is stopping you?

4. What opportunities are you missing because there is resistance to change?

5. Do you have competitors that are seizing those opportunities? What makes them different from you?

6. Create a group of like-minded change advocates in your group. Begin to work on a strategy of tackling the resistance to change. Build a coalition of those who refuse to settle for things the way they have always been done.

3

With the Slightest Nudge, You Can Change Things

*Snowflakes are frail,
but if enough of them stick
together, they can stop traffic.*

Vance Havner

It's probably the sweetest aspect of the Slinky. Even a baby can do it. In fact, a baby may do it better than you can.

Granted, you might have to pry the toy out of the child's mouth a few times, but after a few encounters with those sharp metal coils, that really isn't a recurring problem.

You see, all it takes to set the miracle of a Slinky into motion is the slightest push of an open hand in the right direction.

The Slightest Nudge...

My point? No matter how much you may love this toy, as I do, fanhood won't give you any extra edge when it comes to launching these things. There are no insider secrets, no expert moves to give you any advantage as a Slinky launcher. No "modified European serve." It's as democratic a toy as one could ever imagine.

And so is becoming a change agent in the so-called "real world." No position of leadership, advanced degree, or stratospheric IQ will allow you to nudge change into motion any more skillfully and forcefully than a determined junior clerk, if she or he sets her or his mind to it.

Lech Walesa, the first president of independent Poland, began as a shipyard electrician without a high-school diploma. He was also founder of the Solidarity labor union and ostensibly the man who set in motion the fall of the Soviet empire, the end of the Cold War, and the twilight of the nuclear age. Not bad for a man from the shipyards!

If you let it, history will give you so many examples of this your eyes will glaze over. Great revolutions always come from the fringes. No fancy name on your calling card. Gandhi, King, Mandela, Luther—what did they have in common? No special title, no name recognition, and they all served jail time. As Tom Peters warns however, "Be careful with your great new ideas. You may get sent to corporate Siberia!"

The Genius of Leningrad

How little did I know.

There I stood in a brisk Arctic wind, facing the famous walls of Leningrad's winter palace. It was the dawn of the 1980s. As I stared up at its golden ramparts, all I could think of was how much change this city had witnessed in its *past*.

If you know Russian history, you're probably chuckling already.

Granted, Leningrad did have plenty of past to boast about. The Bolshevik Revolution had begun on this very spot sixty years earlier in a volley of gunfire that had mowed down row upon row of hungry protesters. And for centuries before, the palace before me had been the home of Europe's most powerful royal dynasty. A vast hive of betrayals, conspiracies, counterplots, and both figurative and literal backstabbings. Then, for the last half-century, the city's grand streets had stood as one of Soviet communism's stateliest spoils of conquest.

And yet I had another story on my mind. Because here, beneath the streets of Leningrad, lay a largely unknown yet mighty change-lesson with something to teach every one of us.

Founded in 1703 by Peter the Great, St. Petersburg was built as Russia's new capital. Within ten years Peter the Great built a city that would rival any capital in Europe. Elegant Russian Baroque palaces lined crisscrossing waterways that gave the city the title, "Venice of the North." It was truly a building marvel of eighteenth-century Europe.

Earlier the city's eighteenth-century master planners and architects had drawn up the design for every street and highway into a comprehensive master plan. To accommodate the layout of the new city, numerous large rocks had to be removed. However, one particularly large boulder lay right in the middle of one of this sparkling new city's major avenues.

As good city governments do, the administrators solicited bids for the removal of this massive boulder. Because laborsaving modern equipment and explosives didn't yet exist, the bids came in much too high. This left the city planners with a huge problem bearing no foreseeable solution. How could they move this giant stone without paying a fortune?

As they pondered and wondered what to do, a lowly peasant presented himself and offered to remove the boulder for a much lower price than any of the other bids. A debate ensued. How could this simple man succeed where so many giants of engineering had failed?

Having nothing to lose, the city fathers gave him the job and stood back with smug grins.

The next day the peasant showed up with a small army of other peasants carrying shovels. Right next to the rock they dug a hole deeper than the boulder's height. Next, they simply nudged the huge rock into the hole. They had made their pit deep enough that it swallowed the rock entirely, leaving not an inch above street level. Then, crowning their plain-Jane approach, they filled in dirt around the edges and carted off the leftovers in wheelbarrows to a dump outside the city.

As you can see, their simple audacity was never forgotten—although the names of St. Petersburg's smarty-pants engineers definitely have been.

By thinking outside the box—in this case with *less* sophistication rather than more—these creative change-agent peasants were able to solve a problem none of their supposed intellectual superiors could figure out. In fact, they created a new box.

This should be an encouraging, inspiring story for you, my friend. It means you don't have to be Bill Gates or Jack Welch to stay on the vanguard of today's mind-boggling changes. Even an ordinary person, approaching change in the right manner, can achieve solutions whose impact can last for decades.

The Wall Tumbled Down

Revisiting the peasant's story makes me also relive my trip to Leningrad. It seems like so much longer than twenty years ago. After all, the Cold War was still in force. Leonid Brezhnev was premier. President Reagan had just called the Soviet Union the "evil empire."

Gazed back upon from today's vantage point, those days might have seemed like unstable times, ripe for chaotic change. It might have seemed clear that huge changes were imminent. But since the Iron Curtain had stood for most of my life, at the time it seemed cast in stone—as the present always does.

Today, if I were to revisit the former Leningrad (its name St. Petersburg was restored in 1991), I'm sure the most striking feature I would notice would not be the city's beauty. It would be all the change she has seen in her last twenty years—maybe as much as in her last three centuries combined.

After all, local citizens have restored the city's historic name. The Soviet Union is dead. So is Leonid Brezhnev. So are his next two successors, for that matter. Communism is spent and discredited as a world economic system.

Today, the grand square outside the Winter Palace is filled with young people wearing American T-shirts, hawking everything from Eminem CDs to MP3 recordings of someone called Britney Spears—who was a baby when I made my first trip.

I was there in person to watch the fall of the Berlin Wall in November of 1989. I have a large chunk of it in my office. On a recent return to that great city I hardly recognized the place where so much change has transpired. The citizens' heads must still be spinning! When I think of the peoples of the former Soviet Union and Eastern Europe, the change in their lifetime has been overwhelming. And who was the driving force behind the changes in the last twenty years? All kinds of people throughout their system . . . starting with the peasants.

You Too Can Make a Difference!

Who can really bring about change in behavior from a group of people? The first answer is: anyone who feels the pain strongly enough. Yet you may be asking, "Can *I* really make a difference? Should I just move on?"

I get letters and E-mails from people regularly who ask me that very question. "Here is the situation I am in. What is your recommendation?" someone writes. "Should I try to bring about change? . . . Is there any hope that things will be different, or should I just bale out and find a group that's more satisfying to work with?" I usually try to encourage people to stick with it . . . up to a point. If they don't see any movement or any responsiveness to the suggestions for change, it probably is best to move on.

Many times people ask me, "How long do I keep

trying before I give up and go elsewhere?" Here are a few guidelines to help answer that critical question, "When do I move on?"

- Personal or professional integrity has been compromised—you can no longer accept the actions of management in your conscience.
- The frustration level is much greater than the opportunity if things did change: The juice is no longer worth the squeeze.
- You are viewed as a source of problems—you are the problem. People see you as nothing but a complainer with your continual attempts to push change and you carry around a negative cloud in the organization.
- Great new opportunities knock on your door.
- Contract commitments are completed and you are free to go.

The Bible tells us that our hearts must guide us in times of transition. We have to follow our principles and live with ourselves first. Sooner or later our heart may just convince us it is time to move on. That's particularly true when we feel:

- *Constant frustration and lack of hope.* "Hope deferred makes the heart sick," the proverb says, "but a longing fulfilled is a tree of life" (Proverbs 13:12).
- *Chronic discord.* "A perverse man stirs up dissension, and a gossip separates close friends" (Proverbs 16:28).

- *Issues of integrity that cannot be ignored.* "The integrity of the upright guides them, but the unfaithful are destroyed by their duplicity" (Proverbs 11:3).

Who Can Be Change Agents?

We all expect leaders to look toward initiating change, but it may surprise you who else can act as agents of change. Consider these groups:

1. *Leaders.* It would be an ideal world if leaders always embraced change with open arms. However, that is usually not the case. Leaders often have the most to lose and the least to gain by revolutions that upset the status quo. Their very jobs can be at stake. Their power can be compromised. The humble leader with a servant's heart will relax his or her grasp on the organization and allow for open dialogue about necessary changes. In some cases a leader's attempts to bring about needed change are blocked by a board of directors that won't allow things to change. If possible, try to get new directors into the mix.

2. *Followers.* In corporate America, we have witnessed stockholder revolutions that have brought dramatic change. If you are just one of the members of the group and not a leader, you still have tremendous power to bring about change. I have seen many churches where the congregation has brought about a revolution because of their dissatisfaction with leadership. (Sometimes that is

good news, and sometimes it's not.) Later chapters will deal with the specifics of how to go about being a change agent from the bottom up. When this occurs, the followers become the leaders!

3. *The board of directors.* It is amazing how many passive boards exist, especially in the nonprofit sector. And the early years of the new millennium have seen a rash of irresponsibility at the corporate board level. Many times board members will allow the organization to get away with murder as long as the bottom line is cared for and the numbers look good. Consider the boards that supposedly oversaw developments at Enron and Tyco. How can those directors defend themselves by saying they weren't aware of what was going on? Boards do have the power and authority to bring about change in organizational life, but only through the established leadership structure and the CEO. If they are not happy with the responsiveness of the CEO, then the solution is a no-brainer . . . change the players.

4. *Constituents.* These are the members of organizations. In a volunteer organization, they are the volunteer members. In a school, they are the parents and the students and graduates. In the local church, they are the members of the congregation. In a government, of course, they are its citizens. Constituents have tremendous power of influence if they get themselves organized. Most organizations ultimately exist to serve the constituent base. So constituents definitely have a right and a responsibility to be proponents of change.

5. *Customers.* As customers, you can always vote with your feet. If you don't like a place, you won't give them your business. If a company doesn't provide the products you want, you shop elsewhere. In market-driven economies like ours in the U.S., customers are king. Just take the automobile industry and notice how they have changed entirely the products they deliver to the market because of the customers' desires. Today, people want pick-up trucks, SUVs, and hybrids, and so the auto industry turns itself upside down to give them what they want.

6. *Young and old alike.* Creativity is certainly not a domain dominated by the young. In fact, recent winners of the Ernst and Young Entrepreneur of the Year award were Jack (age seventy-five) and Andy Taylor (age fifty), father and son founders of Enterprise Rent a Car. The company was honored because of its creative culture that treats each employee as an individual entrepreneur. This type of culture has allowed Enterprise to jump to the top ranks of rental car companies in America.[1]

What's the Point? Anyone can be a change agent no matter where he or she fits into the organization. Armed with the right resources, information, skills, techniques, and determination, you too can be an effective change agent. Don't give up or give in just because you are not in a position of influence. You can make things change! You probably have more influence than you realize.

TAKEAWAYS

1. Think about the changes you would like to see happen in your group. Do you have your list? Now think about who might be your allies in the battle. List them and then enlist them. If you are not the leader, start a revolution with your small group of smart peasants! If you are one of the leaders, then listen up!

2. If you are the leader of your organization and don't like what you see, get off the blame game. Start listening to the troops about what needs to be done and join the new crusade to be a part of the solution. There are certainly people in your group who are eager to join such a cause.

3. What little "pushes" toward change can you participate in right now to get things heading in the right direction? Often a whole lot of little pushes will make a big difference.

4. Keep a journal of change. Record the pain of the present and make periodic notes of the progress you see. Again, with many little pushes you can make a difference. Progress is sometimes hard to see until you see it recorded over a period of months and years. The changes that have been made can encourage you in dark times of despair.

4
Change for Change's Sake

Failure is the opportunity to begin again, more intelligently.

Henry Ford

During 1943, as World War II raged on across the globe, twenty-nine-year-old naval engineer Richard James was stuck at the home front, testing torsion springs for use as anti-vibration devices in Navy instruments. Hardly an exciting or promising posting. But during an experiment, he knocked one of the springs to the floor. It began to exhibit a behavior that caused his jaw to drop.

It was almost literally "walking" across the room!

James took the spring home to his wife, Betty, and asked her if she thought this strange phenomenon would make a good toy. Betty said yes. She scoured the dictionary in search of a suitable name and arrived at the word *slinky*, a Swedish word meaning stealthy, sleek, and sinuous.

In the summer of 1945, the war over, James finally found a machine shop in Philadelphia that could manufacture his new toy made of ninety-eight coils. When the Slinky debuted at Gimbel's Department Store in Philadelphia in 1946, both Betty and Richard stood by nervously, skeptical about how well their creation would sell.

They needn't have worried. All four hundred Slinkys for sale were purchased in ninety minutes. By the time of the 1946 American Toy Fair, Slinky was a hit and sales soared. Since then, over a *quarter of a billion* Slinkys have been sold worldwide.[1] Richard and Betty became wealthy.

The Jameses did not change their life for the sake of change. They did it because they refused to ignore the amazement that the wayward spring had sparked in them. Others might have. And still others might have had the same germ of an idea, yet dismissed it by selling themselves short, with a typically self-defeating response: "Yeah, and who do I think I am, Henry Ford?"

In spite of those odds, and despite being an armed forces engineer—hardly a profile considered creative or freewheeling—Richard James proved open to fresh input. He stumbled onto an idea that was fresher than anything he had ever dreamed of. As a result of his mental openness and his wife's willingness to listen to her husband's odd little thought, he went from a navy man tinkering with ship instruments to a major tycoon in the international toy business.

I suspect that if you had pigeonholed Richard James during his lifetime (he died in 1974), he would have shrugged off any suggestion that he was any notable "change agent." That's because he didn't change for the sake of change; he changed because he recognized a true opportunity.

That's a hallmark of legitimate, rewarding change: It comes prepackaged with its own justification, its own rationale. It does not demand to be implemented out of a blind adherence to change for its own sake. It makes its own case. So as a result, it's not necessary to blindly, unquestioningly set out replacing everything before you. Only the things which compel themselves to your attention and present a clear opportunity are great change ideas.

Is It an Age Thing?

Sometimes it seems that the willingness to embrace change falls along generational lines. America today has three large generations, and some in the youngest group harbor a tendency to change just for the sake of change. This group often thinks—even if they don't come right out and say it—"If it's old, it has to be obsolete!" And if you are old, *you* are obsolete. That's not exactly fair or accurate!

A Word to the Younger Generations

If you're part of Generation X or Generation Y (also known as the Millennial Generation), you may believe the line "If it's old, it's obsolete." Yet not everything old is irrelevant, and age alone never made anything discardable. Many people and principles endure the test of time—and many form the very foundation of the world that birthed and sustained you.

By changing just for the sake of changing, instead of doing so for the purpose of remaining relevant and competitive, you will destroy the foundation of our society rather than build on it. Furthermore, you'll mire yourself in needless toil. You don't have to reinvent the wheel— only modernize it. Take the things your forefathers have proven to be true and lasting, then give them a twenty-first-century scrubbing. Throw out what is clearly broken, but only when it has proven itself worthless. Remember, some of our brightest thinkers and innovators today actually have gray hair!

A Word to Those Caught in the Middle

If you, like me, are part of the Boomer generation, you're part of the middle generation, those who are largely today's leaders—in charge of most of our world. You and I need to become a bridge between the old and the young.

Look for enduring values that span the generations. Refuse to get sucked into your sons' and daughters' penchant for change without justification. Use your deepening wisdom to discern between the younger generations' legitimate contributions and their immature conclusions. Keep a sharp eye out for legitimate opportunities in what your predecessors embraced. Above all, have patience with the radical new ideas of the postmodern kids that are nipping at our heels.

A Word to the Elders

If you're part of the Builder generation, today's seniors, yours is the challenge of not developing "hardening of the categories." Show the younger generations you can change and you know the difference between changing methods and enduring values.

Don't give up on teaching the up-and-coming generations the eternal value of all you hold dear. The world needs you more than ever! The highly successful book *The Greatest Generation* (over six million copies sold), by Tom Brokaw, shows the enduring value of what an older generation can contribute to the younger.

A Whole New World

We have to recognize that our children are growing up in a truly different world. On a cool summer evening not long ago, I drove over to pick up my son Mark, to give him a ride home. As I waited for him with my car window open, I couldn't help but hear the teenagers talking with each other around their "cars." My son walked out and, instead of coming over, joined a group of his friends. Mark had just bought his first personal computer with his own money. His friends began to ask him questions about how much RAM it contained, what kind of video cards it featured, how many gigabytes the hard drive contained, what kind of resolution his monitor carried, and how fast his CD-ROM was.

As they stood bantering in the parking lot, bragging about the size of "the RAM under the hood," I had to laugh as I flashed back thirty years to the days when I stood around in the parking lot of my old high school. Back then, we would brag to each other about how many carburetors we had under the hood of our cars. We would get our hands greasy and grimy trying to tune up our street rods and were well versed in things like carburetors, pistons, rods, torque, and the like. We all competed for bragging rights over the number of seconds it would take to speed from 0 to 60 mph. Now Mark bragged to his friends about the speed of his video drivers, or of the broadband connection on his new PC system.

In some ways, this could be considered proof that things stay the same—that only the "vehicles" actually change. After all, you could hold up today's hot-rod computer as the equivalent of yesteryear's hot-rod automobile. But consider this: Mark's computer contains more storage capacity than the Library of Congress did when I was a teenager. It is faster and more powerful than a whole building full of computers was as recently as the 1960s. It contains features that would have graced a far-fetched science-fiction pulp novel back during my own youth.

Indeed, today's change is dizzying.

We as leaders are given the challenge of leading people from generations characteristically far different from our own. Each generation has its own distinct values and culture based upon what life was like during their formative years . . . before each one reached age twenty. If you are older, just compare the world of your teenaged years to that of today's teens.

There *are* real, substantive differences. The world truly is different; not just on the surface, but down deep. And the youth of this new world are our workforce of tomorrow. They will fill the ranks of our organizations, and are wired in new ways we must come to understand.

Save the Baby, Toss the Bathwater

I learned from a trivia-nut friend of mine about the origins of the expression, "Don't throw the baby out with the bathwater." It seems that in the olden days the whole family would take a bath each Saturday night in preparation for Sunday—in the same bathwater! The sequence went from oldest to youngest, with, of course, babies last. The expression was a warning not to throw out that last tiny bather when the water was dirty and the bathing was over.

Many enduring principles and values have passed the test of time and should remain in our organizations. Many practices have worked well in the past and should continue. For example, here's one about personal health and well being: To stay healthy you need to exercise, eat many fruits and vegetables, get the right amount of rest, and drink a lot of water. That is really old stuff—our grandparents knew about it and if they followed the principles they lived a long life. Throw out *that* baby with the bathwater and you'll soon learn to regret it. Not right away—but a few years down the path, when you're overweight and out of breath, ill health will catch up with you.

Think back again to Richard James. He recognized a wonderful, random idea within the framework of a completely traditional, staid work environment. He marketed his toy within the existing retail commercial structure. He didn't need to reinvent everything. He only needed to exploit the one thing in his ordinary world that was obviously radical. The rest he left alone; it was enough of a challenge to build the Slinky brand without worrying about changing the entire universe of retail. He was not interested in reinventing the merchandise distribution systems of America and the world.

I recently received a communiqué from two of our Gen-X employees based overseas. These two newly married young adults who grew up in Chicago were graciously sharing with me some feedback about what they respect in their leaders. After going through our orientation program, they reflected on the type of organization to which they want to be loyal for the long haul. Here is one excerpt from their letter to me:

> We're not bound by what's been done in the past, but prefer to develop our own solutions to age-old problems. Tell me the story of the past problem and how the solution was arrived at, but don't labor me with burdens of rules from past problems. I want a chance to solve the problem in a new, contemporary way—our generation's way.

What's the Point? A word of caution: Don't worship change just for the sake of change. Change is only worthwhile when it is valid and justified. To twist an old cliché, fixing something is only a good idea if that something is broken. Don't dismiss the old just because it is old. Many enduring values and principles stand the test of time. Each generation has a responsibility to discern the enduring from the outdated in the whirlwind of today's world. Not only is it a bad idea to change something just because it's old, it's impractical. There are simply too many enduring principles in our world for them to all be discarded just for the sake of relevance.

TAKEAWAYS

As we embark on the journey of change, we have to be careful that we do not throw the baby out with the bathwater. To avoid that, we should ask ourselves these key questions about things we are inclined to abandon:

1. Are these principles that have enduring value?

2. Is this part of our core values that must not be compromised?

3. Is this an ethic, value, or core belief in our group that is not up for negotiation?

4. Are we dealing with morals that should never be compromised?

5. How do we change things and yet remain true to our original charter?

6. Will our owners agree that these changes do not compromise our mission?

Often the different world of the past created a different set of solutions. It was appropriate for the leaders back then to apply the solutions of the day to their problems. What is different today that demands new ways of doing things?

Your answer reflects change for the sake of new demographics, markets, and technology, not just for the sake of change. The great challenge is to preserve the enduring core values and beliefs but change the delivery systems.

5

A Love-Hate Relationship with Change

The certainty of misery is better than the misery of uncertainty.

Pogo *comic strip*

I remember it like it was yesterday: The day my bank in Chicago changed all the ATM machines and then started charging us two dollars every time we talked to a teller inside instead of using ATMs, an automated phone line, or the Internet. They were forcing us to quit talking to humans! I got so upset that I wrote the president of the bank in disgust about how he was changing the rules and not allowing me the old-fashioned privilege of talking to my favorite teller.

Needless to say, I left the bank and went elsewhere with our family and corporate business. Don't even think about imposing that kind of change on me! If I'm not up on the changes I am probably down on them. This change caused the bank a lot of grief and they lost a lot of customers in a move that they thought was going to actually *help* their bank! The drill sergeants in charge of ramming that decision through were certainly in the dark about customer service.

Resenting the Enemy

Change is a double-edged sword. On the one edge, if we can control the change or can visualize things improving through it, we are all in favor. On the other edge, if we have change inflicted on us by drill sergeants of change, we resist it as if it were a fascist invader.

I'm guilty of this response myself. Since I am the author of a book on change, you might have assumed I am an unqualified champion of the concept. Yet like most human beings, I share the love/hate relationship with change. If I propose the change and can control its implementation—or see its immediate benefits as worthwhile—then I become a gung-ho change agent. But when I feel like its victim—caught by surprise, as is often the case—then I grow as resistant as a stubborn mule digging in its hooves. And to be honest, I have been guilty at times of being that heartless drill sergeant as the leader of my change agendas.

Change imposed is change opposed. When given a direct order, I tend to become a member of the Resistance. I become determined to thwart the drill sergeants of change in my life. I resent the change agents.

It's a paradox. I am a fanatic proponent of innovation,

yet at the same time, a lover of the traditions that matter most to me. For example, I love computers and PDAs and can't get enough of every new technological innovation that comes along. Bring on the changes! I'm your man.

However, if I drive out into the mountains of Colorado near my home, I look up at yesterday's mountain foothills—now turned into suburban sprawl—and I suddenly begin to grow a widow's bun on my head and throw a shawl over my shoulders. I change into a Victorian version of the Luddite, a snarling, sworn enemy of all things modern, a champion of zero growth, an advocate of all real-estate developers leaving the state. In fact, now that I have resided in beautiful Colorado for a few years, I would prefer no one else move here after me. Don't change the landscape any more!

We all harbor this ambivalence about change. We all embrace it when we feel on top of it, when we feel a stake in it, and believe we have had a hand in its development. But when we feel it's an outside force intruding on our lives, we often act like it's a deadly enemy.

Accepting Our Fate

Benjamin Franklin once said that in this world, nothing is certain but death and taxes. A third certainty now asserts itself into our daily reality: *Change is an inescapable part of all of our lives.* There's no going back. Things will not slow down. We will not exhaust this period of change and upheaval in history and revert back to the simple life on the farm. Sometimes I wish we could. But front porches and rocking chairs are sadly in the rearview mirror for most of us.

Change is now the law of life. In an excellent article entitled "Your Job is Change," Robert Reich wrote, "Companies that can't change in this new environment can't play in the new economy. Companies that can't change the way they think about change won't be able to change the way that they compete. . . . Companies that want to prosper over the long term need to practice the art of continuous change."[1] What he says of companies is equally true of not-for-profit organizations, clubs, institutions, and, yes, even churches.

And again, although we enjoy changing the things we are in control of, and we know things have to change, most of the change around us is beyond our command, making us its unwilling victim. Just about the time I have mastered my mutual fund's web site, they pull a major "new-and-improved, revolutionary redesign" intended to make things easier for me. Easier maybe— once I have taken more time to learn the new and kiss the old goodbye. By the time that happens, my blood pressure is hovering almost as high as the International Space Station.

So my question to you is this: Have you ever been fed up with how many things are changing around you? Do you ever grow frustrated at the *pace* of change? After all, even change itself is changing! It seems there remain fewer and fewer constants to which we can anchor ourselves. That bothers me, for although I am all for change, I think life needs a certain predictability to make it bearable day in and day out. And these anchors seem increasingly in short supply.

Managing the Drill Sergeant of Change

Whether they're of the openly hostile variety, or the harder-to-attack smiling kind, drill sergeants of change can be managed. No, I don't mean eliminated from the organization. I mean that they can be worked around, perhaps rehabilitated.

Realize, too, that you could easily become a drill sergeant yourself, if you start to lose your objectivity. It is easy to become oblivious or overly enthusiastic about a newfound love for change. The next thing we know, we are out-of-control drill sergeants cramming changes down the unwilling and unenthusiastic.

Are you unsure whether you actually have such people in your life? Have you become one yourself?

Have you ever worked for a boss who did not grasp the first clue of how to bring about lasting change in a positive and affirming manner? The kind of person who single-handedly runs roughshod over everyone in the way as he or she pushes a personal agenda on the will of the group with little or no input? This is the kind of person who exhibits the following types of behavior:

- Lack of listening before acting
- Dictatorship in decision making
- Hallway decision making
- Secret committees making big decisions that affect everyone
- The team deciding a course of action and then watching the leader "undecide" it
- Implementing unfair policies before dialogue can take place

You're about to learn how to deal with such a person —and, maybe more importantly—learn how to avoid becoming such an oppressor yourself.

It's Time for a Little Advice . . .

My advice? When dealing with the outright change tyrant, resist the urge to outright reject the change, and discover your own reasons for favoring the change; then hold the change tightly. After all, the drill sergeant's ineptitude with moving the concept forward has nothing to do with the notion's actual merits. Figuratively close your eyes, shut out the clamor, and have your own experience with the idea. It just might have merit. Try to separate the idea from the inventor. Write the advantages, or "pros," down in a cherished, private space, and make them your own. Make the drill sergeant irrelevant to your own discovery. Tune him or her out as much as possible, then begin your own process of de-bullying the idea if it truly has merit.

Then do a discreet, respectful end run. Approach colleagues and begin doing the opposite of your nemesis— make oblique suggestions, ask *what if?*, and allow others to wander into the splendors of the idea by themselves.

And how do you deal with the "nice" kind of change pushers? First of all (why not a shameless plug . . . it's my book), buy them this book. Or at least bring it up. Let them read this chapter and see if they recognize themselves.

Of course, make sure you didn't inch over the boundary while you weren't watching and become such a drill sergeant of change yourself.

Are You a Change Bully?

My point is, the nice kind of drill sergeant may be open to persuasion, but will also require much more of it. So we must be careful not to become a change bully. Here's a litmus test you can apply to yourself or anyone you're trying to help see the light. Do you practice one or more of these techniques common to the change bully? Be honest.

- *The seven-mile stare.* Have you failed to see your colleague's eyes light up when you describe an idea for change or a change that has affected you favorably?

- *The hyper champion.* Have you harbored that vague, sneaking suspicion, while sitting in a colleague's cubicle extolling the values of this or that innovation, that maybe you're being a bit excessive in your enthusiasm?

- *The passive-aggressive silent treatment.* Have you failed to stop and objectively ponder the reasons why other people in your organization might not share your own very individual love affair with a particular innovation? In fact, even a cursory think-through might reveal how you were practically the only one benefited. You might find out how others might, rather than share your happiness, actually resent its implementation. Are people avoiding you and your ideas?

- *The living dead response.* If you're not in leadership, and your organization's leader speaks of change, do you find yourself snapping your arm to your forehead with a crisp salute shouting, "Yes Sir! Right away Sir! Whatever you say Sir!"?

OK, that last one was just an attention check. Wanted to make sure you were still with me. But honestly, if you answered "yes" to any of the first three, and saw a bit of yourself in the over-the-top fourth, then you, my friend, might be a drill sergeant of change. Immediately begin thinking of others, and start to back off. They've probably heard the idea by now; let it incubate in their minds. Shut up on the issue and let them arrive at the destination themselves. In other words, let them think it was their idea. Or at least have the enjoyment of a solo discovery. Stop the intellectual bullying.

What's the Point?
Change has become the law of the Medes and Persians in our modern world. It is not always pleasant but we have to try to embrace it emotionally. Even when it is inflicted upon us, we have to try to see the benefits. Avoid being the drill sergeant yourself. Defuse the drill sergeants of change who are in your face by owning the experience for yourself.

TAKEAWAYS

1. Think about some changes that were done to you or in your environment lately that really upset you. List them.

2. Why were you so annoyed?

3. Were there any positive benefits you can now see in hindsight that you missed at the moment of emotional resistance?

4. Who are the drill sergeants of change in your office? Are they the bulldozer kind or the happy kind? And what is the idea they're extolling? Try the exercises listed above to make this idea your own, as if it had fallen into your mind from heaven.

PHASE TWO

Aim Squarely at the Future

1. ACCEPT

2. AIM

Enough of the basics. It is time to start taking aim at concrete change targets and strategies. In chapters 6–10 we will look at how to go about visioning for the future. How do we figure out what needs changing and what is really wrong with the way we do things now? How do we become the kind of person who is change-friendly and agile in our setting?

Sure it is impossible to really aim a Slinky, but we need to try to send it in a certain direction. And when it goes astray, we redirect it time and again until it goes where we want. Change is like that. We aim, then we aim again and then once more. We will learn quickly enough that becoming people who can lead during change requires becoming risk taking dreamers who are not afraid to take off where few have the bravery to follow. And if we misfire, we aim again.

6
Got Vision?

There is no more powerful engine driving an organization toward excellence and long-range success than an attractive, worthwhile, achievable vision for the future, widely shared.

Burt Nanus, Visionary Leadership

Try this: Go out and buy several pounds of steel wire, then find a large open area and unroll precisely sixty-three feet of it in a straight line. Now walk back ten steps, squint your eyes a bit, and try to picture what lies before you as . . .

    . . .a military radio antenna in the Vietnam War.
    . . .a physical therapy tool.
    . . .a new way to find water underground.
    . . .an aid in developing muscular coordination.

. . . a physics guide for teaching wave properties forces, and energy states.

. . . a tightly wound, five-inch-high stack of coils.

. . . the foundation of a lucrative retail empire.

. . . the most popular toy of all time.

OK, so you're not going to go out and buy the wire. But can you picture what I've asked you to imagine in your mind's eye? A little tough? It should be. But consider what you've just done. You've just engaged in the use of personal vision. Yes, it takes internal vision to picture a length of wire as such a wide diversity of objects. You made a mental stretch from what stood before you to an unlikely, yet desired, objective.

Likewise, it took personal vision for Richard James—not to mention his wife, Betty—to see an oddly-behaving metal spring as a profitable toy product. In the year it took for them to bring Slinky to market, both had to cling tightly to their vision while they searched high and low for the proper wire, sought buyers, and borrowed five hundred dollars to fund their enterprise.

At first their product, with no name recognition, didn't exactly roll off the shelves. Desperate to cash in on the Christmas rush in late 1946, the Jameses talked a buyer from the Gimbel's store in Philadelphia into letting them conduct a demonstration. Fearing the worst, Richard slipped a buck to a friend to make sure at least one Slinky was sold.

His concern was needless. As I've described already, all four hundred Slinkys sold out in hours, and the rest, as they say, is history. In February 1999, the first Slinky postal stamp was unveiled to the public as part of the U.S.

Postal Service's "Celebrate the Century" collection. This collection highlights the most significant and influential people, events, and trends of the twentieth century. Who would have dreamed that a vision would go so far?

The Jameses' vision had guided them through—from the proverbial light bulb going off over their heads to a wildly successful product. From sixty-three feet of wire to a cultural icon.

Aiming Ahead

When the Apollo 7 astronauts left the earth in their spaceship on their voyage to the moon, they didn't aim the rocket at the moon. Just like a Kurt Warner football pass or a hunter's bullet, their aim was centered on the place where the target was going to be, allowing for the time needed to get there. (As an interesting sidelight: In 1985, space shuttle astronaut Jeffrey Hoffman was the first person to take Slinky into space and used it to conduct zero gravity physics experiments.)

This is a crucial point of strategic thinking when speaking of vision. If we are going to succeed, we must act in advance of the critical changes occurring in the environment.

Leaders are meant to be out in front. They should take followers to places they would not tend to go on their own. They need to see *farther* than others see, and see *before* others see it. "The only way to predict the future is to have the power to shape it," notes author and philosopher Eric Hoffer. Wally Scott, professor of management at the J.L. Kellogg Graduate School of Management at Northwestern University, says, "The really great leaders have to be able to get ordinary people to do the extraordinary."

However, we must also recognize the danger of getting too far out front. I balance visionary leadership with my own warning:

> DON'T BE SO FAR OUT IN FRONT OF THE TROOPS THAT THEY MISTAKE YOU FOR THE ENEMY AND SHOOT YOU IN THE BACK.

Vision inspires followers. How many people choose a group only because of great administration? I doubt if any do. But if the leader has a powerful vision for the future, the people are attracted and join. Most people care more about leadership than management when choosing whom they will follow.

Authentic Vision

Unfortunately, the word *vision* has become one of the most overused words of the last decade. I wonder how long it will last and be in vogue in our new millennium. For many, the very mention of "vision" is becoming as worn out as "paradigm shift." If you don't feel all that visionary, you probably resent the demand that vision be so important in your leadership. Hopefully this chapter will help you realize that *you do not have to be a visionary by nature, to be an effective change agent.*

Change rule number one is this: *Change is driven by vision.* One of my favorite books on change is entitled *Changing the Essence: Creating and Leading Fundamental Change in Organizations.* Authors Richard Beckhard and

Wendy Pritchard write, "We want to underscore at this point the absolute essentiality of a fundamental change effort being vision driven. The vision of the end state is a statement of leadership priorities and commitments. It is the expression of the context within which goals must be set, activities determined, and commitments secured."[1]

The first thing we have to get out of the way is the fictitious misconception that only a wild-eyed flamboyant entrepreneurial visionary can truly be an effective leader in this day of rapid change. Nothing could be further from the truth. Probably the best proof of this fallacy is found in the book *Built to Last*. In this marvelous book, authors James Collins and Jerry Porras dispel the myth of the visionary and instead emphasize the long-term success of *visionary companies*.

The eighteen companies they found to be effective over the long haul for a period of more than fifty years have been led not by outstanding entrepreneurial visionaries, but by leaders who committed to building *a visionary company*. And all of these organizations have what Collins and Porras term "BHAGs": *Big Hairy Audacious Goals*.

Today it's becoming increasingly certain that the importance of change lies *in the organization*, not necessarily in the makeup of an individual leader. Recently I sat in the office of a leader in Colorado Springs who helps direct a Christian publishing company. On his wall hung a large framed plaque which was the centerpiece of his office decorations. The inscription read, "Attempt something so big, that unless God intervenes, it is bound to fail." I like that. He knows about the vision thing. But I also felt his slogan referred to the company as a whole, not just to himself.

How to Develop Vision

Let's focus in this chapter on how to develop a corporate vision. Job number one as we face the future is to decide where we want to go. Where is your group heading? Have you developed a clear vision and put it down on paper? Does your organization have an intended destination in the future that is, once again, committed to paper? Have you worked out a mission and vision statement? Do you know your leadership's values? If you aim at nothing you will be certain to hit it.

Organizations, whether they are profit or nonprofit, have a leadership group of stakeholders who hold a vested interest in the organization. If yours is a small business or new upstart organization, then ownership issues are easy. A few people can decide the direction for the future.

I have been working for CBInternational, a not-for-profit corporation, for over two decades. Obviously I have developed an incredible emotional stake in our organization. I do not own stock because as a nonprofit we don't issue stock, but I have built up a deep sense of ownership over the direction of the organization.

I am not alone, of course, in that sense of ownership. As the leader, I must respect the views of the other major leaders/stakeholders in the process of developing vision for our group. I am *not* advocating dictatorship, but rather, orderly democracy where key players have input and are listened to throughout the process of developing the vision.

Another one of my all-time favorite books on change, *The Northbound Train* (referred to in chapter 1), agrees with me on this point:

In an organization of any significant size, the executives cannot create the future single-handedly. They must develop the enterprise in a constellation of teams within the overall team if they hope to bring the special talents and resources to bear on the challenge of creating superior customer value and sustaining a competitive advantage in the eyes of its customers.[2]

If you do not have a one-owner shop, the vision needs to be determined as a leadership group. It is a matter of give-and-take consensus building about the ideal future of the organization. Remember that a group's vision, while clinging to its core values, must be dynamic and ever changing for the times and seasons of the organization. If there is a board, they must have buy-in for the vision too.

Every few years, an organization needs to reassess its vision and reevaluate its impact and validity in light of current realities. "The times we are living in are much like a turbulent river," says Joel Barker in his book *Future Edge*, "and in times of turbulence the ability to anticipate dramatically enhances your chances of success."[3]

Do You Have the Building Blocks?

What are the building blocks to creating a vision for your group? Try these steps as a good beginning point:

1. Get books and resources to help you work on vision. One great example is *Visionary Leadership*, by Burt Nanus.

2. Research the best practices of competitors in their vision statements.
3. Be sure to seek input from the stakeholders of your organization as you research and dream about your future.
4. Have a leadership retreat where you can devote a few days to vision, mission, and values. Use a consultant to guide you.
5. Talk with leaders of organizations that have been successful in visioning.
6. Attend some good management/leadership seminars on mission and vision.
7. Take time to reflect deeply on that which you can become passionate about. Make sure that the vision is yours and not merely a passing fancy.

Team Vision

As we were developing a clear vision for the future of CBI, my advisors and I asked ourselves the question, "What do we want to look like fifteen years from now if everything goes perfectly the way we would hope?" This goes along with the following definition of vision:

A vision is a picture of a future state for the organization, a description of what it would like to be a number of years from now. It is a dynamic picture of the organization in the future, as seen by its leadership. It is more than a dream or set of hopes, because top management is demonstrably committed to its realization: it is a commitment.[4]

Although a leader must ultimately steer the group into fulfilling its vision, defining that vision should be determined together by key players of the organization. Then when that vision is clear, the leadership must communicate that vision with passion: "Twenty-first century leaders will lead not by the authority of their position but by their ability to articulate a vision and core values for their organizations or congregations." Thus says Aubrey Malphurs in his excellent book, *Planting Growing Churches for the 21st Century.*

MISSION AND VISION STATEMENTS ARE . .

Like Glue—they help leaders hold an organization together.

Like a Magnet—they attract newcomers as members, employees, customers, or donors.

Like a Yardstick—they allow a leader to measure how his group is doing.

Like a Laser—they point you to your destination.

Change is about future direction. That's why it's the job of the leadership team to offer hope and a brighter future to our followers, as expressed well in the book *Leaders:*

To choose a direction, a leader must first have developed a mental image of a possible and desirable future state of the organization. This image, which we call a vision, may be as vague as a dream or as precise as a goal or mission statement. The critical point is that a vision articulates a view of a *realistic, credible, attractive future for the organization, a condition that is better in some important ways than what now exists.*[5]

Without such a vision, it will be impossible for your organization to weather change. Change is so traumatic, unsettling, and disruptive that it will never be tolerated without a clear vision of a better tomorrow ahead.

What's the Point?

Without a vision of where you want to go—or take your organization—you'll never weather all the challenges and the risks of change. But vision is not a solitary thing. It must be shared by your leadership. It must be built into your company as a whole. It must be realistic, well-defined, and clearly described on paper for everyone to grasp. And it must be far-seeing enough that it reflects where your target will be when you reach it—not where it stands at the present.

TAKEAWAYS

As we embark on the journey of change, we have to be careful as we craft the visions of the future. First of all, if there is a leadership group, the exercise must be done by the group and for the group. Then ask yourselves these questions:

1. Am I aiming ahead of the target—to hit where it will be, not where it was?

2. Have I planted this vision with other leaders in this organization, or just myself?

3. Have I done a good job of seeding the vision within the organization as a whole?

4. Is this vision realistic? Achievable? Desirable? Is it going to keep me awake at night with nervous excitement and anticipation?

5. Have we clearly articulated this vision, in concrete terms, on paper?

6. Is this vision going to galvanize my team to work long and hard to accomplish great things?

With your mind's eye, try to take a picture of five to ten years from now. Put into words what you see so that others can join in the experience and process of making it happen. Take the time to put this vision down on paper. Make a joint journey for those who care most about your group and its destiny.

1
Playing Takes a Dreamer

We don't stop playing
because we grow old, we grow
old because we stop playing.

Wound & Wound Toy Store, Hollywood, California

My ankles were wrenching painfully against the old, rock-hard dirt ruts. Burning wind sliced across a barrage of prairie grass and straight through my flimsy cotton shirt. Overhead, a blistering Midwest sun made a mockery of the straw hat I'd worn to ward off its rays.

Next to me, my wife and children were actually laughing, enjoying themselves. And to be honest, despite my discomfort, so was I.

Hans, what in the world is wrong with you? Fallen prey to some kind of shared, masochistic psychosis?

Sort of, but not really. You see, the year was 1993, and

America was celebrating the 150th anniversary of the Oregon Trail. Seized by an oddly ambitious curiosity, the Finzel bunch piled into a motor home and set out to follow the old path along its entire route, learning its history and its lessons.

History we learned—in spades.

We learned that the Oregon Trail stretches some two-thousand miles—half the width of the United States—from Independence, Missouri to Oregon City, Oregon. At both ends of the trail and all along the route lie informative interpretive centers, where we soon learned of the many who tried and the many who died.

Of the six thousand people who set out between 1843 and 1846, one thousand died along the way. Yet tales of hardship did not deter these early pioneers who settled the Pacific Northwest.

Two thousand miles doesn't sound like much in the age of the Interstate. But try even a quarter-mile of the trail on foot and you get a different picture. Standing where they had stood, braving the elements of heat, humidity, and bugs that they had braved, I found the questions roaring through my head.

What was wrong with you people? Why didn't you quit?

The questions never let up. They only grew louder as our family trail wound on. Our air-conditioned motor home stood ready for us nearby; theirs was a Conestoga wagon with wooden wheels and no indoor plumbing. *Why did they do it? Would we have gone along?*

In the middle of my misery, I started to picture being somewhere else. Hawaii. Alaska. Even the Hampton Inn in the next town over—anywhere but here. And that's when it struck me.

They were *dreamers!*

Their minds weren't showing them this baked-out oven. They were focused on swimming images of Oregon! Of lush green valleys and rows of Douglas firs lining the banks of the Willamette.

"The real voyage of discovery consists *not* in seeking new landscapes but in having new eyes," says Marcel Proust. The eyes of a dreamer.

Slinky, Dreaming, and the Seizing of Risk

What does this have to do with the wisdom of a Slinky? Plenty. Think back, if you can, to the first time you pulled one out of its box, or crouched at the top of the stairs and put it into motion.

How many other things did it remind you of? How many diverse images did you visualize as it started down its wayward path?

A waterfall.

A kitten, bounding the steps.

An alien probe, from a superior planet which had mastered robotic fluidity of motion.

An avalanche.

A gang of baby hula hoops, eagerly running away from home.

A moiré pattern come to life, fleeing this "mortal coil" to moiré heaven.

A dachshund's skeleton, eerily animated like an early Stephen King story.

The list could go on forever.

You couldn't stay entertained for hours with a Slinky without your imagination leading you down such paths. Picturing your toy as simply a coiled strand of metal wire would have left you bored after the first launch. As a child, each mental metaphor lasted for hours, turning each Slinky session into a whole world full of challenges and triumphs.

That's what I found my mind returning to, after my adult reacquaintance with the Slinky. A series of free-wheeling images.

It takes a dreamer to play.

If you weren't a dreamer—even a latent one, whose dreamer potential lay buried under layers of adult cares—you'd be incapable of even launching a Slinky.

That brings me to the other germane fact about the Oregon Trail pioneers: They were risk-takers. I truly believe the two qualities—dreaming and risk-taking—are totally intertwined. Very few people have the intestinal fortitude to take risks (at least the kind of mammoth risks necessary to make a real difference in this world) without possessing the ability to fantasize a desirable destination. "Do not follow where the path may lead. Go instead where there is no path and leave a trail," said Renn Zaphiropoulos, former president and CEO of Versatec, Inc.

We somehow imagine risk-takers as precisely the opposite. We tend to picture them as Type A slave drivers, the emotional and social opposite of a free-wheeling dreamer. Type A people are stereotyped as hard driving linear people with an obsessive-compulsive, objective view of reality. How could they be dreamers?

That stereotype is wrong. Risk-takers come in every shape and size.

Peter Drucker says this about living with risk-takers in our organizations:

> ### EVERY ORGANIZATION NEEDS RISK-TAKERS, TO DISCOVER . . .
>
> 1. Risks one *can afford* to take.
> 2. Risks one *cannot afford* to take.
> 3. Risks one *cannot afford* not to take.[1]

Maybe not everyone was cut out for the Oregon Trail. But creativity and risk-taking in our organizations are not just for the gifted few. They are a necessary component of every learning organization. Your group needs risk takers at every level. Are the leaders allowing them? Here's how they can:

HOW LEADERS CAN REWARD RISK TAKERS

- Reward creativity and pioneering.
- Allow new blood into leadership.
- Crosstrain them/give them leadership opportunities.
- Let them network with others outside the company.
- Site visits: Call on those who do it right.
- Allow failure: trial and error.
- Bring creative people into leadership.
- Make it safe to be creative in your organization.

- Celebrate creative acts in your group.
- Relax the controls that stifle coloring outside the lines.

How to Develop Personal Creativity

You don't have to start wearing a beret or tossing a foulard around your neck to unearth your personal creativity. Even if you've never been thought of as a dreamer, you can spark creativity. It lies within all of us, because it comes directly from our Maker.[2]

I heard an advertising writer speak of participating in a direct-mail campaign targeted at tax accountants. Someone in the brainstorm session made an offhanded wisecrack: "Can I depreciate my cat?" And someone else, seizing on the moment, responded, "Hey! Sounds like a perfect cover slogan for our mailing!"

A fierce debate ensued. On one hand stood a dubious contingent which insisted that because accountants were notoriously boring people, doing a boring job, they couldn't possibly respond to a whimsical and creative letter.

On the other hand, another group insisted that even supposedly "boring" people had the innate capacity to respond to humor.

A compromise was struck. As good direct mailers do, the organization conducted an A/B split test between a traditional, staid cover and a picture of a feline over the contested slogan.

As I hope you'll expect, the kitty version won the test hands down.

What's the point?

That again: even a supposedly boring (or bored) person harbors the embers of creativity within himself. Even an ad agency account manager targeting accountants can be a dreamer. Everyone can if they try.

The Number One Skill for Creativity

The number one skill necessary for exhuming and then honing your individual creativity is to learn how to *think associatively*. What does that mean? It means abandoning the linear model of Western thinking, first of all. Am I leading us down a path of Eastern mysticism? Not really. But I do think we can learn something from cultures that refuse to think of life in terms of straight lines stretching from Point A to Point B. We can benefit from picturing it instead, if only temporarily, as a series of circles, or even meandering paths, which not only intertwine but educate each other.

One of the best companies around that does this as a mission is IDEO, the designers of, among other things, the coolest versions of the Palm Pilot. America's leading design firm takes free thinking and imagination to whole new levels, as described in *The Art of Innovation* by Tom Kelley, IDEO's general manager. Grab that book for your change arsenal.

Again, I'm not going to launch into instructions for the lotus position or the latest trendy form of yoga. But I will say that when you start free-associating in a non-linear manner, you allow parts of your thinking to latch onto others they might never have approached before.

ARE YOU READY TO HEAR "EUREKA!" IN YOUR GROUP?

That's when you enter that zone where true genius is possible. Instead of A following B, it might follow T. And "A after T" might spark innovations and ramifications no one ever expected. The kind of "eurekas" that change organizations, and our world, forever.

Our world and its culture are in a zone of their lifespan where it seems every slogan, every pitch, every idea has been thought of ten times before. So where does true originality come from, in our day and age? Is there room to invent the next great thing like Velcro, duct tape, or bungee cords? You bet there is. Right in your organization!

It comes from ordinary people free-associating their brains off. Visualizing a better way. Dreaming of heaven.

How safe is it to be a dreamer in your group? Is change rewarded or is preserving the rituals of tradition more important?

If tradition is your mantra, you'd better get to work.

LATTES, ANYONE?

Anybody who gets to know me for any length of time learns pretty quickly that I am a coffee lover. I come by it genetically. My father was born and raised in Leipzig, Germany, in the state of Saxony, and Germans are world renowned for their love of coffee. In fact, every year they reserve for themselves the top choice in coffee beans from around the world. And of all the coffee lovers of Germany, they say the folks from Saxony are the most fanatical. The

German citizenry actually calls them "Coffee Saxons."

When Starbucks came along here in the United States, I became their perfect customer. Donna and I grab Starbucks lattes together nearly every afternoon after work so we can catch up on our day. We have our own table and they know us on a first-name basis!

Years ago, when Howard Schultz bought the Starbucks franchise and began to dream about bringing the European café culture to America, countless skeptics and critics scoffed. "No American will ever pay more than a dollar for a cup of coffee!" He proved them massively wrong. Everywhere I go, not only in the United States but also around the world, I have seen that familiar green-and-white disk. On a recent trip to New York City, I found a Starbucks on almost every street corner. In Vancouver, the taxi drivers claim there is only one street in the downtown area without a Starbucks!

Heed the Starbucks Creed

It's a lot more than coffee. Howard Schultz actually changed the habits of modern America. What he had seen in the streets of Milan he grafted into his home culture. Schultz tells how in his book *Pour Your Heart Into It*. I love the four principles upon which he operates as a coffee evangelist:

- Care more than others think wise.
- Risk more than others think safe.
- Dream more than others think practical.
- Expect more than others think possible.

Caution: Don't Kill the Dreamers

I'll finish this chapter with some blunt thoughts on how to kill dreams. Are you killing the best dreams of others that will bring you the future? Are others killing your dreams?

In my first book on leadership, *The Top Ten Mistakes Leaders Make*, I have a whole chapter on "making room for mavericks." I think they are our dreamers. Here are a few observations about how to kill dreamers:

THE THREE DEADLIEST PHRASES FOR THE MAVERICK

- "We tried that before and it didn't work."
- "We've always done it that way."
- "We've never done it that way."

I also have in that book what I call the *Eleven Commandments of Organizational Paralysis*, or "How to put people in their place if they try to bring us into the future with their great new ideas."

ELEVEN COMMANDMENTS OF ORGANIZATIONAL PARALYSIS

1. "That's impossible."
2. "We don't do things that way around here."
3. "We've never done it that way."

4. "It's too radical a change for us."
5. "We tried something like that before and it didn't work."
6. "I wish it were that easy."
7. "It's against policy to do it that way."
8. "When you've been around a little longer, you'll understand."
9. "Who gave you permission to change the rules?"
10. "Let's get real, OK?"
11. "How dare you suggest that what we are doing is wrong!"[3]

What's the Point? Not only are dreamers essential to an organization's survival, but each of us are dreamers-in-training. If you're not one, get on the ball and quick. Today's radical innovations require organizations with nonlinear thinkers and dreamers to help them survive.

TAKEAWAYS

1. Rate your "dreamer quotient." Would people call you a dreamer? When was the last time you stuck your neck out for a truly "random" idea?

2. Here are several exercises for creating dreams and just being creative in how you see things. Practice these approaches during the next couple weeks.

- *Get out your Slinky, send it down the stairs, and come up with six new ways to picture the toy.*

- *Identify at least one true dreamer in your*

organization. Think of ways you can make his or her mission easier.

- Try to come up with one truly random, non-linear association of ideas.

- Take a different route to work every day during the coming week. Make a note of how many different sights, sounds, smells, colors, and patterns you observe.

- Next time you eat out, order something that you have never tried.

- Go to your favorite bookstore and buy ten magazines outside your interest area. See what else is happening in the world. What new ideas can you find from these outsiders?

- Take a stroll through the mall and notice what is hot and what is not. Who is opening new stores and what recently closed? What are the hot boutique stalls in the aisle of the mall?

- Read books like Mozart's Brain and the Fighter Pilot, by Richard Restack, or The Art of Possibility, by Rosaline and Benjamin Zander, to learn about how the brain works and how you can encourage creativity in yourself and others.

- Consider networking as an opportunity to not only promote yourself and what you are pushing, but to get great new ideas to cross-pollinate with your own.

8
Follow That Bouncing Change!

You think you understand the situation, but what you don't understand is that the situation just changed.

Ad copy from a mutual fund company

Growing up as a boy in Alabama, I spent summer vacations in Daytona Beach. We always occupied the same motel, the Swiss Colony, right on one of those beautiful, sandy Florida beaches. I earned the worst sunburns of my life on that beach. I also learned the dangers of swimming in the ocean. One danger was riptides, that powerful undertow many of us have experienced. And at Daytona there was often a sideways current that would carry you down the beach when you weren't even aware of it.

As a young boy of eight, I swam one day just a few hundred feet offshore in that pleasurable, warm Atlantic water. I glanced back occasionally to make sure my mom and dad were onshore, reading their magazines, lying out on the lawn chairs at Swiss Colony. The side tow was worse than usual. Because it seemed as though I had been swimming for only a few minutes, I did not bother to look back to shore. When I turned around and glanced at the beach, my parents had disappeared. Swiss Colony had vanished. In fact, there was nothing recognizable in sight! I panicked. Terrified, I swam quickly to shore and ran up the beach back in the direction of our motel.

In the space of what seemed to me like just a few minutes, I had drifted probably a good half mile down the beach.

WATCH OUT! YOU LIVE IN A SEA OF CHANGE.

I have sometimes recognized twinges of that same disoriented panic as an adult. That's because we live in a sea of change. Change subjects us to the same kind of drift. We expect and account for change in relation to our familiar vantage points. But while we're not even looking, everything changes, behind us and around us. The anchors of security we use as reference points suddenly vanish. That which we always thought would never change is suddenly changed forever. A panic can set in as we are swept away in the tide.

Even change is changing. You've probably encountered this brand of statistic before, but it bears repeating . . .

From the time of recorded history until 1900, information doubled.

By 1950, it doubled again.

Starting in 1975, it began doubling every five years. Presently, it's doubling every two years.[1]

You've heard it before: we're in an era not of incremental, inch-by-inch change, but of exponential growth. In the world of computing and the Internet, even the established patterns of exponential forecasting are being shattered. John Seely Brown, chief scientist of Xerox, recently predicted that computing storage capacity will multiply by a thousand times in the next eight years. This obliterates the traditional law of storage, which merely states that we are capable of doubling storage at the same cost every year.[2]

This development is no abstract calculation; it will have a huge, tangible impact on our lives. "We now have to start thinking," Brown warned, "about a whole new game, thinking about your telephone, your Palm [PDA], your cell phone, carrying literally everything you have ever done with you. Every movie you have ever seen, every book you've ever read, every paper you have ever read or written, is something with you." Can you imagine carrying that all around with you in a handheld device?

IT'S TIME FOR SOME "AGILE EXPERIMENTATION."

The solution, Brown offered, "the key to survival, maybe the only place where you can get a sustainable edge in the enterprise that you are in, or the industry, has to do with how you learn faster than your competitor. How do you share those learnings more rapidly, within your firm, how do you in fact engage in *agile experimentation*, and *reflection*?"[3] (emphasis added).

How does one learn to learn faster? I'm convinced one of the key methods is to, once again, corporately abandon all attachment to prevailing views of "the way things are." You may have never thought of your cell phone as a repository for every bit of data you've ever produced. But once you embrace the fact, you can start to master all sorts of opportunities and possibilities the innovation will trigger. The sooner you learn to discard ingrained views like thinking of your cell phone as just a wireless telephone, the sooner you and your organization are off to the races. As you aim toward your ideal future, lay aside your current paradigms.

I like Brown's term, "agile experimentation." Once again, the term takes me back to that navy science lab where Richard James invented the Slinky so many years ago. (You didn't think I was going to omit the Slinky, did you?) I think "agile experimentation" refers to James's mental habits quite aptly.

In retrospect, it may not seem so hard for us to imagine a very ordinary spring as a toy, but that's with sixty years of hindsight to aid us. Richard James had every reason to stay rooted in his concept of the torsion spring as an instrument cushion, a tiny military device with unusual walking habits. After all, everything around him served to reinforce the military application of all he did. How many of us would have chuckled at the spring's idiosyncrasies, then turned back to our work and forgotten about them?

Yet James abandoned the view of his contraption as a Navy instrument cushion in a matter of milliseconds. That's agile experimentation—research and development with flexible objectives. I wonder if even James would have possessed the imaginative agility to recast his sixty-three feet of coiled wire into the incarnations they would later embody: becoming a component in pecan picking and in assorted machines, a drapery holder, an antenna, a light fixture, a window decoration, a gutter protector, a pigeon repeller, a birdhouse protector, a therapeutic device, a wave motion coil, a table decoration, a mail holder, and countless more.

After all—he did OK by positioning the Slinky as a toy. Why go further? One change seemed enough. Yet change has swept along the Slinky like everything else. Today you can buy hexagonal and pentagonal Slinkys. Plastic butterfly-shaped, and oddly-colored ones. Even brass or gold-plated ones for the executive who wants to release tension.

Look Within for Anchors, not Without

Last in John Brown's proffered solution came "reflection." I can't guarantee what he meant by that, but the term has great import for me.

After all, you might be tempted to mumble at me, *Great. So nothing I've looked to as a guide is valid. All permanence is a mirage. All vantage points are temporary. So what do I do? How do I learn to live and think, year after year, like someone on a life raft?*—Indeed, you may think of yourself as stranded as Tom Hanks on the nameless island in the movie *Castaway*—someone completely bereft of navigational aids, reference points, and guidance tools. Someone at the mercy of the current.

You might think this new world requires living like someone completely adrift, trying to cultivate some kind of mental aimlessness or at best, split-second adaptability.

Certainly, adaptability is a desirable trait, but I don't think it's necessary to live without anchors. I just believe today's challenges are forcing us to hearken back to the anchors that were unchangeable all along—and discard ones which were never worthy of our trust in the first place.

To put it bluntly, anchors that lie without us, outside of us—in the marketplace, the culture, technology—are not anchors at all. They're just temporary signposts, the kind that a road crew can come and move at a moment's notice. Today's unpredictable environment only proves what was always true: that these external, so-called touchstones have always been temporary. And it has always been a mistake to put one's trust, or even orient one's worldview, according to their positions.

Anchors are about core values, those unchanging deep commitments that endure in the shifting sands of our changing world. Here is a good example. Donna and I are now into "buying healthy," and we love shopping at a chain called Whole Foods. A new store just opened a few blocks away. While unpacking the groceries the other day, I noticed their core values printed on the brown paper sacks. They're shown below.

THE CORE VALUES OF WHOLE FOODS

- Selling the highest quality natural and organic products available
- Satisfying and delighting our customers
- Team member happiness and loyalty

- Creating wealth through profits and growth
- Caring about our community and environment

How do core values work? To change with every new idea but not go adrift from core principles? It is about changing on the outside in our nonessential methods and delivery systems, while striving on the inside to maintain the deep internal commitments of core values. Whatever happens in the future at Whole Foods, I suspect the leaders will watch the values carefully. They seem to be doing a great job so far.

As a follower of Christ, I'm compelled by the pace of change to reiterate what my faith has told me all along: that the only valid, lasting anchors are those found within. Like a personal relationship with an eternal God.[4] An inner faith that stands the test of time. Regular immersion in a Bible that has defied two thousand years of shifting societies and cultures.[5]

Faith in an unchanging God offers a concrete and practical alternative to spiritual rootlessness. In order to survive in a world without dependable external anchors, we don't have to throw out the idea of anchors altogether. We just have to rely on other ones, different and internal. That's why I say,

DON'T ABANDON ALL ANCHORS! JUST FIND THE RIGHT ONES.

Ironically, the right anchors are timeless. They have stood for millennia. In a book like this one heralding change and embracing the future, I realize this is one of the great paradoxes. But no one can survive without anchors of some kind. Left without them, we'll eventually patch together our own pathetic imitations. Even the aimless can turn their aimlessness into an anchor of sorts—only an anchor that will ultimately fail and disappoint.

Abandon the false, unworthy anchors and see them for what they are. Viewed in the proper light, they're perfectly useful—just not as true anchors. Again, to mix my metaphors, instead of anchors, they're temporary road signs in a rapidly-changing construction zone. Road signs are awfully important. They're just not proper foundations upon which to orient your personal life-map.

As those created in God's image, we need to anchor our spiritual needs in our Creator. For me, there is no greater rock for a foundation than the rock of Jesus Christ and His Word. When one is so grounded, "He is like a man building a house, who dug down deep and laid the foundation on rock. When a flood came, the torrent struck that house but could not shake it, because it was well built."[6]

So what if technology is not a reliable vantage point? So what if the speed of computing, the cost of data storage, the uses of data—all of these mutate at the speed of bacteria in a petri dish? You can remain calm and personally oriented in the sea of change by aligning your personal navigation with the stars, as it were—with vantage points that have occupied the same positions for time everlasting.

Ideas: Today's Hottest Currency

Once you have anchors to sustain you during change, you're ready to face changes. But you also need to welcome ideas. The pace of today's change has led to ideas—the most ethereal, unquantifiable, mutable, and fleeting commodities of all. Ideas are becoming the most valuable commodities on the planet. The individual with the best ideas wins the day. In the search for tomorrow's roadmap, the trophies go to the idea champions.

Think about the magnitude of this shift. America was built on broad shoulders, endless prairies, and the strikes of a million hammer blows. In other words, visible, physical, solid manifestations of work and value. We strung barbed wire, railroad tracks, and telegraph lines in the nineteenth century. We built cities and roads to connect them in the twentieth century.

Today, these mammoth constructions pale next to the value of a really good idea in the addled brain of the most scatterbrained, skateboard-riding, ponytailed corporate savant.

This intellectual capital—innovation, imagination, and creativity—must be valued and sought at all costs. Percy Barnevik, chairman of the giant ABB Corporation, says that his first and foremost challenge as leader is "releasing the brain power." In the words of Michael Eisner at Disney, "My inventory goes home every night." People have always been our greatest resource. And today that is truer than ever.

"You usually can't win by doing the exact same thing as your competitor, but 10 percent better," says Chris Peters, a Microsoft vice president. "You need to change the rules to get ahead. Offer something else." The Microsoft rules are simple: Pay attention to ever-changing market forces so you can jump on new opportunities or pull the ripcord on losing propositions. Let your employees know they can fail every now and then so they take the right risks.[7]

So if you're not winning, do the Microsoft thing, and make your own playing field. Microsoft does not believe in firing the people who fail now and then. They believe such firings only serve to throw away the value of the learning experience. One Microsoft programmer who found a bug in their new release of Excel, which meant a recall costing $250,000, thought for sure he would be fired on the spot by Bill Gates. He was on the team responsible for creating the error. Instead, when he walked into Bill's office he heard, "Well, today you lost $250,000. Tomorrow you'll hope to do better."[8]

In the designing of your change strategy for the future, remember that it is not programs you are seeking but ideas. It is not boilerplate templates that others are using but a brand new way of seeing things that make for the truly inspiring breakthroughs.

What's the Point? Even change is changing. We have to be people of change and we have to learn new skills like rapid-fire learning, agile experimentation, and inner anchoring. We have to relearn our view of tangible assets, seeing ideas as the currency of success. While changing on the outside with nonessential methods, we strive to maintain the deep internal commitments of our core values.

TAKEAWAYS

1. *Ask yourself and your organization the following questions about taking risks and honoring core values in the midst of change:*

- *Are we judging our progress by guides that are themselves gliding past us in a sea of change?*

- *Are there agile experimenters in this organization? Who are they?*

- *Does my organization allow people to fail without destroying them?*

- *Are we still anchored in external reference points that are no anchors at all?*

- *What are our core values? Do you have a list? If not, get busy writing them out. Do your people know them? Do they believe them?*

- *As leaders, are we reminding our people of what the core unchanging beliefs are in our organization?*

- *Is my organization geared for rapid learning?*

2. Take some time to reflect on what is truly important to you and your organization. What values emerge as directional pointers? What are the values that determine your practice? Where do they come from? Are you satisfied with them? Are they a rock-solid basis for both personal and organizational life, or are you in shifting sand and caught in a side tow?

3. Understanding that your college education is outdated within five years, what are you doing to keep up in your marketplace? Build your own office library of books, tapes, journals, web sites, magazines, clippings, seminars, and contacts. Be sure to always plan enough time just to read to keep abreast of the changing tide in your world.

4. Do you allow people to just sit around in their offices and daydream? Is it permissible to do nothing but exchange ideas, think, and reflect?

5. When thorny issues arrive, schedule time for quiet reflection. This is a great opportunity to face the new changes that are affecting your organization. Too often we get caught up in the day-to-day time crunch and do not give ourselves permission to take the time to reflect on the important issues before us.

9
Become a Futurist

The best way to get good ideas is to get a lot of ideas.

Linus Pauling, two-time Nobel Prize winner

Even though I have passed the benchmark of midlife, my wife still accuses me of being a teenager at heart. And of course, part of every teenager's dream is to own a convertible. A couple of years ago, I finally had the chance to scrape up enough money for a used Mazda Miata. It's nimble, bright red, and loads of fun. No, it's not my midlife crisis, but my therapy. I love driving in the mountains with the top down and the breeze blowing through my hair (the little I have left!), forgetting my worries, concerned only with what fresh curve and unknown landscape the next turn will bring.

Sometimes I think being a leader is a lot like driving a small sports car over a narrow, winding mountain road. As the leader, I am in the driver's seat, holding the steering wheel, and I find myself continually asking these two questions: "What's around the next curve?" "What is just over the horizon?" It could be good news or bad news; either way, it's my job to see it coming.

Just around the next corner could lie the greatest opportunity we have ever been handed. It could be the next great thing for our organization—or on the downside, it could be a huge obstacle capable of destroying us. It could be a huge cow in the road! Remember that obstacles can become great opportunities!

To fully exploit this imagery of an organization driving down a road, you also have to think about the past. One leader has described the past as a foreign country; people do things differently there. The world of 1984 was dramatically different from the world of 1964. . . let alone 1944! And the world of 2004 is certainly different from the world of 1984. Our past successes can be our greatest roadblocks to future accomplishments, because what worked in that foreign country of the past will not necessarily work today.

Three great technological innovations have had a historic impact on humankind's methods of information dissemination. Probably none was foreseen by any but a few visionaries, yet each created mega-shifts for all of humankind. Their impact reminds us of a universal truth that remains today:

THE FUTURE IS ALWAYS FUZZY.

First, the Roman Empire engineered a vast network of roads of more than fifty thousand miles. For the first time, merchants and citizens of the world could travel great distances on these roads instead of traversing stormy, pirate-ridden, difficult-to-navigate seas.

The next development, the printing press, allowed great ideas to circulate to the common people, including the printing of Bibles and other religious pamphlets for distribution all over the known world. Interestingly enough, the church fought the press, though it eventually put the Bible in the hands of all. The entire Renaissance owes most of its power to this invention.

In more recent history, the Internet, a technological revolution still in progress, became the third major innovation. Whole economies are forming themselves, as we speak, around the decentralizing, destabilizing, entrepreneurial, anti-monopolistic juggernaut that is the Internet.

Imagine the surprise of those who smirked at the last two innovations on that list. I doubt either of those developments was anticipated except by a few futurists who endured laughter and ridicule. Most people actually take the opposite stance when it comes to the future: They resist it and consistently think small. Look at the limited vision of these five statements about the future made by leaders during their day:

- "The photograph is of no commercial value."
  Thomas Edison remarking on his own invention in 1880.

- "There is no likelihood man can ever tap the power of the atom." Robert Millikan, Nobel Prize winner in physics, 1920.
- "It is an idle dream to imagine that automobiles will take the place of railways in the long-distance movement of passengers." American Road Congress, 1913.
- "I think there is a world market for about five computers." Thomas Watson, chairman of IBM, 1953.
- "There is no reason for any individual to have a computer in their home." Ken Olsen, president of Digital Equipment Corporation, 1977.[1]

These people were all experts and leaders in their days, but they, like the rest of us, had a fuzzy view of the future. No matter how cloudy the future seems, we must press forward to explore and anticipate.

From Existing to Exciting

Recently, General Motors engineers were given a challenge: to design a new car completely from scratch, instead of starting from existing models. They ended up with the AUTOnomy, a radical and exciting new concept car that has already won several of the automotive world's most prestigious awards. They built a skateboard-like chassis that can hold a pick-and-choose variety of modular car and engine designs. The AUTOnomy is the first car ever built around environmentally friendly fuel-cell technology, and the first to control its steering, braking, and other functions electronically rather than mechanically.

It's a whole new car, possibly the most thoroughly re-vamped design since Henry Ford.

Yet none of the AUTOnomy's breakthroughs would have happened if its creators had merely been asked to refine an existing model. Instead, they took a new look, going outside the lines. No idea was out of bounds. It reminds me of the wise advice of chemist and Nobel Prize winner Linus Pauling, "The best way to get good ideas is to get a lot of ideas."

Time for New Wineskins

We must become accomplished authors of a new way of doing things. Too many years have been wasted on one effort after another attempting to adapt old procedures to new realities. We see such a parallel in the New Testament. When Jesus was challenged by the religious leaders of that day for not following the traditional way of doing things, He responded with the admonition not to put a new patch of unshrunk cloth on an old garment. He said the patch would pull away and a worse tear would result.

Wanting to be sure they got the point, He provided another example. "Neither do men pour new wine into old wineskins. If they do, the skins will burst, the wine will run out and the wineskins will be ruined. No, they pour new wine into new wineskins, and both are preserved" (Matthew 9:17).

The future requires us to think within totally new wineskins. That's a great metaphor for the challenge lying before the typical organization. New rules, new players, and new boundary lines call for new strategies and structures. However, too many corporate leaders are standing sheepishly in pools of spilled wine, having relied on the methods of past successes to navigate them through present turbulence. As I have repeated before and will say again, our past success may be the biggest barrier to future survival.

FIND YOUR TRAIN TO THE FUTURE!

During my interview to become the president and CEO of my organization, the board of directors asked me about the future. Of course, they were concerned about what I thought of the future of the organization and whether our future would be successful if the organization was entrusted to my leadership. "How do you see the future?" they asked. "What is your greatest fear?" I shared with them a decade ago what I still believe today: "My greatest fear is becoming irrelevant." And I went on to add, "Irrelevancy is a bigger risk than inefficiency." We have become so efficient at doing things right, instead of being effective at doing the right things. Leading the charge toward the future always means trying to stake out the territory of effectiveness and relevancy.

The future is coming quickly! Stake out your territory and decide the direction you will take. Once you figure out where you are going, then get on board. Warn others that if they don't want to go with you they should get off the train! In the book mentioned previously, *The Northbound Train,* Karl Albrecht talks about the concept that is the title of his book. *The Northbound Train is the fundamental, driving idea of the business, for which all resistance crumbles.*

This is the future direction you have chosen and no

other. This is your northbound train. If others don't feel they want to go north with you, there are other trains they can ride. If your particular train is going north, then expect anyone who rides it to commit his or her energies fully to the journey.

What's the Point?

What's the Point? The future is rushing toward us at breakneck speed. Are we ready for it? Change agents have to become students of the future. You have got to be a futurist. Figuring out change is all about the future. We have to start living in the future and figure out as best we can what lies around the next bend for our group.

TAKEAWAYS

So how do you figure out the future? Here are a few concrete suggestions:

1. Give yourself lots of "staring at the wall" time. Or as Peter Drucker advises, spend 10 to 25 percent of your time as a leader staring out the window. Remind yourself that especially in a leadership position, you don't have to be sitting before a keyboard to be working. Sitting back in your chair with your eyes closed and your mind engaged can be far more productive than anything else you could do. Take "thinking retreats"—time to yourself where your sole task is to contemplate the future. Properly anticipating the future is one of a leader's most important tasks.

2. Brainstorm for all possible ideas about where

the future might be heading—even the most out-
rageous. Make "what if" or "what then" your refrain.
Constantly think five to fifteen years in the future,
picturing the impact of every development you learn
about. Take every new step ten steps further.

3. Read books and magazines that are future ori-
ented (i.e., Fast Company, Wired, Cyber Magazine,
Nanotechnology *magazine, and more), even if they're*
not publications you would have ever dreamed of
reading.

4. Learn to think laterally, or associatively. Men-
tally combine trends, ideas, and innovations that
otherwise fall far apart on a linear continuum. Refuse
to think only in Western-style, linear terms and spend
time thinking in circular and lateral directions. In
other words, don't segregate ideas merely because
they fall on different points of the historical or topical
scale.

5. Make visits near and far. In this country, visit and
study the competition—what do they think about the
future? Overseas, study other approaches. How are
things different there? What can we learn? (You can
develop contacts in other lands over the Internet.)

6. Study past failures—how other folks, convinced
of their gravy train's eternal lasting power, ended up
swept away by change. What precise skills did they
lack? What lie did they embrace? What was their fatal
mistake?

Finally, and above all, listen to your daydreams!

10
It's All About Alignment

Business basically is run by the economic rules of the marketplace, but organizations are run by the cultural rules of the workplace. They are often not in alignment.

Stephen Covey

Like countless other boys of my generation, I learned the concept of alignment at the top of the stairs, Slinky in hand. The trade-off was simple. If I launched the toy with so much as a nudge in the wrong direction, the Slinky would end the descent with an ignominious crash against a wall or side rail. If my older brother or sister distracted me at the last second and caused my aim to go astray, I might have to fish my toy out of a buffet-top vase near the landing or worse yet, cause a precious piece of porcelain to crash.

Perhaps I should have provided my sons with a

Slinky, because alignment is a concept one of my teenage boys does not appreciate. He enjoys the sport of cornering his car on a long hill in our neighborhood by coasting to see how far he can go. I've learned from his secret-informant little brother that the teenager does not always make some right angles and *bam!*—the wheels hit the curb. And last summer while I was out of town, according to the informer, his older brother actually knocked the tire off the rim on one corner job. I figured out something was wrong when I recently drove the car and, you guessed, . . . strange wobbling and noises coming from the front wheels. Forty-five dollars later, we had the wheels fixed with an alignment job. "Son, have you no appreciation for alignment!?"

Alignment jobs are what many groups need. You can't be sure what is wrong, but the organization is not running well. The wheels are wobbling. Different pieces of the organization are not in sync with each other. Only through launching the processes of change in the right way can alignment issues be rightly addressed and corrected.

Organizations "are often not in alignment," says Stephen Covey. How can you tell if your organization lacks harmony and needs an alignment? See if your group exhibits any of the "Symptoms of Nonalignment."

SYMPTOMS OF NONALIGNMENT

1. General confusion exists about where you are heading as a group. Goals are fuzzy.
2. People say they believe in the mission statement but don't act like it in day-to-day activities.

3. The leader talks a lot about the vision of the organization, but few people follow it in practice.
4. Management is not in coordination and harmony with the leadership folks.
5. Management is not in coordination and harmony with the "followership" folks.
6. A gap develops between the dreamers and the implementers.
7. Different departments or working groups are in silos with insufficient coordination between each other.
8. Your business can be described as, "The right hand doesn't know what the left hand is doing."
9. People do not tend to line up with each other and march in the same direction at the same pace toward the future.

We have to walk in full harmony if we are going to have organizations that work in today's world. Never is that more true than when you attempt bold changes in your group. Change guru John Kotter puts it all out there for us with this insight:

> A central feature of modern organizations is inter-dependence, where no one has complete autonomy, and most employees are tied to many others by their work, technology, management systems, and hierarchy. These linkages present a special challenge when organizations attempt to change and thus the process of leadership; unless a large number of individuals line up and move together in the same direction, people will tend to fall over one another.[1]

Another apt metaphor for these alignment issues is to picture the parts of an organization as strings in a piano. Unless each string produces a precise pitch, and most of all, in perfect position relative to each of its peers, your playing will not result in beautiful music but a cacophony. There is no room on a piano for the errant string that wants to "do things my way" or forego the rigors of tuning. If that happens too many times, you may have a pretty piece of furniture, but it certainly does not function as a melodious piano.

Here is another example of nonalignment. My family and I were eating in a great restaurant which claims that its patrons are king and that service is its mantra. Core values were plastered everywhere on walls and menus. Yet, despite all the plastered assurances, we found ourselves treated harshly by the waiter!

There was no alignment from the top to the bottom of the organization. Management should spend more time in customer-service training and less time making posters!

Every time a company makes a promise to you that they do not keep—it's an alignment issue. The leaders wish and pray that it is so, but without alignment from top to bottom, success at keeping the promises of the company is only wishful thinking.

Checking the Alignment

Actually, a great way to figure out how well you are aligned is to perform a vision audit. One of the best books out there on vision in leadership is *Visionary Leadership*, by Burt Nanus. Pay special attention to his fourth bullet.

He says the best way to gauge momentum is to do what I call a vision audit. The four questions of the audit help determine whether the organization really has the vision and knows what it is:

1. Does the organization have a clearly stated vision? If so, what is it?
2. If the organization continues on its current path, where will it be heading over the next decade? How good will such direction be?
3. Do the key people in the organization know where the organization is headed and agree on the direction?
4. Do the structures, processes, personnel, incentives, and information systems support the current direction of the organization?[2]

Nuts and Bolts

OK, you nuts-and-bolts people are asking yourselves about now, *When is he going to get to a plan of attack? How can I really take aim with an action plan for change?* Let's turn to the change expert for the answer. Why completely reinvent the wheel?

The book *Leading Change,* by John Kotter, is my number-one book on the topic of change. I wish I had written it myself! I'm not aware of any better change bible in print. I use this template constantly in our own change programs at CBI and in consulting with other organizations. It is suicide to miss any steps in his eight-step process.

THE EIGHT-STAGE PROCESS OF CREATING MAJOR CHANGE

1. Establishing a sense of urgency
2. Creating the guiding coalition
3. Developing a vision and strategy
4. Communicating the change vision
5. Empowering board-based action
6. Generating short-term wins
7. Consolidating gains and producing more change
8. Anchoring new approaches in the culture

SOURCE: John Kotter, *Leading Change* (Boston: Harvard Business School Press, 1996), 21.

In our own organization we have formed a long-range change team to tackle issues of alignment. Their charter is to represent all the stakeholders of our group and recommend bold changes in all the arenas needing alignment. We use Kotter's eight-stage process as the rails on which to ride. No compromise. We recognize that for us it is a long-term process because of the size of our organization (eight hundred people spread through seventy countries) and our age (sixty years of traditions). If your group is younger or smaller, it can of course be compressed. Since I, the chief executive officer, and our chief operating officer are both a part of the change team, there is bite to the group, and it does have the authority to actually see that things get done. Form a group like this with neither teeth nor authority and it is just wishful thinking and a waste of time. Haven't we all been on committees with no power that decided nothing of any merit that anyone adopted?

Feeling the wobble of your Slinky? Maybe it is time for an alignment job. Remember that the quest for alignment is a key rationale for change but so very difficult to pull off. I suppose that is why Kotter writes that the majority of change programs fail.

If you do happen to be at the head of your organization—you are the leader—then you have a special role to play in promoting change. Recently someone asked leadership guru Stephen Covey if it's possible for a leader to actually change culture, or does she or he actually have to just adapt to the culture that already exists? He answered in this way:

> I think both. He has to adapt in the sense that he deals with where the culture is now. And therefore he cannot just artificially and unilaterally impose a whole new system and a bunch of new guidelines.
>
> But a CEO also has a vision and a mandate . . . to make some fundamental changes that, deep inside the bowels of the organization, people have known for a long time should take place. . . . A CEO also should respect that you don't announce a culture, you don't mandate it, you don't legislate it. It happens naturally inside the hearts and minds of people.

Then Covey was asked a second question: What sep-

CHANGE is like a SLINKY

arates the CEOs who fail from those who succeed? His answer makes a lot of sense to me:

> They don't know how to bring about a change in the culture. You see, business basically is run by the economic rules of the marketplace, but organizations are run by the cultural rules of the workplace. *They are not in alignment.* A lot of people over time have become dependent on the old cultures and systems, and it takes a lot of courage to change the structures and systems.[3] [emphasis added]

Alignment has become a huge issue to me as a leader. Many of the problems that plague us and keep our organizations from really working are alignment issues. Change processes are meant to move us toward the harmony of the parts like those strings in the piano. How is the alignment in your organization? In my checklist of symptoms of nonalignment, how did you do? How many of those bullets plague your group?

What's the Point? Embarking on a road to change is not change just for the sake of doing things differently. As we have already seen in a previous chapter, there are many reasons to change. One of the biggest is to address lack of alignment in an organization. Proper alignment is the quest to make sure that your group functions coherently, consistently, and cohesively from top to bottom.

TAKEAWAYS

1. Take my list of "symptoms of nonalignment" and have a discussion with your key leaders. How much agreement is there even about this list? It should be a lively discussion. First have each person rate the organization privately; then have each share his or her score for the group.

2. Finish this sentence: "The lack of alignment in our group can be seen in . . ."

3. Repeat steps one and two with some of the rank and file in your group. Form some focus groups and measure alignment. You will be surprised at the views of the followers.

4. Being in proper alignment implies conforming to an established set of standards. To have organizational alignment, you must have identified your standards, i.e., values, goals, vision, and practices. Have you taken the time to do this for you and your group?

5. Try asking a random selection of your customers what they think you stand for. Can they tell you what your standards are? Do they sense alignment with those standards as the end users?

Later chapters will offer more specifics about moving toward alignment and forming your own change teams.

PHASE THREE
Anticipate Your Adversaries and Allies

1. ACCEPT

2. AIM

3. ANTICIPATE

Part of warfare is a plan of defense. You have to know your offensive plan of attack, but you also have to study the enemy. You just might be fighting for your very survival in your organization. Or you may be fighting for the survival of the organization. *Those who oppose change at any cost are truly the enemies of survival.*

You are convinced that you must change or die (Phase One: Accept). And you have dreamed about a vision for the future (Phase Two: Aim). Now in these chapters we will explore the issues related to those who help the change program and those who resist. You will learn about creating a case for change and building allies as well as how to get people to buy into the change plan.

As you anticipate your progress in the dream you pursue, do not underestimate the challenge. Something that never changes is *resistance* to change that is a part of human nature. As Niccolo Machiavelli wrote about change in 1532:

> There is no more delicate matter to take in hand, nor more dangerous to conduct, nor more doubtful of success, than to step up as a leader in the introduction of changes. For he who innovates will have for his enemies all those who are well off under the existing order of things, and only lukewarm supporters in those who might be better off under the new.[1]

11
Create a Sense
of Urgency

**The few projects in my study that
disintegrated did so because the
manager failed to build a coalition
of supporters and collaborators.**

Rosabeth Moss Kanter

In 1973, Betty James implemented one of the only two
basic changes ever made to Slinky's design. She decreed
that both ends of the toy be crimped, softening the sharp
point that had marked Slinky for decades. The first
change had been to move away from the dark blue steel to
a less expensive, lighter variety.

I have no idea whether this change was met with internal opposition, but if it was, Betty would have possessed
an instant, irrefutable defense: "Children could get hurt!"
There was an apparent real danger of children being

poked and their skin broken by the toy's previously sharp wire point.

Betty held one of the rare aces-in-the-hole in contemporary business: a change that needed no lobbying, that carried its own compelling rationale. After all, what is a more compelling motive than to keep children from being injured? Surely any potential opposition within the company wouldn't have stood a snowball's chance.

But what about the rest of us, who face the challenge of mustering support for a change before ever beginning the task of implementing it?

Jumping the Gun

I've done it—and I'll bet you have too. Tried to fix something before support for the fix was in place. Move an office. Redo the stationery. Adopt a new logo. Complete a major asset purchase. Upgrade the computers. Undertake facility improvements. You name it. You think it needs some tweaking, so you undertake the changes impulsively, "half-cocked." You decide to do it yourself.

And then something doesn't turn out quite right. So now comes the scorn. "Why did you mess with it? It was fine." And of course the classic of all, "If it ain't broke, don't fix it!"

Here is where I learned one of my most painful lessons on change. If you roll out and announce big changes before you have created your case for change, it's like scratching people where they don't itch. Selling people things that they don't want to buy. Fixing things that people are convinced are not broken.

> **DEFINITION**
>
> **A Case for Change:** the rationale you articulate to explain why things are broken, how things are not working right, and the urgency of the risks if solutions are not addressed. It is the first homework of any change agent.

In his book *On What Leaders Really Do*, John Kotter claimed that most executives rarely push the urgency factor hard enough. Earlier, in his classic, *Leading Change*, Kotter argued that creating a case for change and its urgency are the first essential steps in the change cycle. "With complacency high, transformations usually go nowhere because few people are interested in working on the change problem," he wrote.

The case for change and the case for urgency are non-negotiable. "Sooner or later, no matter how hard they push," Kotter argued, "no matter how much they threaten (if they are the leaders), if many others don't feel the same sense of urgency, the momentum for change will probably die far short of the finish line."[1]

My father always used to tell me, with his rich German accent, "Son, vee get too soon old and too late schmart." He was right. You would think I had learned a few things about implementing change during my years in leadership and as a CEO! In my passion for change, I am still not smart enough to avoid the common mistakes of putting these ideas into practice. Just recently I did it again—underestimated the fallout of changes among our people. In a major, recent reorganization launch, a large and unexpected outcry of opposition rose up against me. The reaction was based on four objections to my poor plan of building a case for change. The rank and file people who would have been most affected by the changes had four negative reactions to our new organization chart. Their reactions are common to most recipients of surprise changes and are summarized in the following chart:

WHY PEOPLE RESIST CHANGE ANNOUNCEMENTS

1. We did not know there was a problem. (The "it ain't broke" syndrome)

2. We are in shock about your solution to a non-problem. ("Don't fix it")

3. We had no idea any change was coming. ("We felt ambushed")

4. We offered no input for the solutions imposed on us. ("We might have had really good input for you to consider— a better solution")

Each of these arguments reflects a failure in creating a prevailing sense of urgency. Because the benefits of this change were so glaringly clear to me, I failed to anticipate possible opposition and therefore overlooked setting the stage for a well-received "roll-out." Each of these four reactions could have easily been answered if I had taken the time to address them with the right people.

This brings me to a cardinal rule of managing change:

> **FORGET ABOUT THE "OBVIOUS" BENEFITS WHEN PLANNING YOUR STRATEGY. ASSUME THAT EVERYONE BUT YOU WILL ABSOLUTELY HATE YOUR PLAN, AT LEAST INITIALLY.**

So how do you proceed in introducing the planned change? It pays to be systematic when deciding to proceed.

Draw Up Your Game Plan

That means drawing up a game plan. First, determine what kind of an organizational procedure will be required to implement your proposal. Is it a vote of the board of trustees? A vote by others? A simple committee decision? Consensus of the leadership team? Or the arbitrary fiat of a single executive? Each of these will offer vastly differing strategies for success. Of course, there is also the question of whether the formal or the informal leaders hold the keys to change. Just about every group has both kinds.

Second, draw up an actual chart of individuals along this decision map whose support will prove crucial. (As a visual learner, I favor this map-like approach for perhaps personal reasons, but I can vouch that it works.)

Now rank these people in order of their authority over the choice you seek. It pays to know the pecking order in your hierarchy-within-a-hierarchy.

Third, determine how to reach each of them. What is each one's personal inclinations? Does he or she have key lieutenants whom you know well? Does the person have personal agendas that could be thought to benefit from the implementation of your change? Each individual will have differing aversions to change—the higher theirs is, the stronger must be your description of the stakes involved. Remember that even an "old stodgy" can harbor enough personal love for an institution to favor profound change if he's convinced the group's survival is at stake.

Finally, go to work impressing these people of the dire need for the change you're proposing. Simply "keeping up with the times" isn't enough. Simply pointing out that the status quo has been in place for a long time won't work either. You have to make a case that the organization will not survive—that it will not continue to succeed at its stated mission—without a change like the one you're advocating.

And you have to go further: In the most delicate way possible, you need to make sure this person understands that his or her own professional future could lie in the balance.

If you encounter resistance, remember that nothing disarms opposition like a request for help. Instead of charging in to inform someone of impending doom, you can come with a solicitous posture, asking for advice and help in your endeavor.

Liberate the Elephants

In his book, *Teaching the Elephant to Dance*, James Belasco uses the analogy of liberating the elephants. Trainers shackle young elephants with heavy chains to deeply embedded stakes. In that way the elephant learns to stay in its place. Older, powerful elephants never try to leave—even though they have the strength to pull the stake and move beyond. Their conditioning has limited their movements. With only a small metal bracelet around their foot attached to nothing, they stand in place. The stakes are actually gone!

Like powerful elephants, many companies are bound by earlier conditioned restraints. The statement "We have always done it this way" is as limiting to an organization's progress as the unattached chain around an elephant's foot. Remember my list of eleven commandments for organizational paralysis?

Yet when the circus tent catches on fire—and the elephant sees the flames with its own eyes and smells the smoke with its own nostrils—it forgets its old conditioning and changes. He physically escapes the fiery death!

Your task: Set a fire—or at least point it out—so your people can see the flames with their own eyes and smell the smoke with their own nostrils.[2] And anyone can set the fire at any level of the organization.

The pioneers and mavericks you enlist to help you in your change process are obviously risk takers. You as a leader are a purveyor of hope as you paint a picture of the future that others can believe in. But you must paint the picture—or start the fire, as the case may be—and then ensure that others in your organization find it as compelling as you do.

What's the Point? A sense of urgency is the critical first step in the journey of change. If there is no case for change, and no sense of urgency built into the system, then you have to begin with some homework. Go back to the beginning and do what is necessary to promote discomfort among enough people to get things moving in a new direction.

TAKEAWAYS

1. Change is the river that must be traversed between the land of opportunity and the land of pending disaster. Here are things you can do to help the troops see the need for change:

- *Walk that fine line between being a negative complaining whiner and someone who sees both the opportunities and the pending disaster if things do not change. If one is not careful, he can begin sounding like the boy who cried wolf—someone who others dismiss. Be positive in your approach.*

- *Clearly define the opportunity or problem as you see it, from the perspective of those over you and those under you. For that group most affected by your proposed change, make sure you are considering the issues from their position. Is it a real problem, an alignment issue, a keeping-relevant need, a matter of a cus-*

tomer base deserting to the competition if no changes are made? Or is it just something you want to do for the sake of change?

• Discuss with those potentially affected the opportunity/problem as you see it/define it. Do they concur? Do they see a problem or missed opportunity if no change is made?

• Recruit and enlist these people as partners in the coming change process. What ideas and solutions can they bring to the table? Can they help you implement the mutually desired change?

• Communicate, even over-communicate, with the organization the opportunity/problem and pending change process with ways of contacting and giving feedback to those involved in the change.

2. Try making some lists here of experience with false starts in change:

• List some change initiatives that have utterly failed which you have watched from the sidelines. Why did they fail?

• Now list some examples of changes that you have personally implemented without support that backfired on you. What can you learn from these mistakes?

• Draw up an actual chart of individuals along the decision map whose support will prove crucial for changes (more on this in the next chapter).

12
Build Consensus from the Inside Out

The less I have to do with it, the less I like the idea.

An anonymous employee

When Slinky inventor Richard James and his wife decided to demonstrate their new toy at Gimbel's Department Store in Philadelphia for the Christmas season of 1945, they feared that their discovery was too simple and few would buy it. As mentioned earlier, they were so worried that they gave a close friend one dollar to buy one. Yet ninety minutes after the first demonstration, they had sold four hundred of the toy springs.

Richard knew the first rule of effective consensus building: Get an insider to step up and commit himself publicly to the change.

As we have already said, leaders have much responsibility in making change happen. And when times demand it, leaders have to change the way they lead. Back in 1991, Warren Bennis prophesied that managers had to change their way of leading. "Move to maestro from macho in the way we are thinking," he challenged. That means shelve the old autocratic "command and control" thinking. Be a real leader who both listens and guides people to get the job done.

Dump the old-style bullying of "control, order, predict (COP)," he said. Adopt the approach of the results-getter known as the "ACE: acknowledge, create, and empower. People in charge have imposed change rather than inspiring it," Bennis lamented.[1]

We have to build the coalition for change from the inside out. Start with those closest to you that have a kindred spirit. Build a team that is committed to moving in new directions. Allow the circle to expand outwardly to other people who can influence the future. Try to get as many stakeholders into those ever-expanding circles before any change is ever publicly announced.

Why do people resist change? Before we proceed to the positive steps needed to make it happen using consensus building, let's review some of the top reasons why people do not want to change. (We'll look at the complete list in chapter 13, "The Anatomy of Resisters.")

> ## TOP REASONS WHY FOLLOWERS RESIST CHANGE
>
> 1. *Fear:* The unknown is a threat to their comfort zones..
> 2. *Insecurity:* They may be worse off after the changes are implemented.
> 3. *Power:* They may lose power in the shuffle.
> 4. *Inertia:* It is easier to maintain the status quo.
> 5. *Energy:* It takes a lot of work to change things.

Change will face many detractors. It is up to leaders and influencers to turn around the five resistances noted in "Top Reasons"—showing that each one will be served by supporting the change, not opposing it.

SAVING FACE IS NOT JUST AN ASIAN CONCEPT.

Another way to say that you need to work from the inside out is to invoke the principle of *persuading individuals before selling groups.* One of the basic, fundamental principles in change dynamics is that groups respond differently to change proposals than do individuals. When seeking to change the direction of a group, you have to sell its individuals first—especially its key influencers. When an idea is presented to an entire group, everyone's reactions are publicly registered. Everyone sees where everyone else stands in the initial reaction. Once you have gone on record, you lose face if you change your initial reaction. So people who initially reacted negatively are not going to want to lose face and change their mind publicly.

Losing face is a huge issue in the quest for change. People who privately change their minds from rejecting an idea to embracing it will seldom let anybody know of their shift once they have gone public with an opinion. Selling an idea to individuals before presenting it to the entire group makes it easier for people to change their minds.

So the next time you're seeking to build a consensus for change, remember that "saving face" is far from an exclusively Asian concept. In fact, no one in an organization wants to look like a vacillating, uncertain "waffler." By identifying and addressing opposition on an individual level, you give people the chance to consider your points, then, quite possibly, change their minds in privacy and safety.

Test the Waters

Learn to test the waters, or, in a more patriotic phrasing, "run it up the flagpole to see who salutes." It is crucial that you try to find out how people will react to the changes you propose—before the official period of staking out territories.

Government leaders are great at this. Long before making an official proposal, they will leak it through back channels. They will figure out a rough sketch of their idea or proposed legislation, then let it leak out so as to see the reaction it evokes. They stand back and watch news reports and other responses from their constituents. In so doing, they gain invaluable data about the lay of the land.

In the process, they answer for themselves countless vital questions. Was the idea embraced? Did people react to it violently? Why did they not like it? Were there any good points that they did like? If they rejected it, what were the reasons they did so? What can be learned from their reaction to make it a better proposal?

This is called *beta-testing* your proposal before it is launched in earnest.

Work the Circles from Inside Out

When mapping out how to lead your group through major changes, be careful to work the process through the circle of ownership from the inside out. In other words, look for consensus first from within the organization's most powerful and effective circles, or your idea for change will be DOA. (See the "Circle of Ownership" chart on the next page; notice that the rank and file form the outer circle in every organization.) "Successful companies have a consensus from the top to the bottom on a set of overall goals. The most brilliant management strategy will fail if that consensus is missing," remarks John Young of Hewlett-Packard.

This may sound elementary, yet an amazing number of innovators waste their intellectual capital by blabbing their ideas either to the nearest willing ear, or to their ideas' likeliest supporter, regardless of the person's position within the organization. Unfortunately, status matters. You must be brutally perceptive in ascertaining who can help you the most, and dole out your disclosures accordingly. This applies, of course, to both the formal and informal networks.

CIRCLES OF OWNERSHIP FROM THE INSIDE OUT

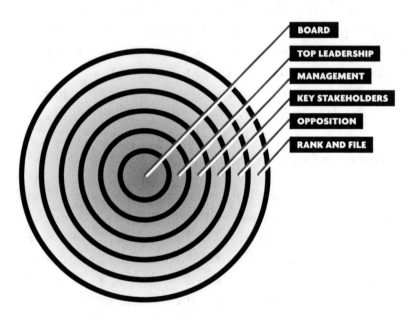

- ***The board circle:*** the decision-making boards of your organization.
- ***The inner circle of top leadership:*** the inside members of the executive team
- ***General management circle:*** the managers—middle-level leaders
- ***Key stakeholders circle:*** other key people who should be in the loop and have influence
- ***Key opposition circle:*** those identified as opponents
- ***The rank and file members:*** the general members of the organization

If you are not in these inner circles, look for ways to win your superiors' confidence. Leaders ultimately have to buy in and drive the process forward. But good leaders are listeners, and they can be radically influenced. You simply have to master your pitch, be sure it conveys great urgency, and show where the leaders' self-interest lies. Do so, and you'll win their support.

What's the Point? Without consensus building, ideas for change are dead on arrival. Consensus building should start privately and move to the public forums. And it should move from the inner circles of influence to the outer rings. Everyone is important in the circles, but timing and sequence do count.

TAKEAWAYS

1. Make your own circles of influence for your group. Label each group. Who are the key individuals of each circle of ownership you will need to work with to build consensus for change? Draw them in a diagram like the one in this chapter.

2. Study the key stakeholder groups in your organization:

- *Rank them in order of influence in your group.*

- *Which groups are most critical to win over with new ideas?*

- *Who are the real brokers of influence?*

- *Who is the single most important person in your organization who has to give the nod for ideas to move forward? Or is it a small group of leaders?*

3. Now make a list of the small group of individuals who you can count on to share your passion about change. Those become your inner circle as you build consensus from the inside out.

13
The Anatomy of Resisters

**In short, a change imposed
is a change opposed.**
Spencer Johnson in Who Moved My Cheese?

Like all objects, the Slinky tends to resist change in its motion. Because of this dynamic, known as inertia, if it were placed at the top of the stairs it would stay at rest without moving at all. At this point it contains potential, or stored, energy.

But once it starts down the stairs and gravity affects it, the potential energy is converted to the energy of motion, or kinetic energy. The Slinky gracefully tumbles coil by coil down the stairs.

Some people in your organization are there to help the company along in the new right direction with increased kinetic energy. Others serve to keep it heading in the same old wrong direction.

In his book *Principle Centered Leadership,* Stephen Covey says this about making your adversaries your allies by bringing them into the process: "When people become involved in the problem, they become significantly and sincerely committed to coming up with the solutions to the problem."

That's why we put together a change team at CBI. We are attacking huge chunks of unsolved, recurring problems with aggressive doses of "change medicine." In the process, we're finding that personal investment is the key to implementing change and increasing commitment. If we are not involved personally, we will likely resist change altogether.

Bringing about change in people and organizations is not simple; or if it is simple, it's not easy. We are dealing with a blend of momentum, attitudes, skill levels, perceptions, and established patterns. People cling to old views, old ways, and old habits. Old styles and habits are hard to change.

There is definitely a downside to involving people in problem-solving. Whenever you involve people in the problem, you risk losing control. It is much easier, simpler, and safer—and seemingly much more efficient—not to involve others but to simply tell them, to direct them, and to advise them. That's why "most chief executives slip into authoritarian roles without realizing that the process is going on," notes former ITT president Harold Geneen. "They change because it is easier and less time consuming to be authoritarian."

HOW STRONG IS YOUR FORCE FIELD?

Curt Lewin, a great social scientist, contributed enormously to our understanding of the processes of change when he came up with his force field analysis theory. Developed more than fifty years ago, it states that driving forces are pushing organizations for change; at the same time, restraining forces or discouraging forces are at work that cause people to resist change. We can picture these forces as arrows pushing in opposite directions: →forward/driving and ←reverse/restraining.

The current state of things is the equilibrium between the driving forces and the restraining forces.

The question is, when you are embarking on a major change program, *do you put more energy into increasing driving forces or into decreasing the resisting forces?* That's the great debate. It seems logical that if you added more push, you would reach your desired outcome. But that's not necessarily the case. Forward thinkers want to be involved in solutions, but it is also very important to reduce resistance as well. One of the reasons many change efforts fail is that barriers to change are not removed.

It is easy to polarize people with too much push. Cynicism is likely to develop rapidly. Trust levels can drop so low that any new effort designed to push toward change is viewed as manipulation by management.

One way to see these forces is to picture a gas pedal or brake pedal. It doesn't do any good to continue to push harder on the gas pedal if the brake is on. It might be easier to deal with the brake than to deal with the gas pedal.

HAVE YOU DRIVEN A BUICK LESABRE LATELY?

Let's use an example to illustrate the facilitating forces and the restraining forces of change. My father-in-law has been driving a Buick LeSabre for the last decade. Actually he just bought a new one, but it's just like the last one he had. He is retired, has no mortgage, has raised his children, and is relatively well-off financially. I have been on his case for a long time to drive a cooler car. Why not? Why not consider a Porsche Boxster? Or a nice Audi A-6?

The *current state* is that he is driving a Buick LeSabre. No offense to Buick and General Motors, but there are cars that are a lot more fun to drive. The objective is to drive a new Porsche Boxster. That is what I would call the *ideal state*.

The chart below shows the *facilitating* and *restraining* forces in his change to a Porsche Boxster:

FACILITATING FORCES	RESTRAINING FORCES
The Boxster is a pleasure to drive.	I can't get the grandkids into the Boxster.
The Boxster looks great in the driveway.	People might criticize the opulence.
The Boxster is a German-built marvel!	It's too much money.
The Boxster is much more dependable.	It's too much for insurance coverage.
The Boxster has a better sound system.	I will worry about it being stolen.
I would look great driving around in a Boxster.	Am I too old for a sports car?

As you can see, when the facilitating forces overcome the restraining forces, you move from the present level of reality to the new ideal state. I am still working on my father-in-law!

ARE THEY REALLY REBELS?

Many times we view the people who oppose our ideas as adversaries. Actually that is probably not the best way to see them. *See them as advisors.* They are a necessary piece in the process of transforming a good idea into a great one.

You might view your opponents like the funny sounds your car makes when it is out of tune and in need of repair. Those sounds can be your allies and not your adversaries in the process of tuning your car to make it run better. Use your adversaries to tune up your ideas to make them much more workable and saleable.

Reasons People Resist Change

I have thought long and hard about all the reasons that people resist change. This list comes from years of observing human nature in real-life situations. See if I have missed any as you read through the litany.

- *Fear of the unknown.* We feel more comfortable in the known than in the unknown. "I know the rules, boundaries, strengths, and weaknesses of our current system. How can I be assured that the land toward which we are headed will flow with milk and honey better than where we are now? I am afraid that the changes do not make sense for our organization."

- *Fear of loss.* We do not want to lose something of great value, which is what the current state of the organization is to most of the people who enjoy working here. "I am afraid that I will lose what I am comfortable with."

- *Surprise.* Spooked like a horse! If management announces change at a staff meeting without proper preparation, then people will be startled and spooked. This guarantees that they will dig in their heels and react negatively to change by the leadership team.

- *Insecurity.* It's hard for most people to see how they will be better off under the new system than they were under the old. They believe they have a lot to lose and very little to gain. Some people feel insecure by thinking that under the new system they won't be needed any longer or somehow they will be demoted in their importance or role in the group.

- *Uncertainty and confusion.* People don't know enough about what the next step will be or how it will feel out there. There is simply not enough information to enable them to emotionally "put their arms" around the new order of things. They misunderstand the intentions of managers and leaders.

- *Loss of power.* Change is exciting when it is done by us, but usually threatening when it is done to us. "I know what power and influence I have under the current order of things, but I'm doubtful about where I will end up when the dust settles in the new order of things." Change tends to create winners and losers. Some people may lose status and others may gain status. This is a political reality in any organization; it is real and demands recognition.

- *Inertia.* The status quo is strong. Overcoming initial inertia is always one of the great challenges of any change process. Everyone is settled in their own ruts and routines; dislodging them takes effort.

- *Energy.* The major change program simply takes more energy than to leave things the way they are. And, if you are exhausted and overextended, there is no energy left to give to a change process. Some fear such expenditures and cry out, "It will take more work!"

- *Steep learning curve.* There is resistance to learning new ways of doing things. "I have to learn new stuff." A great deal of work in organizations is done by routine. Most people will fail if their routines and habits are forced to alter significantly. Employees and members of the group also display self-doubt about their own competency to perform. No one likes to look inadequate; no one likes to feel that he or she has to start over again.

- *Time Pressure.* Change involves increased workload. It takes more energy, more time, and greater mental concentration to go about a process of change. Many times change processes end up giving people more work, especially if it is a downsizing situation. Some cry out, "Who has the time?"

- *Ignorance.* There has to be a whole lot of communication and handholding during the change process. People will sit at their desks, or sit in their meetings, or go through their routines and not know how to

161

navigate the new order of things. Even if they are committed to change there is a great deal of ignorance about how to go about it. Some cry out, "How will I know the right course?"

- *Disruption of the comfort zone.* Who wants to move from the comfortable to the uncomfortable? "I like having new shoes, but they make my feet hurt. I don't wear new shoes on Saturdays when I want to relax." Most people really enjoy the comfort zone they have grown used to, even if they know that a new order of things will be better for the entire group. A lot of us have a low tolerance for change.

- *Loss of face (also known as organizational embarrassment).* Most people feel that by accepting change, they have to acknowledge that the way things were done in the past was wrong. That's embarrassing for them. People will go to extreme lengths to save face and try to protect the old order of things.

- *Historical baggage.* People will run into disgruntled employees who are bitter over some unresolved past grievances or leadership sins that were not cleared up. Gripes from the past can fuel resistance to new ideas for the future. It can take the form of a conspiracy of silence, or a malicious resistance to the new order of things. Don't underestimate the negative power of passive-aggressive behavior.

- *Lack of trust.* Those who don't trust the leadership are certain to oppose new changes supported by those same leaders. If there is a history of poor change management, there will be resistance to trying it again. People have become skeptical, embittered, and entrenched in the status quo. They passively rebel against future attempts to improve the organization.

What Resisters Can Teach Us

When we listen to our opponents, we can learn two things. First of all, we can recognize the flaws in our ideas. It's amazing how our resisters have the ability to see right through the weakness of our proposal. I've seen this with my own wife: I'll tell her about a proposal that I'm getting ready to launch in our organization, and she will immediately cut to the heart of the matter and raise an objection that I find quite uncomfortable. But if I really think about it, I realize that she spotted the proposal's weakness. We discover both obstacles and fundamental flaws in our proposals.

The second thing we learn from the resisters is the hidden psychological barriers we have to overcome among members of the group. Just because an idea is a great one doesn't mean that people are going to buy it. There are many below-the-waterline reasons why people don't embrace incredibly great ideas. Look at how much initial resistance there was to people owning personal computers. That's why even Ken Olsen, the head of Digital Equipment Corporation, once said, "I can't imagine any reason for the family to have a computer in their home."

Was Olsen's attitude based on logic or sub-logic? We often have to get down to the arena of sub-logic to really understand why people are resisting change. And, by the way, why did people begin to buy computers and put them in their homes? *Because they saw little pieces of personal advantage.* They didn't buy a computer because someone told them to, but because all of a sudden they saw others gaining great benefit and they realized that they personally would have advantages for adopting this new idea.

In every change situation with groups, there are the resisters and promoters. Make sure you understand the world of the resisters and what they can do to help you in your journey.

What's the Point? Count on resisters and promoters in any change program. There are the early adopters and late joiners. Some people will fight you all the way, but with the right strategy you can transform your rebels into apostles. And you can learn a great deal from those who initially oppose you.

TAKEAWAYS

Here are some tips for bringing along your resisters through strong communication strategies. Practice these approaches as you get ready to present your next (or present) plan for change:

1. Educate people beforehand—change is about information! Get as much to the right people beforehand. Show the costs and benefits. Let them know that this is not being attempted lightly without forethought.

2. *Have town meetings with all key stakeholders before and during the process of change.*

3. *Write memos and reports to keep people informed.*

4. *Produce videos, in-house web sites, and PowerPoint presentations on the major themes of the change process and the progress to date.*

5. *Involve potential resisters in the change team that is directing the change efforts; participation often leads to commitment, not just compliance.*

6. *In some cases, management will need to enter into negotiation and agreements, including incentives for rewarding people as they adopt changes.*

7. *Ask how those involved would like to be kept informed—memos, E-mails, group meetings, teleconferences, copies of meeting minutes, sitting down over coffee, even an interactive web group.*

Remember, over-communication is a good thing. When you think you have said it enough, there is always someone who needs to hear it again.

14
The Next Big Thing

You manage things; you lead people.

Grace Murry Hopper,
Admiral in U. S. Navy (retired)

Alas, in 1960 the Horatio Alger story of Richard and Betty James turned tabloid tale. Concluding that being the Slinky King wasn't enough, Richard James left Betty to journey to Bolivia, pursuing what she describes as a spiritual quest. (He died there in 1974.) She, meanwhile, was left with the company, six kids, and a load of debt. He simply left the picture. It was Betty who rescued the toy and carried the company until her retirement in the late 1990s.

When Richard first came up with his odd little toy, perhaps Betty ridiculed the idea as an off-the-wall waste of time. We don't know if she was an early adopter. But in the end Betty saved Slinky. When Richard left her alone with the company, she sold the Philadelphia factory and moved the operation to the small, western Pennsylvania town of Hollidaysburg.

She steered its comeback with co-op advertising and a simple jingle that remains lodged in the brains of Baby Boomers everywhere. There have been few other changes. The prototype blue-black Swedish steel was replaced with less expensive, silvery American metal; later a plastic model was added. An original 1944 vintage blue-black Slinky is worth one hundred dollars today! Over three million miles of steel wire have gone into making Slinkys since 1945.

Betty James, now in her eighties, sold the company to Poof Products in 1998. And business is as good as ever, thanks in part to a strong supporting role for the Slinky Dog in 1996's movie *Toy Story*. This was not, however, Slinky's big-screen premiere; the toy claimed a cameo in John Waters' *Hairspray* and an even more memorable role in Jim Carrey's *Ace Ventura: When Nature Calls*. It also appeared in *Demolition Man*, *Other People's Money*, and *The Pink Panther*. On the small screen it has been seen in *Law and Order*, *Wings*, *Happy Days*, *St. Elsewhere*, and *Spin City*. It is so deeply engrained in our culture now that not only is a $130 gold version available (by mail order) but also, according to a recent survey, 90 percent of Americans know what a Slinky is.

As crucial as he was to its development, Richard James was only the early pioneer. It took a faithful and enterprising late-bloomer like his wife, Betty, to keep Slinky alive and thriving for the future.

I have a colleague working close with me who is a daily delight (every leader needs a few of these). I am sure if I said to Bruce, "Let's go jump off that mountain," he would be very open to the idea. I have never floated an idea that I felt he shot down. He is the essence of an early adopter. He loves change. Don't get me wrong; he is not passive nor indifferent. He is a man of convictions. But he also is built to love the Next Big Thing. He is my go-to guy for change. He never met a cool idea he didn't at least consider.

Then there is another person who I will not name, who provokes in me the opposite reaction. I am reluctant to even talk to him about my ideas, because I just get the sense that he will be against them. If it is new, forget it. "Everything is fine"; "It ain't broke," etc. It seems to me that he never met a new idea that he actually let into the front door.

You can guess who I enjoy being around. And you know who I enlist first in my personal or corporate campaigns for change.

We're All on the Curve Somewhere

Some people love to get on the bandwagon early; they jump on every new idea like a hungry dog on a juicy bone. They are out waiting for the NBT, the *next big thing*. Other individuals—just as valuable in the long run—take the wait-and-see approach. Both are essential and part of the equation for successful change. Between those two extremes lie a host of other players with varying degrees of buy-in to new ideas. Check out "The Buy-In" curve, which is based on recent research.

THE "BUY-IN" CURVE

1. "YES!" These are the *inventors and innovators*. They see the future first: 6 percent.

2. "I'm willing to be convinced." These are the *early adopters*. They are ready to jump on the bandwagon right away: 10 percent.

3. "I'll do a gradual buy-in." These are the *early majority*. They follow the crowd when it seems like the right direction to go: 34 percent.

4. "I'm somewhat reluctant." These are the *late bloomers*. Once the idea has been mapped out and proven in early beta tests, they are willing to get on board. They are often your valuable process people who want lots of data: 34 percent.

5. "Over my dead body!" These are the *laggards and holdouts*. They may never get on the program for a new order of things: 16 percent.[1]

THE "INVENTORS AND INNOVATORS" TO "LAGGARDS AND HOLDOUTS" CONTINUUM

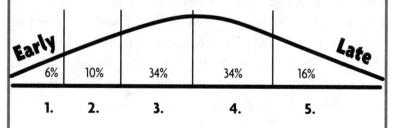

Early				Late
6%	10%	34%	34%	16%
1.	**2.**	**3.**	**4.**	**5.**

SOURCE: Everett Rodges, *The Diffusion of Innovations* (New York: Free Press, 1997), n.p.

Every organization has its share of laggards and hold-outs. Many become involved in keeping things the way they are. They have a set view of reality and tend to stay in predictable ruts on how things are done.

When we begin to talk about changes, the early adopters will gladly get on board. They are the kind of people who are open to change and become your cheerleaders because you are the champion of change.

However, just because someone says he or she is on board with the change process doesn't mean the person truly is. Often I will sit in a meeting where talk will center on what we are going to do differently; then everyone goes out and subconsciously continues to operate under the old scheme of things. Amazing. Like those wagon wheels that fell into the well-grooved ruts on the Oregon Trail, we always go back to our natural normal pattern of doing things.

A Strategy for All Kinds

So what do we do with the people who fall at various places on the adopter continuum? Actually you have all kinds in your midst; the key is to identify them and then work with them accordingly. Build your change strategy on those that can help you the most, and try to be gracious to the rest.

Here are strategies for dealing with the big five players in the change game:

- *Inventors and innovators.* Build on them. They are the foundation for your inner circle of change. They are the idea bank that you harvest for your change strategies. They help you cook up the future.

- *Early adopters.* These are the first to get on board. Treat them well and care for them, because they are going to be there for you when you need them.

- *Early majority.* Be patient with the silent majority. There is nothing wrong with following the crowd. This is the great majority of your people who support change once they have been convinced and, more importantly, when they see that others have gone before them.

- *Late bloomers.* Don't burn your bridges with these who will hopefully come along in the long run.

- *Laggards and holdouts.* I have to be careful here, but most are relics of yesterday who tend to love life with their heads in the sand, away from the action. At times we need to ask them to get off the bus.[2] Tom Peters and radical change proponents like him suggest that you fire these 16 percent that never get on board with you. Brutal but worth considering. Sometimes housekeeping has to be done—even a family member or a close friend might have to go.

A word of caution about the last group is needed. I have seen some groups hamstrung by vocal holdouts. Churches are sometimes the worst in this regard, because pastors are too kind to deal with the people who are being human roadblocks. I have a pastor friend who told me of three families that have held his church hostage with their continual resistance. No one has had the courage to stand up to them for years . . . so by resistance they run the church. They keep the church entangled in the cobwebs of the past.

Many organizations have these informal gatekeepers that tie the group to the past and powerfully resist any attempts to radically change things.

Do you run from conflict like a cat from a bath? Some of us as leaders have an incredible temptation to keep peace at any price. That is leadership at the lowest common denominator. If we are only willing to take actions when everyone can agree . . . we will never bring about change. We cannot let a vocal few hold us hostage! Work with the early adopters and help bring the others along, but never allow yourself to be held hostage to that final group that refuses to budge at any price.

What's the Point? This is similar to the chapter on resisters and promoters, but goes into more depth about the five different responses to radical change. Don't persecute people for not jumping on every NBT. Give them time and move with the movers. You eventually need the majority to move your organization forward as you build consensus and alignment. Finally, don't allow the "holdouts" to paralyze you from action.

TAKEAWAYS

1. Where are you on the adoption continuum? List some of the change initiatives in your organization where you responded as an early adopter. Now how about proposals that you resisted early on but they became the NBT? What can you learn for yourself about adoption from those experiences?

2. Here is a bold suggestion. Make a list of all the key players in your group. Now sort them on the continuum of the five major reactions to change ideas. It is especially important for you to recognize who are your key allies who can be counted on to go boldly with you into the future. Spend the bulk of your energy working with them as you build your change coalition.

3. Identify the inventors and innovators and the laggards and holdouts. Use each group to develop and refine your change ideas and the process. The inventors/innovators will help grow the idea and get the wagon rolling for others to join. The laggards/holdouts can force you to seriously consider issues you may have overlooked (blind spots). Look for the gems of wisdom in their reluctance/resistance. They may never become enthusiastic drum-beating proponents, but your change can be made better from their input. If you can win their support, so much the better for the organization.

4. There may come a point where conflict is unavoidable. The issue must be forced and the laggard/holdout must choose to join in the change or follow somewhere else. As a leader, are you sufficiently committed to the changes to ask someone in your organization to leave? Are you prepared for the resulting fallout of terminating the relationship of an "old faithful" who cannot let go of the past to move into the new tomorrow?

15

Don't Forget Your FAQs!

He that won't be counselled
can't be helped.

Benjamin Franklin

Most in the business world know two abbreviations for dispensing information and acting as soon as possible: FYI and ASAP. Thanks to ever-growing influence of the Internet, we can add a third: FAQ. Most of the computer-literate world recognizes this final abbreviation as the place for answers to common questions; more precisely, Frequently Asked Questions.

FAQs have always held a warm place in my heart—whether asked and answered on the Internet or at the office. In fact, FAQs are a bit of a secret weapon of mine.

I have the kind of personality that leads to making

decisions based on logic. I think things through, come to my conclusions, and then expedite. I have what is called the typical CEO personality: hard driving, results-oriented, logical, inspirational, and driven to creativity and change. Yes, I am a proverbial High "D." The "D" stands for dominant.

For all the strengths this entails, this also means I have a tendency to run over people who fall into the "follower" category. I tend to make decisions without truly thinking how the so-called rank and file will feel about my decisions.

That's where FAQs come in. Part of what I have learned about unveiling change programs is the importance of forcing myself to think through how people will react. That may sound like a no-brainer, but for some of us leaders, especially those with personalities like mine, such basic logic does not come naturally. We figure if it's logical and right, people will just have to accept it. But there is the softer side of change. Sub-logic is a powerful force I have learned to reckon with.

Anticipating the Common Questions

One way to squeeze my headstrong perspective into "someone else's moccasins" is to formulate Frequently Asked Questions—even before they're asked. At our organization, every launch of a new effort which clashes with the status quo begins with a group of leaders sitting down and going through the process of creating its FAQs. It never fails to amaze me how many questions we can come up with. In one recent change, we came up with thirty-five questions along with their answers that people were sure to ask.

Part of this is motivated by a desire to head off objections at the pass. We anticipate the questions so that we can roll out our defensive responses prior to the change itself.

But that is far from the whole reason for the exercise. In fact, it may be the least profitable. Those questions that make our FAQ list alter our own planning in the first place. It helps us think altogether differently—carefully anticipating how people will respond. What will be their spin? What motives will they read into the leadership? One recent change we implemented blew up in our faces because we failed to field test the idea with real live users. We should have FAQ'd!

At times, the demands of FAQ drafting have led us to involve various stakeholders in the process firsthand. After all, *the more people who give you an initial impression of how a change will come across, the better you'll fare.* This move has invariably resulted in our changing the proposal altogether.

FAQs in Action

I watched this firsthand at our high school recently. As my son Jeremy entered his final weeks before graduation, the principal decided it was time to change the procedures surrounding the senior prom and graduation exercises. He was tampering with the whole process of guiding the seniors through the final stages of high school.

Now, our principal is a smart leader. Before he met with all of us parents, he ran through some of the proposed changes with a group of parents who serve as his regular sounding board. Then he called a special, required meeting of all graduating seniors and their parents.

Once he had things adjusted right, and had taken into account the needs of the parents, he called all parties together for an assembly to roll out the new graduation procedures. Instead of alienating parents by simply writing us and informing us of the final changes, he carefully explained point by point with PowerPoint, giving ample opportunity for questions. He gained all manner of goodwill and defused criticism with a clear communication strategy. It was obvious to me that he had done his homework and had come up with his own personal set of FAQs before the rollout. Well done!

Investing in the brain work of thinking through frequently asked questions is well worth the effort. It will save you a lot of backpedaling and embarrassment down the road of change.

What's the Point? You need to make your FAQs a part of any change rollout in your organization, be it major or minor. Think through how people are going to react. Put yourself in their shoes. Try to anticipate their questions. This is the necessary homework for all successful change. It will sharpen your defenses, smooth your rollout, and best of all, force you to think through the implications of what you're about to do.

TAKEAWAYS

The application to this chapter should be obvious. Before you try to sell a group on changes:

1. Make a list of the possible questions they might have.

2. Write your answers. The best way to do this is with the leadership group that is responsible for rolling out the change.

3. Show the list to a few people who will be affected and see how they react.

4. Ask them what other questions they have that you did not include.

Try these four actions the next time you are planning for change.

Advance the Plan With Courage and Tenacity

1. ACCEPT

2. AIM

3. ANTICIPATE

4. ATTACK!

Sooner or later it's time to step up with bold leadership. As Ken Blanchard notes in *The Heart of a Leader,* "Good thoughts in your head not delivered, mean squat!"

Whether you are a follower or a leader, there comes a time when some aggressiveness has to appear. We can't allow a few to hold hostage the many. That resembles a bus with one accelerator and fifty brake pedals. Don't allow a handful of resisters to hold off an army of revolutionaries who support your ideas.

In this section we are going to look at the launch phase. After you have accepted change, thought about the future and what you would like to see different, and anticipated allies and resistance, it is time to act. In the words of Ross Perot, "If you see a snake, just kill it. Don't appoint a committee on snakes."[1]

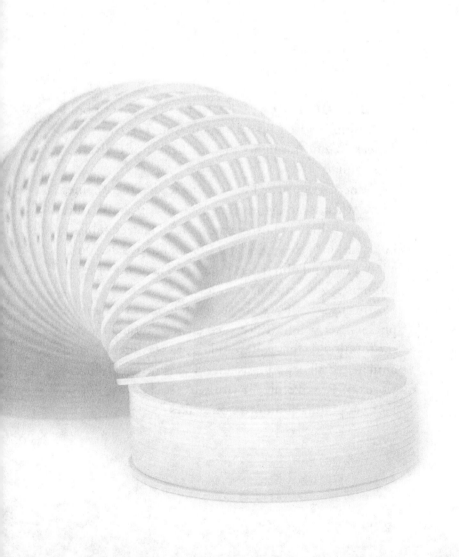

16
Launch with Courage

Take time to deliberate, but when the time for action has arrived, stop thinking and go in.

Napoleon Bonaparte

In the thirteenth century, Sir William Wallace, hero of Scotland and true patriot, desired peace and freedom by uniting the clans of his country. He gained the loyalty of the people, struck fear into his enemies, and defied the cruel hand of an evil, warring, and invading king: Edward "Longshanks" Plantagenet I of England. Never heard of William Wallace? Well, you probably do know an actor by the name of Mel Gibson who portrayed Wallace. Gibson's movie and direction landed the best picture and best director Academy Awards in 1995 for the movie named after William Wallace: *Braveheart*.

As the second son of a minor Scottish laird (lord), William Wallace seemed an unlikely candidate for the label "hero." He was pointing toward being a clergyman, a common path for second-born sons in thirteenth-century Scotland. His older brother would inherit what little wealth the Wallace family had; William would be a priest.

Yet Wallace's stature soon would command attention and a following; he stood 6 feet 7 inches at a time when his peers averaged less than six feet.[1] At age twenty, after English invaders had already killed his father and older brother, his passions stirred. At the abbey, William learned about the "idea" of freedom in a poem that today is part of the Wallace monument in Stirling, Scotland:

> Freedom is best I tell thee
> Of all things to be won
> Then never live within the bond
> Of slavery my son.[2]

Wallace's rage grew as he watched English efforts to control the region. Eventually he acted. As one historical account noted:

> Longshanks had required a mere six years to crush Wales. Wallace would see to it that his Scotland would not be completely subjected as Wales had been. But his efforts would result in a trial that was a gross judicial sham. And in his efforts to "legally" crush Wallace, Edward I created a Scottish martyr whose heroism is still honored seven hundred years later.[3]

The Marks of True Warriors

"Braveheart" did not just taunt the enemy with a war dance. He was a man of deed. The war dance was a ritual dance around the campfire by American Indian warriors before riding off to battle; it became an integral part of mustering the courage to risk their lives. Occasionally, though, a young, untested brave enjoyed the chest-beating machismo of the dance, and the relative safety of the fire circle, more than the actual departure. And he delayed that departure.

This metaphor offers us a potent and very helpful question to ask ourselves at any point of the change-making process. *Is this war, or is it the war dance? Is it the real thing, or is it just the chest beating that precedes the real thing? Are we going to actually get around to using live ammunition?*

In his speech, "The Man in the Arena," given at the French Sorbonne in 1910, Theodore Roosevelt said of moving on to the real thing:

It is not the critic who counts, not the man who points out how the strong man stumbled, or where the doer of deeds could have done better. The credit belongs to the man who is actually in the arena; whose face is marred by the dust and sweat and blood; who strives valiantly; who errs and comes short again and again; who knows the great enthusiasms, the great devotions and spends himself in a worthy course; who at the best, knows in the end the triumph of high achievement, and who, at worst, if he fails, at least fails while daring greatly; so that his place shall never be with those cold and timid souls who know neither victory or defeat.[4]

The true danger is in losing the ability to discern the difference between achieving in the arena and posturing in the war dance. I can't count the number of folks I've met who've mistaken the war dance for the war. They never actually developed the ability to jump on a horse and ride off to the fray. Instead, they spent their whole lives beating their chests and mistaking preliminaries for the real thing.

My own closest brush with the war dance came in my decision to marry. Before I finally got up the courage to ask Donna to marry me, I pondered the decision long and hard. I knew it would be great to have a life mate, and that I was deeply in love. But I also knew that married life would bring huge changes to the independent world I enjoyed as a twenty-three-year-old.

We danced the dance around the issue for awhile. And one day, I just knew it. It was time to *act*. Thank God I did—or I would have missed out on one of His highest blessings in my life.

Sooner or later all great plans amount to nothing without flipping the decision switch and going into action.

Telling the Dance from the War

As part of our change plan at CBI, we hired a consultant to give us a SWOT analysis of where we stood at that moment in history. It was part of our preparation for action—a necessary part of the war dance.

You may have heard of SWOT analysis. It stands for

"Strengths, Weaknesses, Opportunities, Threats." The exhaustive breakdown gave us a complete and objective picture of where we stood.

What did we do with our SWOT? First, the board of directors had to have assurance that we would not destroy the ship in the process. But once we as the leadership team had that in hand, it was time to act. After six months of pondering, we flipped the switch. We implemented a major reorganization. We put our money where our mouth was.

First, we immediately set aside $25,000 as a seed fund for change. Not a lot for big corporations, but for us as a nonprofit, that was a sizable chunk. We restructured the international headquarters staff, so that I had one of my brightest stars released to be our full-time vice president of organizational change. Then we organized a change team of major stakeholders to drive the process forward.

In other words, despite much careful preplanning, and some requisite war dancing, we actually went to war.

I heard someone put it this way: "Plans are nice . . . but money talks." Talk is cheap. Many organizations are long on talk. But show me your budget—how you spend your discretionary money—and I will show you your real priorities.

Here's another handy measuring stick. Who are your hotshot people, and where are they working? That's also your real priority. Regardless of the intentions expressed in the strategic plan, where you put your key people and money is the direction in which your organization is going to move. Back your new tomorrow with money and people, or else your plan will be consigned to the shredder.

DO YOU EXPERIENCE SLINKY PARALYSIS?

Did you ever suffer from Slinky Paralysis? The tendency to crouch at the top of the stairs before a ready Slinky and become so obsessed with launching it perfectly that you never actually flipped it over?

Once or twice, I remember struggling with this ailment. I wanted so desperately to have a smooth, unobstructed, floor-reaching trajectory, exactly like the one on the TV commercial, that I could not bring myself to flip mine over and give myself over to fate.

Eventually the hesitation would drag on so long that another toy or situation would pull me away. Later that day someone would complain about the Slinky sitting forlorn at the top of the stairs, and I would be reminded of my defeat.

OK, so maybe I am pushing the imagery a bit here. But there is no denying the fact that it takes action to make things change. No method, however clever, can hide the fact that it takes massive determination to drive the change process forward. "Nothing worthwhile can be accomplished without determination," wrote Admiral Hyman Rickover, father of the modern nuclear submarine fleet. "In the early days of nuclear power, for example, getting approval to build the first nuclear submarine the Nautilus was almost as difficult as designing and building it. Good ideas are not adopted automatically. They must be driven into practice with courageous patience."[5]

Ray Kroc, founder of McDonald's, had a favorite saying about persistence. The message, first spoken by

President Calvin Coolidge, adorned not only the wall of Kroc's office but the executive offices of every McDonald's headquarters. Today, it has become a classic—a worthy one. You may have read it already; I repeat it here for its undiminished value.

> Nothing in the world can take the place of persistence. Talent will not; nothing is more common than unsuccessful men with great talent. Genius will not; unrewarded genius is almost a proverb. Education will not; the world is full of educated derelicts. Persistence, determination alone are omnipotent.[6]

The Preeminence of Passion

Courage is rooted in passion. How strong is your passion factor? It will make or break your holy war of change. In his book, *Organizing Genius*, Warren Bennis analyzes great groups. Using illustrations like Apple Computer and the Walt Disney Company, and even the Manhattan Project, he emphasizes how much *passion* plays a role in change.

> Great groups are engaged in holy wars. The psychology of these high-minded missions is clear. People know going in that they will be expected to make sacrifices, but they also know they are doing the monumental, something worthy of their best selves. When you are frantically writing computer code, fueled by Coke and pizza, you don't wonder whether your work is meaningful. You are fully engaged, absorbed by the problem, lost in the task. But people in great groups are different from those

who spend countless hours enthralled to video games or other trivial pursuits. Their clear, collective purpose makes everything they do seem meaningful and valuable. A powerful enough vision can transform what would otherwise be lost in drudgery into sacrifice.[7]

Bennis goes on to explain that leaders of great groups recruit people for crusades, not jobs. Are you able to frame your change proposal in terms of a crusade? I hope so. Hopefully, the work of your organization has much merit, fights some worthy adversary, and leaves a legacy capable of being woven into the language of crusade.

If you wonder whether you have the courage to lead a charge for your organization, consider this poem on the subject of risk.

THE DILEMMA

To laugh is to risk appearing a fool.
To weep is to risk appearing sentimental.
To reach out for another is to risk involvement.
To expose feelings is to risk rejections.
To place your dreams before the crowd is to risk ridicule.
To love is to risk not being loved in return.
To go forward in the face of overwhelming odds is to risk failure.
But risks must be taken because the greatest hazard in life is to risk nothing. The person who risks nothing does nothing, has nothing, is nothing.
He may avoid suffering and sorrow, but he cannot learn, feel, change, grow, or love.

Chained by his certitudes, he is a slave.
Only a person who takes risks is free.[8]
Anonymous

What's the Point? Sooner or later it is time to act. There is no substitute for courage in that moment that you flip the switch of change. Courage will need to be the fuel of your risk taking as you act on your plan.

TAKEAWAYS

Do you consider yourself a courageous person? Are you a risk-taker? How about your allies? Can you build a team of courage with some of your colleagues? To help you answer those questions, respond to the following projects and questions:

1. Make a list of some of your bold ideas that you have already thought of in previous chapters and have a passion about. What is to keep you from moving from the dance to the act of implementation?

2. What are the "war dance" behaviors of your organization? What are the early warning signs or signals of your patterns of circling the fire of change?

3. Is there an individual who consistently recommends waiting, preferring nonaction?

4. Is there a policy or established procedure that holds you back, slows you down? Does the system keep the dance going, sticking speed bumps in the highway of change? What can be done to remove them?

5. Understanding the need for research and thinking through an issue, is it now time to act? If not now, when?

17

Communicate, Communicate, Communicate!

Communication pathways are the veins and arteries of new ideas.

James M. Kouzes and Barry Z. Posner in The Leadership Challenge

Face it—it's just sixty-three feet of coiled wire. The first toy magnates to witness the rocket rise of this amateur, simple product must have smacked themselves on the foreheads and exclaimed, "I could have made that! Why didn't I think of that?"

And, as usual, they would have missed the point. That's because it wasn't the product alone that propelled the Slinky's remarkable rise to popularity. No, the true secret weapon was the lady whom I highlighted in earlier chapters: Betty James.

Betty not only visualized a marketable product in her

husband's strange workplace experience. She also made the product successful with some shrewd planning in a field her engineer husband probably found alien: communication.

Fresh on the heels of their toy idea, Betty began to scour the dictionary for a name. Like any homegrown marketing genius, she realized that a toy as simple and obvious as theirs should have a catchy name. That's when she ran across the Swedish term "Slinky," defined as "stealthy, sleek, and sinuous."

Can you imagine the toy without the name? I can't either. That's because without the name, the toy would probably not exist.

That's not the end of Mrs. James's forays into communications strategy. The multitalented Mrs. James also saw to the development of the Slinky Song, one of the most popular and beloved songs in advertising history. (You can listen to the song at the company web site: www.pooftoys.com.)[1]

The moral of the story? When you have a formidable challenge ahead in selling your view of something—such as convincing the world that five feet of coiled wire is actually now a $2.99 toy packed with a lifetime of entertainment and dozens of mind-boggling uses—you have got to communicate, communicate, communicate!

The Submerged Giant

An old farmer once said, "Go slow. People are a lot like horses. They don't like to be startled or surprised. It causes deviant behavior."

You can almost picture the weathered face of the man

saying that, can't you? Probably chuckling sagely at the thought of that vicious kick he took from an old mare he once startled.

And as many old-timers are, he was right. When you talk to people about change, you have to look below the waterline. Both the conscious and the subconscious are simultaneously at work in people's minds and hearts—and it's the one you don't see that will rear up and kick you.

I recently spent considerable time with a particular employee to share with him some of the major changes going on in the organization and how they would affect him. I knew it would be a delicate conversation, because these changes involved moving him to a totally different place in the organization. I knew that many circumstances surrounding the decision would make it difficult. He felt that he was being demoted.

During this meeting I spent over an hour trying to carefully explain to this employee what the decisions were and why they were made. I allowed plenty of time for feedback and conversation. When I finished and the conversation was over, I was surprised at his reaction. He took it very well—very calmly, almost stoically. I remember thinking to myself, *This doesn't add up.*

In fact, I was so bewildered that I told the person to go home and think about it—that I wanted to meet him again in a couple of days. I was convinced that a whole minefield of issues lay under the waterline; issues that would sooner or later erupt and explode to the surface.

No, the person assured me, it was fine. It all made sense. "No problem."

But sadly, I was right. The man went home that night

and barely slept. Sure enough, issues exploded onto the surface within twenty-four hours. He later told me that he wandered the streets of his neighborhood at 3 A.M. that next morning, upset about what I had shared with him.

We did have the follow-up meeting, where we finally got to the real issues at hand. I learned again a valuable lesson from that episode. Don't assume people are going to take what you tell them at face value. They have a sub-conscious, which they usually don't even realize they are dealing with. Once they think things through, then the implications and ramifications begin to dawn on them. If they are married, they will go home and process it with their spouse, who will have a whole different spin on the event.

During such times . . .

A LEADER IGNORES "BELOW THE WATER-LINE" ISSUES AT HIS OR HER OWN PERIL.

What would have happened if I had never had the follow-up meeting? I would have wrongly concluded that everything was fine . . . and an explosion would have occurred down the road.

In retrospect, it was important that I got back to the person and allowed him to go through another layer of processing. In fact, since that time, we have had numerous discussions, as I have tried to help him on the journey of accepting the change. He is coming along well *after a lot of communication has taken place.*

Leaders have to be there for their followers to help them process decisions. It's part of the good, hard work of implementing change. As change guru John Kotter says,

> Without credible communication, and a lot of it, employee's (and follower's) hearts and minds are never captured. Repeat, repeat, repeat: The most carefully crafted messages rarely sink deeply into the recipients' consciousness after only one pronouncement. Our minds are too cluttered and any communication has to fight hundreds of other ideas for attention. In addition, a single airing won't address all the questions we have. As a result, effective information transferal almost always relies on repetition.[2]

What to Communicate

Never assume that anyone knows anything. We cannot overcommunicate, so what exactly should we be talking up during times of intense change? And what kind of communication should we foster between different teammates during the process? Here are six basics:

- *Big Vision.* Be able to articulate the grand vision in one minute. People have to be constantly reminded about the dream: "Tell us again, where are we going?" In Donna's business, they are trained to give the vision of their product in thirty seconds! In some cases that is all the attention span you may have from listeners.

- *Concrete Plans.* Most people hate surprises. The more they know about plans that will affect them, the better. My leaders give constant updates on the progress of our Change Team (and on the projects groups working on chunks of the change process).

- *Tiny Details.* The smallest change can set people off, like a married couple whose argument ignites over something as small as where Bill drops his socks. Again, the more they know, the better. As much as possible, no surprises.

- *Legitimize Doubt.* It is OK to doubt; go toward the natural doubt that will linger in your people's minds. Don't run from it or deny that it is there. Speak to it and allow it to be verbalized.

- *Legitimize Grief.* It is OK to grieve the loss of the old way. It is human nature for people to react to change with a personal sense of loss. To move forward, we have to allow those feelings to exist. People need a chance to mourn by talking freely about their loss to their leaders and to fellow teammates.

- *Legitimize Questions.* It is OK to question; it's only natural for people to examine your motives and your methods. Allow it. Indeed, welcome it. Be vulnerable and transparent and allow the questions to flow. I have an ironclad commitment to answer every question (they usually come via E-mail) personally and thoroughly. It sends a healthy signal to those who work with you.

We have too many meetings but too little effective communication. For that reason,

NEVER ASSUME ANYONE KNOWS ANYTHING.

Once is not enough. Communication has to take place over and over and over again. Communication happens when the person has finally heard what you have tried to get across . . . not simply when you have opened your mouth and spoken. In fact, communication truly takes place when your heart has connected with the heart of the listener. This isn't to say he or she is going to necessar-ily accept and agree with you. It means that communication has taken place when you have been truly understood on every level. That usually takes several cycles of communication. Be available to communicate with key stakeholders in the processes of change.

REAL COMMUNICATION

Communication takes place when the person has finally heard what you have tried to get across and can repeat back to you, in his or her own words, what you have said.

What's the Point? Be available to communicate with key stakeholders in the processes of change. We have too many meetings but too little effective communication. Never assume that anyone knows anything. Communication has to take place over and over and over again. Communication takes place when the person has finally understood what you have tried to get across as he or she now repeats what you said back to you and to others.

TAKEAWAYS

Learn to sharpen your own communication strategies. Most of us undercommunicate by a factor of ten. Try some of these suggestions:

- *Assume that people do not really understand where you are heading as a change agent. Assume that they have not gotten it. Repeat it in different settings and from different angles.*
- *Make sure you meet face-to-face with key decision makers and give them time to just talk. Don't program every minute. Troll for issues under the waterline.*
- *Communicate in writing with newsletters, E-mails, and postal mail about what you are planning/thinking.*
- *If you are trying to influence the leaders in your group, be gracious and yet doggedly determined to keep communicating your dreams.*
- *List how many different ways you can communicate your changes.*
- *Determine and enlist anyone who can help in getting out the message.*
- *Think in terms of word pictures and stories. How can the goals of change be presented in the form of story? How can the goals of change be presented in the form of pictures? Word pictures?*

Patrick Lencioni offers four disciplines for "making any organization world class."[3] Try to practice these disciplines:

1. Build & maintain a cohesive leadership team. Do so by:
   (a) knowing one another's unique strengths & weaknesses,
   (b) openly engaging in constructive ideological conflict,
   (c) holding one another accountable for behaviors and actions, and
   (d) committing to group decisions.
2. Create organizational clarity. Do so by answering these questions:
   (a) Why do we exist?
   (b) Behavioral values?
   (c) What specific biz are we in
   (d) Plans? Achieve what?
   (e) Who is responsible for what?
   (f) What goals? Month, quarter, year, next year, 5 yr.?
3. Overcommunicate organizational clarity.
   (a) Repeat. Repeat. Repeat again the vision, values, plans, and goals.
   (b) When asked, how do employees answer?
4. Reinforce organizational clarity through human systems.

Finally, read these books: *Managing by Storying Around,* by David Armstrong, and *The Story Factor,* by Annette Simmons.[4]

18
Think 1-3-5

Are you fast enough and slow enough to work in what David Allen calls "weird time"?

Fast Company *magazine*

As a boy, I rarely set out to play Slinky intentionally on any given afternoon after school—beyond the first day I took it home. No, playing Slinky was always a secondary or tertiary activity. By its very nature it's a spontaneous toy. It was an unscheduled pastime I landed on by accident, after first pledging to do something responsible, like chores, then moving on to the toy chest after my mother's back was turned. (Maybe that's why I still think of Slinky with that carefree thrill of childhood—because it still carries that clandestine cachet of favorite diversions like playing hooky or planning a glorious runaway.)

Now that I bought a new batch of Slinkys, I dig one out from time to time in my home office and play with it. I especially like the oversized neon orange one. Swoosh, swoosh, swoosh. Love that sound! What a great diversion from the mundane chores of life! As an adult, I still experience this aimless, "Slinky spontaneity" as a joyous diversion. People come into my office, see the Slinky box, and without permission take it out and revert for a few moments to their own childhood. It is fun to watch.

DON'T PLAY WITH THAT SLINKY!

Playing with Slinky as an adult is silly. It is irresponsible. Life after all is working hard and getting things done. And I really love getting things done at work and at home. For instance, there's my Saturday morning routine that I'm certain I inherited from my father. In fact, I think list-making is encoded somewhere on the German DNA. I get up and make my list for the day. (To be honest, I've been working on the list all week.) And then it's time to get things done around the house. Probably a trip to Home Depot will be a highlight of my day. I love that place . . . paradise for weekend honey-do lists!

But I start with cleaning up the garage, and I get distracted with another project I'd forgotten about. One leads to the next, like a butterfly hopping flowers, and before I know it my day is gone with only a fraction of the list checked off. I did it again: overestimated, and under delivered.

Getting things done with the right timing is the challenge of every change agent. Spontaneity will not cut it.

Let's consider timing and priorities as you tackle change in your organization.

The 1-3-5 Paradigm

We usually overestimate what we can accomplish in a given year and underestimate how much change we can see happen in five years.

My organization has learned from its consultants to think in terms of one-, three-, and five-year chunks of change. What can we get done immediately this coming year? What has to take a little longer but needs to be in place in three years? Five years is a long time in today's world, but we do need some long-range vision, and that is probably as far out as we can think. By the time that day arrives, the world will have moved again . . . of course.

As a result of conducting our SWOT analysis—our major organizational assessment—we were glad to learn that we possessed seven strengths that rank as tremendous assets to our organization.

Some of those strengths are legendary. One of our notable strengths is having great people. There is no substitute for having great people . . . and good people attract good people. If you don't have good people, it's hard to attract them and vice-versa. We also learned that integrity is a great strength of our sixty-year-old organization. That was tremendously heartening, for integrity is a virtue you cannot go out and buy.

We had strengths. That was good news. The bad news was that we had twenty-three identifiable weaknesses. Twenty-three crying needs/issues! And some of them contained many subpoints under each main point.

I experienced a variety of personal reactions to the presentation. One was depression. Another was despondency. I wanted to give up. Then on a practical level, I began to consider what it would take to tackle all of these problems. Their sheer number started to overwhelm me.

Where do we begin? What do we start with? What saved us was thinking in one-, three-, and five-year increments. That's the 1-3-5 paradigm. We don't have to solve everything at once. We can ask ourselves, *What has to be accomplished first?* At our organization, that meant of the twenty-three identified weaknesses, we could ask, *Which of these do we need to tackle during the first year of change?*

We did that; we began to prioritize those issues with sticky notes. *Which can wait a few years? What do we just want to make sure we've resolved five years from now? What do we have to undertake in this coming year?* We came up with four large weaknesses/issues that needed immediate attention in the first year.

- Restructure the corporate headquarters for better accountability and span of control.
- Develop a solid proposal for a strategic planning process to present to the board of directors by year-end.
- Seek new funding sources for our change initiative under the direction of our vice president of advancement.
- Appoint a task force project team to focus on issues of recruitment of new talent into the organization.

Making it Happen

A good example of a five-year goal was our implementation of a thorough, revised worldwide strategic planning process in our organization. That will take a lot of time, a lot of training, and a lot of buy-in. It will probably take us a year just to come up with a strategic plan for the future that has the ownership of all of our stakeholders. Then it will take a good year to roll out the communication process. Implementing it down to the grassroots level in the seventy countries where we work will take added time because of the vast gaps in culture and language, not to mention proximity. So we have classified our strategic planning process as a long-range change objective, one that we intend to have fully implemented within five years.

As you can see from the preceding bullets, the one-year target sheet contained the reorganization of our corporate headquarters. It became obvious to us that we were unable to embark upon a process of change without a corporate structure that works *for* us instead of *against* us. Later we added to the immediate list a corporate name change.

One thing became certain: We would self-destruct if we tried to accomplish all these goals on the same timetable.

Change Compression and the Speed Team

Even though we have to think in chunks of time one, three, and five years out, we must nevertheless get used to a more rapid *pace* of change. Call it *change compression*.

Things change faster, and only the nimble survive.

In early 2000, Dell Computer Corporation, the world's number one computer company, set out to upgrade its world-class manufacturing infrastructure with a bold yet simple premise: "Build more systems with less inventory."

In about one hundred days, Dell conceived and implemented an approach allowing them to operate on *no more than two hours of inventory* at a time. From the time parts enter the building until the time they are put into the flow of production is two hours! Nothing collects dust on shelves. It is called *just-in-time* inventory. Now in place at Dell plants around the world, this system has already generated a 500 percent return on investment, while enabling Dell to adapt more quickly to rapidly changing technologies.[1]

Two hours of inventory!

Maybe we should be speaking one, three, or five *months* instead of years!

Are we fast enough to compete in Internet time? Can you move your project from idea to market in four months? That's the estimated time of survival in the fast-paced world of the Web, where startups nest themselves in incubators and hatcheries, soaking up talent and ideas.

WATCH OUT! RIVALS ARE READY TO RUN YOU DOWN!

Are you slow enough to worry that you're losing ground to a batch of fast companies in hot pursuit, ready to run you down? Maybe you need your very own *speed team*. I am constantly pushing our change team to be a "speed team." Urgency is one of the essential values of our change process. We do not have the luxury of years to make changes, but months at most. It usually boils down to resources. The more resources you have to devote to change, the faster you can move. To free up these resources, we appointed one of our top leaders as a full-time VP of organizational change and freed him from other responsibilities that would distract him.

Are you fast enough to set a world record in the 100-meter dash? World-class sprinters offer advice in the art of going fast, mentally as well as physically. Are you slow enough to appreciate the beauty and style that come with taking your own sweet time? Are you fast enough *and slow* enough to work in what Microsoft cofounder David Allen calls "weird time"? It's that strange balance we are all seeking between going fast and taking our time to do it right. It is sort of like what some people call "making haste slowly."

At a time when everyone has more to do than time to do it, the real trick is to maintain your focus: Think of what projects need your attention most in the immediate future and what can go on the back burner. Perhaps one good idea is to have three sets of project teams: immediate, midterm, and back burner.

What's the Point? Change projects have to be tackled with a sense of the right priorities and the right timing. Some issues are urgent and others must take longer. Don't bite off more than you can chew. As you plan your attack on the problems in your group, think 1-3-5. Determine what can be done in the coming year and what will take three to five years to turn

around. Be mindful that in some industries three and five years is an eternity too long in which the competition will consume you. Timing has to be weighed with the specific factors of your situation and external environment.

TAKEAWAYS

Make a list of all the things you have been itching to work on for change that could be described as change projects. Be thorough. Brainstorm the list with your leadership team if you have one. As a group exercise, have everyone choose their three top issues. Now sort them into three groups using the idea of one-, three-, and five-year increments. Then within each grouping number the lists in priority. Now you have the building blocks of timing for a change calendar.

19
Think Leaps, Not Tweaks!

**Incrementalism is
innovation's worst enemy.**

*Nicholas Negraponti,
Head of MIT's Media Lab*

Have you ever seen a Slinky at rest? Pretty boring object. In fact, there's no indication from the dormant stack of coils what all this amazing toy can do. Only in motion does Slinky acquire life. Without motion, it's nothing more than a small metallic pile. A postindustrial relic at best.

And the motion Slinky needs had better be fluid and consistent. A jerky stop-and-start does not produce the desired effect. Motion cannot be forced or faked. It must be 100 percent genuine and constant for the metal to keep moving.

Stop-start is just as incomplete a solution in business. Incrementalism, stop-start's organizational counterpart, is as dead as a doorknob.

Sooner or later you too will get frustrated and realize that gradual, slow evolutionary change will not cut it. It is time for revolution—not from one paradigm to another, but as a constantly evolving process.

Revolution has innately negative connotations: upheaval, unrest, displacement, even war. But when things get bad enough, everyone accepts revolution. In fact, they're accepting every minute of the day, with or without consciously assenting to it. We have to change from a planning model of the future to a preparedness model. Instead of focusing on *plans* for an unpredictable future, we build an organization that is *prepared* for anything.

WE HAVE TO BUILD CHANGE INTO THE DNA OF OUR ORGANIZATIONS.

In some ways we have to act as though we are constantly under siege, every minute of the day, from now into perpetuity. John Kotter wrote, "Too many people have been trained for and raised in a stable world, a world that for the most part, no longer exists. Too many people have been trained only to manage the current system or to make incremental shifts. They have not been shown how to provide the leadership to make bigger leaps."[1]

The Ever-Restless Auto Market

It seems lately the only time I really enjoy newspapers is when I'm on the airplane. There I actually get to read every article I want and ponder some of the things happening out in the world. I usually spot many parallels to my own organization.

On one of my recent business trip flights, I enjoyed a leisurely read of *USA Today.* The business section reported on why the automobile industry has been doing amazingly well in such a weak economy. Sales have been red-hot in many areas of the country. But one product segment has been seeing explosive growth. It's not the old standard products of the car industry, such as family or luxury sedans. Lexus, for example, has suffered an almost 30 percent decline in sales of its bread-and-butter model, the LS 400, and the other large luxury sedans. So where's the market hot?

SUVs and trucks! And combo vehicles that are part SUV, part truck, and part minivan.

Lexus is 50 percent ahead of previous years in selling SUVs. The hottest market in vehicle sales is small SUVs, then large SUVs, followed by pick-up trucks.[2] Who would have thought? Donna and I each drive an SUV.

If Lexus had rested contentedly with its past success in luxury sedans and failed to "read the tea leaves," as it were, they would be hurting badly today.

And what's even more amazing to consider is that if you're reading this book more than three years after its first publication, you're probably rolling your eyes. *SUVs. How yesterday!* you're probably telling yourself. Because the market has moved on and SUVs are yesterday's news.

If Lexus stops to congratulate itself on its prescience about SUVs, it will miss the next boat. Again, change is not a destination. It's a never-ending process.

Our organization has a new member on the board of

directors who has shown himself to be a refreshing man of change. The first refreshing fact about Bud is that he is of retirement age. He has already made his success in the corporate world and is now serving on our nonprofit board. Creativity is not in the domain of young people alone. I find people of all ages with hearts for change.

Bud joined our board recently and made an interesting observation as we embarked upon a radical program of change. He said, "Hans, we don't need to be thinking outside of the boxes, we need brand-new boxes!"

THINK OUTSIDE THE BOX, OUTSIDE THE BUBBLE . . . EVEN OUTSIDE THE GALAXY!

I thought long and hard about his statements, and I couldn't agree with him more. Sometimes we try to take the old and somehow tweak it and adjust it to make it work in the new order of things. That approach used to work, when change rolled along at a much more stately and staggered pace.

Today, however, what we really need to do is simply throw out the old altogether in order to usher in the new. *We need to think leaps, not tweaks.* In fact, "new boxes" may not even be enough. Boxes may themselves prove entirely unusable within a short period of time. We may need to start thinking outside the bubble . . . or the galaxy. We need to take the "blank sheet of paper" approach. If we didn't have this particular program or approach and started from scratch with a blank sheet of paper, what would we do? If we had the luxury of starting over, what would be our approach?

Of course, it's so much more difficult to change aging

organizations as opposed to starting brand-new ones. It is easier to bring about new life than to raise the dead. But it can be done.

Build ADHD into your organization!

I have to start this section with an apology. For those reading this chapter who have suffered from Attention Deficit Hyperactive Disorder (ADHD) or have a child suffering from this condition, there's nothing funny or lighthearted about ADHD. I know it causes untold distress to families and children. I realize that, and I would never want to be flippant about something so serious or add to anyone's pain through something I wrote.

It's only in the most superficial way that I advocate "building ADHD" into an organization. But I happen to think it's an analogy worth making.

You see, what I'm trying to say through this analogy is that a restless quest for something more, an inability to sit still and sink into the morass of the status quo, is absolutely essential today. We need to be restless, on the move in our quest for change.

In my current situation, I have become increasingly frustrated year after year. My whole leadership team agrees that we face challenges. We also agree we need to change. We even agree on what the changes will be and who will do what. Yet somehow, it seems that's where the process stops in the actual implementation. An incredibly powerful inertia stops us just at the point of progress. And what we need is the opposite of inertia: restlessness. An unwillingness, even inability, to stop.

And that's where my ADHD analogy comes in.

Planning for the future is great, but we will never change unless we actually build change processes into our DNA; unless we graft ADHD into our organizational synapses. Picture your organization's feet, shuffling and moving constantly, never at rest, never satisfied. Change is like that in today's marketplace. It can never be an objective which you reach and then sit back. Change is as relentless and demanding as your need to generate income.

Listen to these words of wisdom from James M. Kouzes and Barry Z. Posner, a couple of the great leadership thinkers of the last decades:

> Standard operating procedures are the habits of organizations. Even the loosest organizations adopt practices that become second nature. These cultural norms operate in subtle but powerful ways to box us in and restrict our thinking. These norms are especially potent barriers at times when innovation is required.[3]

As I mentioned in the last chapter, our organization decided to appoint a vice president of organizational change. This person's sole responsibility is to be the "pit bull" of change in our organization; constantly nipping at our heels to make sure we don't give up on the process. So many of us are buried in our own silos and overworked with our own tasks that we never stick our heads up out of our cubicles to act and work on the priority of change. You will never think in leaps if there is not someone around doing the thinking!

Then, of course, there's the issue of the actual expertise it takes to do the job properly. How many of us really know how to rearrange the fundamental building blocks, dismantle the old, start from scratch and build something brand-new? That is difficult for an older organization.

It's not easy—someone said that *the unlearning curve is steeper than the learning curve.* But it can be done. Any sized and aged organization can infect itself with corporate ADHD and become a restless, never-satisfied changing organism. And that's a healthy infection!

Mega Leaps and New Boxes

As we look to the future, we have to do much more than catch the "next wave." The whole "next wave" concept, branded in the eighties, smacks of incrementalism. We have to prepare for an onslaught of new waves that will never stop, and whose frequency will only increase with time. In order to survive, we have to think less about making tiny little improvements and more about mega leaps to the new way of making change a part of daily life.

This approach to problem solving is really nothing more than good old-fashioned creativity. Every time you face a great challenge, make a list of ten possible solutions, no matter how bizarre or off-the-wall they might seem. Don't stop until you have at least ten solutions. Then, work your way down that list until you've come up with something that will work. That's creativity. And make sure that some of the ideas on the list are leaps.

Don't let impatience become the enemy of change. It takes time to be creative. Sometimes the first solution is not the best. While I do believe in raw intuition and instinct, I'm not necessarily an unqualified fan of the "go with your instinct" idea. A first instinct can often be just as lousy as the next. We often go with the first idea hatched because we are busy and things need to get cleared off our desks.

Building tomorrow's boxes takes time, takes people, and is messy by its very nature. If you want to solve a problem quickly, apply the first solution that comes to mind that you believe will work. But if you want the best solution, ask others for input. Doing that immediately slows down the process, which at times is very difficult to do.

But it's usually worth it. Take another lesson from the Slinky. After its initial, enthusiastic development as a toy, other applications eventually were discovered. The Slinky has been used as an antenna by soldiers in Vietnam, as a therapy tool, and for coordination development. The possibilities are endless.

There are great rewards for those who help us build tomorrow's boxes. Not only will those who build them survive, but those who lead the way will go on to achieve levels of success completely unimagined by yesteryear's leaders.

Here is lesson one of creativity in times of change: *Think leaps, not tweaks. Take time to think of more than one solution to your problem.* Rarely is the first instinct the best.

What's the Point? If you think in increments of challenge-and-success cycles, you're dead already. Change is not a single project, with a beginning, middle, and end. It is a whole new way of looking, and reacting to, the world of today and tomorrow. Build

restlessness and dissatisfaction with the status quo into your very organizational DNA.

TAKEAWAYS

1. Identify the last time your organization went through a traditional, project-style major change. How differently would you make it today?

2. Picture, then answer for yourself: How would a vice president for organizational change fare in your organization? Are your colleagues ready for him or her?

3. Remind yourself and your organization of where and what you want to be in one, three, and five-plus years/quarters—with a focus on the dynamite project, the big dream, the inspiring vision, and the grand goal, instilling a dissatisfaction with today and a restless desire to live out those dreams.

4. At the risk of overcommunicating, tell them and then tell them again the story of the big bold future you have in mind for the organization. Then put it into print, building restlessness on one hand and heightening the desire for the new you on the other.

20
Be Sure to Issue
Flak Jackets

If I were to read, much less answer, all the attacks made on me, this shop might as well be closed for any other business. I do the very best I know how—the very best I can; and I mean to keep doing so until the end.

Abraham Lincoln

During World War II, the Germans waged serious warfare with one of their most potent weapons: their sleek, black underwater vessels of destruction called "the U-boat." (U stands for *untersse,* which is the German word for *undersea,* a typical literal German functional description.) These U-boats wreaked havoc in the Atlantic as the Allied forces attempted to close in.

The great war movie *Das Boot* illustrates the incredible

stress of life underwater for weeks on end in one of those German submarines. When the Allied Forces detected one of these underwater warriors, they began to pummel the U-boats with depth charges. For days on end the German sailors would be shaken up like gravel in a cement mixer, being pounded with explosives, rolling from side to side, mortal danger surrounding them on literally all sides.

It is hard to imagine that they lived through that kind of beating, but many did live to tell about it.

Ironically, it was just a few years after the war that an American engineer was working to develop naval instruments that retain their stability during just such turbulence when he accidentally knocked over a coiled torsion spring, saw it "walk" down the table, and . . . well, you know.

There are times during major change initiatives when criticism can get that intense, and remaining stable is a near impossibility. Beware: *Resistance will come.* And it will hurt. If you have bold plans to shake things up, you'd better strap on that army-surplus flak jacket right away.

It has been said that leaders need to have thick skin. But that's easier said than done—and actually, as I'll explain later, it's not even a desirable goal. Criticism cuts deep and hurts terribly. The cute little saying, "Sticks and stones may break my bones but words will never hurt me," is a bald-faced lie.

When we are pounded by the missiles and depth charges of friends or enemies, it has a devastating effect on our emotions. It can bring our work to a screeching halt as we ride out the barrages of the criticism. Old Abe was probably right to ignore the criticism and just do the best he could.

Coping Mechanisms: How People React to Change

People rely on one of five coping mechanisms when responding to change. The five coping mechanisms of any transition are: *hold out* (hope that the past returns), *keep out* (hunker in the bunker), *move out* (relocate and hide in nostalgic yearnings for the status quo), *close out* (toss in the towel and admit defeat), and *reach out* (change with a direction toward the future).[1]

So how do you, as a change agent, respond to these tactics?

In his book, *Post-modern Pilgrims*, Leonard Sweet wrote of a recent poll that found an astonishing 49 percent of business executives taking the most radical position they could about the future. They conclude that that we are living in revolutionary times and at the dawn of an entirely new economic era, requiring a fundamental reinvention of how we live, work, and play.

Perhaps there is one more reaction Sweet missed: *dish out*, as in dish out opposition in open hostility! Dramatic times of change require dramatic choices that will likely provoke dramatic reactions. (Though I am not recommending this.)

If people in the organization think you are fundamentally changing the values of the organization in a bad direction, they will oppose you most openly. I have had numbers of people tell me, "Well, this is not the organization that I signed up for."

What are they driving at? Simple. They feel that the changes being made are eroding what they perceive to be the organization's bedrock values dearest to them. I am messing with their culture. Their sense is that I am removing the anchors we discussed in an earlier chapter.

But they are confusing means with ends. They are turning a methods issue into a values issue.

Change will at times fail because the new directions are just too radical for the organization. Many change efforts fail because the proponents of change have underestimated the opposition.

Of course, at times proposed change may involve or impact values of the organization. As Burt Nanus points out,

> Leaders must always understand their own values as well as the values and culture prevailing in their organizations because these values determine whether a new sense of direction will be enthusiastically embraced, reluctantly accepted or rejected as inappropriate. Values and cultures are deeply rooted, persistent, and often constrain possible new directions."[2]

Protecting Your Own Skin

How do you survive the rough and tumble of change warfare? Is it by developing a thick skin?

No. In fact, developing a coarse emotional hide is the worst thing you could possibly do. Making yourself impervious to pain means shutting yourself off from most of the nuances and intricacies of life—and business. I've seen leaders become thick-hided and insulated before, and it only led to their demise. Before long, they became so well-insulated that they could not hear the whispers of common sense, interpersonal resentments, or even approaching trouble. For a leader whose greatest responsibility is to sense how the proverbial wind is blowing, that is the kiss of death.

Rather than a thick hide, the thing to develop is a resilient one. One that can absorb the blow, not deflect it. Instead of trying to develop ways of never feeling the attack, work on ways of processing it more painlessly and efficiently.

First, identify a core group of allies. These are the first people you came to with your radical idea, and who not only "got it" but asked how they could pitch in. They are the ones willing to endure with you the endless bombardments. As such, they are your allies.

When the sniping gets too hot, gather these supporters in your office, close the door for awhile, and unknot your tie. Find things about the situation that you can laugh at with them. Be irreverent, as long as it stays behind that closed door. Lower your blood pressure. Without a single friend of this kind in the organization, you're doomed. Find at least one; cultivate one, if you haven't already.

Second, try to visualize the attacker's world; what is going on in their world that leads to this type of response? Why do they feel threatened by the changes? How does the relative viciousness of the attack reflect on your foe? Ask yourself, "How would I feel if I saw things the way that person does?"

At this stage of the attack, it is imperative to listen. Play the role of an empathetic person who is trying as best as he can to put himself into the shoes of the attacker. What is going on inside the person's head? Inside his or her emotions? Leaders must develop the art of listening. As the Scripture says, "Everyone should be quick to listen, slow to speak and slow to become angry."3

Third, let the criticism make you better. If a particular attack has left you stung, don't react defensively to its message—instead, absorb the blow by going back to see if it has any merit. You'll never gain anything by denying legitimate criticism. Use criticism as a tool for improving your proposals. Then move forward with your modification. You'll have a better plan and you'll disarm your opponent.

Nothing could improve—or perhaps repair—an internal reputation faster and more thoroughly than that sort of response on your part.

Criticism helps us see our blind spots and recognize personal weaknesses. We learn to be better leaders through the process. Recently I was reminded again through a sharp personal attack, for example, that I am a conflict avoider. The attack showed me that avoidance is not an option for leaders that need to deal with problems in the organization. James says, "Consider it pure joy, my brothers, whenever you face trials of many kinds, because you know that the testing of your faith develops perseverance. Perseverance must finish its work so that you may be mature and complete, not lacking anything."4

Fourth, reshape your self-image. Enduring an attack in your role as an organizational leader hurts the most when your job determines how you see yourself. Go back to bedrock and remind yourself who you are: your parents' offspring, a person loved by God, possibly a father, mother, husband, or wife. Aren't these more meaningful and significant realities than the job you hold?

A solid grounding in who you are is the best flak jacket you could ever don during difficult times.

What's the Point? Get ready for opposition and develop coping skills as you push forward with change. Some people will not sit on the sidelines quietly but will dish out hostility to your plans and actions. Don't reject their words out of hand; let them make you better, stronger, and your proposal for change that much more coherent. Learn from your adversaries.

TAKEAWAYS

As far as your own identity, make sure that you are grounded deeper than just your job description.

- *Identify some of your anchors and values that will carry you through the tough times of change warfare.*
- *Identify and nurture your leadership change-agent team. Whether it is a formal committee or a casual group of coworkers, make sure they are on board with you in the change process. Talk often, polishing the dream.*
- *Remember, the pain of another's words often comes from the ounce of truth buried in the criticism. What can you learn about the criticizer and his or her perspective? What can you learn about yourself in developing as a leader and change-agent? How can the change process be improved as a result of the painful criticism? Often those who seem most passionately opposed to the change merely passionately want to be heard.*

Set aside the pain and fear of the opposition and listen for what can be learned.
- Go back to your journal or notes to review your own personal values and those of your organization. While you may be passionate yourself about the criticized change, you are not that change—there is much, much more to you than that; your own life, your family, your relationships and friends, your God.

And when you do face criticism:
- *Who in your life can you talk to in order to vent and get help? Make a list of the people that you can use to process the criticism fairly. Allow them the freedom of being honest with you— sometimes the criticism is fair and has grains of truth. Are you willing to hear those?*
- *Develop relationships with a few key individuals both inside and outside your organization or industry. Consult them during the turbulent times; they will be objective and provide wise counsel and perspective.*
- *How do you personally tell the difference between accurate and inaccurate criticism? What is your sifting process?*
- *What type of criticism most easily upsets you and gets under your skin? Why?*
- *Always have an E-mail cooling off period before you push the send button in your response to written criticism.*
- *There are some who seem to gain joy and satisfaction from inflicting pain with their words.*

Learn who these people are, remove them from your organization, and steer clear of them in your life. Their purpose is not to advance change in the organization, but to protect and advance themselves at the expense of others.

Adjust Course As You Listen and Learn

1. ACCEPT

2. AIM

3. ANTICIPATE

4. ATTACK!

5. ADJUST

One thing we learn quickly in the change game is never to use quick-drying concrete! In fact, don't use concrete at all. Perhaps sand is a better material to place your moorings in because you will be pulling them up and changing them again soon.

We are well on our journey of change, and it is now time to consider midcourse corrections as we listen and learn. I learned in science when I was in elementary school that for every action there is an equal and opposite reaction. This is true in the world of people working and planning together for their future. Just about the time you launch something new, an unanticipated reaction takes place. So we adjust. We live and we learn. In these chapters we consider the learning that has to go on throughout the life cycles of change.

21
Change Is Like a Box of Chocolates

Blessed are the control freaks, for they shall inhibit the earth.

Rev. Will B. Dunn, in Kudzu *comic strip*

Push the Slinky down the stairs and you never know where it will land. By the same token, launch a major change initiative and you never know what you'll end up with. It all reminds me of that movie character, Forrest Gump, sitting on the park bench, musing about his mama's "advice": "Life is like a box of chocolates; you never know what you're gonna *get!*"

The deepest wisdom is often found in the oddest places. Forrest Gump and the Slinky's trajectory both point to a lasting truth.

Their lesson? Don't try to control change. You simply

cannot. Instead, unleash it among your people like a carefully nurtured and controlled firestorm. Then, cultivate flexibility, rapid response, and excellence, and the future will take care of itself.

The Space Program and Chaos

My father learned this well as a member of the United States space program in the 1960s. Dad had the privilege of working with Werner Von Braun as part of the original group of rocket scientists who came to America after World War II. The pioneering days of the U.S. space program were a lot like a giant runaway Slinky heading down a massive set of stairs.

In the mid-1960s, after the Russians embarrassed the U.S. by launching the first satellite into orbit, President Kennedy laid down this challenge: "We will beat the Russians to the moon. And we will do it before 1970."

They asked Dr. Von Braun how they could build a missile of sufficient size and launch power to heft a lunar module out of earth's orbit and on the way to the moon. He told them that with current resources, personnel, and procedures, it would take *eight years.*

Kennedy told the rocket team that eight years wasn't fast enough. They had to do it in half that time. So Von Braun came up with an incredibly ingenious solution. Instead of remaining strapped to the bureaucratic paradigm of building a brand-new giant rocket from scratch, he "rode the chaos" and improvised. What if they could take some of their current rockets and strap the engines together into a bundle with the necessary horsepower for the desired launch vehicle?

The Saturn 5 rocket was the solution to his ingenuity. It was the biggest rocket America had ever built, before and since. And, sure enough, the U.S. did beat the Russians to the moon by landing there in the summer of 1969.

CAN YOU RECALL MANKIND'S GIANT LEAP ON ONE HOT JULY NIGHT?

I will never forget that hot July night in the summer of 1969—same summer as the infamous Woodstock music festival—when we all sat glued to our TVs to watch Neil Armstrong's "giant leap for mankind." The United States space program deserves credit for that accomplishment—one of the greatest in the history of mankind. They basically broke every rule in the book along the journey. That is particularly difficult among different government agencies and with the military, which all had to cooperate!

What's the point here? Had they been obsessed with getting things right and remaining glued to a set of pre-described rules and predetermined solutions, they would have failed. It was their out-of-the-box thinking, their fearless management of an out-of-control juggernaut, that gave them the ability to change whatever they needed in order to make solutions work. And the people in charge—an important point here—had to give them space (excuse the pun) to think creatively for the right way out. Control freaks were their worst enemy.

Years later, the National Aeronautics and Space Administration had another great example of innovation, creativity, and resourcefulness in the process of getting things done in crisis.

That happened in the early 1970s, when NASA was saved by duct tape.

DUCT TAPE STRIKES AGAIN!

If you saw the movie *Apollo 13,* you know the scenario. When an accident threatened the lives of three astronauts, a group of engineers on the ground created solutions to one of the crisis' most life-threatening episodes with the use of duct tape! They used the gray marvel to improvise a seal for air filters that did not fit—providing enough oxygen for the astronauts to make the journey home.

They didn't have time to go back to the engineering books. They didn't have time to form a committee. They had to throw their heads together and come up with a creative solution on the spot.

The heroic story of Apollo 13 was all about creativity and improvisation. If you are willing to lay aside the normal ground rules and procedures, and let people change and flex to get things done, it's amazing what can be accomplished. In this case, billions of dollars, years of painstaking planning, and the prestige of an entire nation were saved by a roll of duct tape and creative thinking.

Duct tape? $5.95. The liberated mind? Priceless.

Harvesting the Greatest Chocolates

Whenever I get a box of gourmet chocolates—See's from California is our favorite—I do what you do. I go hunting for my favorites. I like the chewy caramel ones with nuts inside. I really don't care for those fruity tasting, gooey ones. Over the years, I've developed a finely tuned "choco-radar" for the precise candy I want. I aim my finger at the box and let it find its way unerringly to the target.

Where is a person with that kind of nose for great ideas in the quest for change solutions? I'll tell you where to find him or her: among the rank and file. The people on the front lines, who do the work day-in-and-day-out, find our greatest "chocolates."

"Take away my people but leave my factories and soon grass will grow on the factory floor. Take away my factories but leave my people and soon we will have a new and better factory," observed Andrew Carnegie a long time ago. He built a great industrial empire on the belief that people are our greatest resource.

It is the job of leaders to listen and learn (more on that in chapter 23). Harvest the great ideas that are brought forth by regular folks. And it is your job, if you are not the leader, to keep pushing your ideas up the food chain until they are heard. If the people running your company think they have all the answers, it's time to find a better place to work!

In a recent *USA Today* poll, 50 percent of all employees surveyed said that their company's number one time waster was poorly-run, inadequately-focused meetings. Not long ago one of our people out in the trenches came to me with a simple solution for saving time and money along these very lines.

Why not move certain decisions down the line to where they could be made with more intelligence? One of our teams asked, "Why do you have to make these decisions at the home office when we are fully capable of handling them?"

Good point, I thought. So we rewrote the rule book (policy manual), cut it into about a fourth of its former size, and bang—things are working much better. It is amazing what people will do if you treat them like adults! These steps saved us hundreds of wasted meeting man-hours and thousands of dollars.

People are our thinkers. They are our greatest re-source. They will find the prized solution in the box of chocolates.

What's the Point?
Never assume that you know where the change process will end. You don't know and it doesn't matter, as long as you stay anchored in your core commitments. Simply stay true to your organizational values, put people first, and stay focused on flexibility in the midst of chaos. More on that in another chapter.

TAKEAWAYS

1. *Can you name something that you produce or a service you provide that you stumbled on by accident?*

2. *Can you name a solution that you came up with by accident to a big, hairy problem?*

3. *Recognize these four truths:*

- *You will not end up where you thought you would in the journey of change. Your best solutions are yet to be discovered.*

- *Followers can be as smart as leaders when it comes to creative solutions to plaguing problems.*

- *Brainstorming with everyone often leads to finding the best solutions.*

- *No idea is a stupid idea!*

22
Read the Seasons

**A company is never more vulnerable
to complacency than when
it's at the height of its success.**

*Herb Kelleher, founder and
CEO of Southwest Airlines*

Just about the time we think we are on top of the world
with everything working right—bam! We get dethroned
by the next one to come along that has figured out the
future better than we have. Just when we thought we were
in our prime, we became geriatric and the new teens
passed us by. It just isn't fair.

We all live in and around organizations. While they
are man-made, they are also living organisms. That's why
groups of people working together—organizations—
have seasons of life just like in nature. They are born,
grow, enter middle age, and eventually reach the calcifi-

cation of old age. Their milestones roughly correspond to those of our own lives: infancy, childhood, youth, adulthood, midlife, the graying years, old age, and, yes, death. Many great organizations that accomplished so much good have passed their prime.

We see them everywhere. Their past is full of great ideas, products, and services, but they are rapidly becoming irrelevant in the third millennium.

What did they do wrong? *Nothing.* That is the point. They remained static while the world changed. If you always do what you always did, you always get what you always got.

Many leaders become stuck in the proverbial ruts, remaining within organizations that boast few new ideas and new products. Places where new programs and new initiatives find a fallow field. Actually, the threshold for falling victim to complacency has fallen even below such obvious failure. Stagnation once required actual indifference and intellectual laziness to infect an organization; now it only takes a less-than-relentless commitment to the mastery of change.

Yet organizations are like organisms. As such, they need our attention and nurture so they may develop and adapt.

ORGANIZATIONS AS ORGANISMS

Organizations are organisms. They experience life cycles.

Organizational life cycles lead ultimately to death, if we don't tamper with the DNA.

We naturally evolve in man-made organizations:

From Inspiration to Institution

From Passion to Policy

From Movement to Machine

From Bravado to Bureaucracy

The Tale of Two Industries

In the book *Nuts*, we read the extraordinary story of the most successful airlines in the world. Southwest Airlines has consistently turned a profit every year for thirty years. It has one of the most unique and inspirational corporate cultures I have encountered. It refuses to grow old and institutional! In a time when the major carriers are on the brink of bankruptcy, Southwest has a creed about change that is worth replicating. It is exactly because they have built flexibility into their DNA that they have survived and thrived in a cutthroat industry. In their life cycle, they have stayed as a thriving adolescent.

Southwest Airlines has always resisted the temptation

to be something it's not. Perhaps this is because the people of Southwest Airlines know that arrogance is the quicksand of success. Herb Kelleher, who is the founder and CEO of Southwest Airlines, says repeatedly, "A company is never more vulnerable to complacency than when it's at the height of its success." He began his 1993 letter to all of his employees outlining the major threats to Southwest Airlines during the decade of the '90s by saying, "The number one threat is us!" He went on to say: "We must not let success breed complacency; cockiness; greediness; laziness; indifference; preoccupation with non-essentials; bureaucracy; hierarchy; quarrelsomeness; or obliviousness to threats posed by the outside world."[1]

Kelleher later explained how to keep a company's structure conducive to innovation and in a perpetual state of youthful enthusiasm:

"The bigger you get, the harder you must continue to fight back the bureaucracy and preserve the entrepreneurial spirit. Sure, you need more discipline and more systems, but they are adjuncts. They are not masters; they are servants. You have got to keep that entrepreneurial spirit alive in the company no matter how big it gets."

Herb Kelleher of Southwest Airlines does not put much stock in the traditional strategic planning. His concern is that writing something down in a plan makes it gospel. When the plan becomes gospel, it is easy for people to become rigid in their thinking and less open to new, perhaps off-the-wall ideas. Kelleher explains, "Reality is chaotic; planning is ordered and logical. The two don't square with one another. The meticulous nitpicking that goes on in most strategic planning processes creates a mental straitjacket that becomes disabling in an industry where things change radically from one day to the next."[2]

Then there is an opposite story, about watchmaking and ingenuity. In the 1960s, if anyone had asked the question, "In the decade of the '90s, what nation will dominate the world of watchmaking?" the answer would have been unanimous: "Why, Switzerland, of course!"

Switzerland had dominated the world of watchmaking for the past sixty years. The Swiss made the best watches in the world. Anyone who wanted a good watch, an accurate watch, bought a Swiss watch.

And the Swiss were constantly improving their watches. They had invented the minute hand and the second hand. They led the research in discovering better ways to manufacture the gears, the bearings, and the mainsprings of modern watches. They were on the cutting edge of research in waterproofing watches. They brought to market the best self-winding watches. They were constant innovators.

By 1968 they had done so well that they had more than 65 percent of the unit sales in the world watch market and more than 80 percent of the profits (some experts estimate as high as 90 percent). They were the world leaders in watchmaking by an enormous stretch. No one was even a close second.

Yet by 1990 their market share had collapsed from 65 percent to less than 10 percent. Their huge profit domination had dropped to less than 20 percent.[3] By all significant measures, they had been ignominiously dethroned as the world market leader.

WATCH OUT—PARADIGM SHIFT AHEAD!

What happened? Something profound. They had run into a *paradigm shift*—a change in the fundamental rules of watchmaking.

The old-age mechanical mechanism was about to give way to the infant of electronics. Everything the Swiss were good at—the making of gears and bearings and mainsprings—would become irrelevant to the new way.

In less than ten years, the Swiss watchmaking future, which had seemed so secure, so profitable, so dominant, had been destroyed. Between 1979 and 1981, fifty thousand of the sixty-two thousand watchmakers lost their jobs. In a nation as small as Switzerland, it was a catastrophe.

For another nation, however, it was the opportunity of a lifetime. Japan, which had less than 1 percent of the world watch market in 1968 (even though their mechanical watches were almost as good as those of the Swiss), was in the midst of developing world-class electronic technology. The electronic quartz watch was a natural derivative. Seiko led the charge, and today the Japanese and other Asian nations have well over 50 percent of the market, with an equivalent share of the profits.

The irony of this story for the Swiss is that the situation was totally avoidable if only the Swiss watch manufacturers had known how to think about their own future. If only they had known the kind of change they were facing: a paradigm shift.

It was the Swiss themselves who invented the electronic quartz movement at their research institute in Neuchâtel, Switzerland! Yet, when the Swiss researchers presented this revolutionary new idea to the Swiss manufacturers in 1967, it was rejected.

ALWAYS THINK YOUNG AND STAY FLEXIBLE.

After all, it didn't have a mainspring, it didn't need bearings, it required almost no gears, it was battery-powered, and it was electronic. *It couldn't be the watch of the future.* So sure were the manufacturers of that conclusion that they let their researchers showcase their useless invention at the World Watch Congress that year. Seiko took one look, and the rest is history.[4]

One company stays young to keep profitable and ahead of its competitors. No matter how old your group is in real years, strive to stay young at heart. Build youthfulness into the DNA of your organization. Do whatever it takes to think young and be flexible.

The cause of organizational old age is not a hardening of the arteries, but a hardening of the *categories*. I like what Henry Ford said years ago, "Anyone who stops learning is old, whether at twenty or eighty. Anyone who keeps learning stays young. The greatest thing in life is to keep your mind young."

What's the Point? Organizations go through the normal cycles of life just like people. The problem is that they tend toward midlife and then old age with passion being overtaken by policy. Inspiration is replaced with institution. We have to work at staying young by not allowing calcification to take root in our DNA.

TAKEAWAYS

1. Read magazines that push the envelope of creative thinking. Three top recommendations are Red Herring, Entrepreneur and Fast Company.

2. Think about your own group or organization or company. Answer these questions to analyze where you fit in the life cycle chart.

   a. How old is your organization in real years?
   b. Which of these states best describes your group? Why?

   - infancy
   - growing go-go years
   - adolescence
   - young adult
   - adult
   - mature/prime of life
   - aging
   - elderly
   - almost in the grave
   - decomposing

3. Usually others see us differently than we see ourselves. How do outsiders view your organization using the categories in 2b? Why?

4. What thoughts do you have after reading this chapter on how you can move toward being a more youthful, vibrant organization? What rules and policies should you abandon as part of a restrictive bureaucracy?

5. Consider other organizations in your industry in light of life cycles. Compare yourself with them. Be fair with yourself; compare like organizations. But also be brutally honest; stretch and push yourself to be ever young.

6. How open are you to doing or trying things new or different?

7. How long has it been:

a. since a new product or service was introduced by your organization?
b. that you've "always done it that way"?

8. Look at your environment and answer these questions:

a. What technology is being ignored?
b. What political events are taking place around you, demanding a new way of accomplishing your goals and vision?

23
Listening Leaders

In times of change, learners inherit the earth, while the learned find themselves beautifully equipped, to deal with a world that no longer exists.
Eric Hoffer

Let me tell you a story of an awesome opportunity missed. It starts with a beginning that by now you're quite familiar with.

Engineer Richard James accidentally knocks over a spring, and then he watches with ever-increasing amusement as the coiled wire proceeds to "walk" down his shelves in an orderly and graceful way. Then he picks up the spring and puts it back in its place.

That night, he tells his wife, Betty, about the odd behavior of his very simple object. "I think I can make a toy out of this." Remember my conjecture in an earlier chapter that she thought he was crazy? Well, that is not what happened at all. Actually, Betty, being of a non-engineer mentality, but being a wife and a mother, furrows her eyebrows, peers for awhile at the ceiling, and then shakes her head with a loud laugh.

"You know, Richard, that sounds like it would make a *great* toy!"

[Now, reader, up until now what you've just read was a reasonably faithful adaptation of what really happened. What I describe next is a what-might-have-been deviation from fact.]

Richard then lowers the radio volume on *The Shadow* and growls, "What? What are you gabbing about?"

"Richard, I'm telling you, kids would love a toy like that! And think how simple to make and cheap it could be!"

"Are you talking about that stupid spring again?"

"Yes! Would you listen to me?"

"Yeah, honey. Whatever. Stick to the kitchen, OK?"

That scenario, had it really happened, would have cost the James family of Philadelphia, Pennsylvania, untold millions of dollars, the satisfaction of owning their own business, and the applause of having created one of the most beloved toys of all time.

Fortunately, Richard James listened to his wife. Even though he heard an unusual, even farfetched idea (how many people get excited for three minutes about some product idea they never act on?), he listened.

He really listened. He listened enough to act on the suggestion.

ARE YOU LISTENING?

Leaders who fail to listen can cause a world of hurt for their followers. When the signals for change go unheeded, the captain can take the whole ship down with him. How many times have we seen this scenario repeated in recent U.S. corporate accountability scandals? If you are a leader, you must stay tuned to the outside forces that threaten you—as well as the opportunities that could make you great.

What greater story of a leader who would not listen than that of Captain Edward John Smith and the *RMS Titanic?* Edward John Smith had been a ship captain for twenty-five years when he piloted the *Titanic* in its maiden transatlantic passage. Somehow, Captain Smith did not listen solely to his boat on that crucial voyage. He ignored all kinds of data that were coming his direction. Once he was on his voyage, he never looked back and his pride seriously got in the way!

THE TITANIC MISSTEPS OF CAPTAIN SMITH

- He was blinded by his natural instincts.
- He underestimated his enemies—the icebergs.
- He overestimated his strengths—the toughness of the ship.
- He took too many risks—with his crew and his ship.
- He became reckless—pushing the ship's engine too hard.
- His pride got in the way of effective leadership.

- He took ill-advised counsel to charge ahead from the ship owner.
- He left subordinates in command at a dangerous time.
- He was overconfident of technology—the latest in ship engineering.
- He relied too much on past experience.
- He did not know his ship as well as he thought he did.
- He ignored repeated warnings of impending danger.
- He ignored the natural realities of the environment of that sea.

In times that call for change, times in which we certainly live today, leaders must be superb listeners. They must pay particular attention to those advocating new or different images of the emerging reality. Sometimes it simply takes others to see the icebergs ahead.

In their excellent book *Leaders: The Strategies for Taking Charge,* Warren Bennis and Burt Nanus note that many effective leaders establish both formal and informal channels of communication to gain access to these ideas. "Most leaders spend a substantial portion of their time interacting with advisors, consultants, other leaders, scholars, planners and a wide variety of the people both inside and outside their own organizations in this search. Successful leaders, we have found, are *great askers*, and they do pay attention."[1]

Leaders by their very nature tend to be removed from the front lines of battle in the organization. Therefore they must be quite intentional in their efforts to interact with those in the trenches. Then they must rely on that information to make wise decisions. *The greatest innovations and forward strides we will make in our calling will arise from ideas generated at the fringes of our organization. And how can we be aware of these ideas if we spend no time at the fringes?*

Leaders don't have all the answers. When it comes to the organization's future, leaders don't even know many of the questions. The answers come from those doing the work. And how will we leaders ever harvest those profound ideas if we do not listen long, hard, and often? Leaders trying to preserve the status quo close themselves off and listen only to those voices that agree with them. Learning leaders listen genuinely and relentlessly to the voices around them.

Create an Interactive Culture

The ranks of today's companies and organizations are now full of a new breed called *postmoderns*. In a great treatment of the inner workings of this new phenomenon in our culture, Leonard Sweet remarks, "Postmoderns are not simply going to transmit the tradition or the culture they have been taught. They won't take it unless they can transform it and customize it."[2]

Sweet calls postmoderns an "EPIC" culture: *experiential, participatory, image-driven,* and *connected.* This is why eBay has been such a smashing success and so addictive in our postmodern culture. Those on eBay's Internet web site can participate in an auction and feel connected even though they may be thousands of miles away from the seller; it is a unique and yet dynamic experience. The auction web site fulfills all four criteria; it is truly an EPIC company.

This concept has been a great help to the change team in our own situation at CBI. It helps us understand why postmoderns in a change environment want to be so interactive. As Sweet writes, "Postmoderns don't give their undivided attention to much of anything without it being interactive." He adds:

> It is no longer enough to possess things or to enjoy positive events. One now has to be involved in bringing those events to pass to brokering those things into the home. People want to participate in the production of content, whatever it is. One reason why democracy has triumphed around the world is partly because of its interactivity. It is the most interactive model of government ever invented, but even democracy [must] shift from representative democracy to participatory democracy if it is to survive in the future.[3]

Can you have an interactive culture in your organization without a leadership that listens? I don't think so. My experience is that postmoderns run like deer at the sight of humans from traditional top-down organizations. They greatly resist leaders who do not have the ears of the people. They run toward the new interactive organization that is a learning culture (dealt with in our next chapter) with a listening leader.

WILSON AND MAXWELL ON LISTENING LEADERS

The ear of the leader must ring with the voices of the people.

Woodrow Wilson
U.S. President

A good leader encourages followers to tell him what he needs to know, not what he wants to hear.

John Maxwell
In *The 21 Indispensable Qualities of a Leader*

What's the Point? Listening leaders are the key to organizations capable of effective change. Listen to the followers, usually at the fringes, who will actually bring the future to pass. Postmoderns demand cultures where the leaders create an interactive environment.

TAKEAWAYS

1. Think about how postmoderns are changing your organization. Thinking of Sweet's EPIC—experiential, participatory, image-driven, and connected—how are you seeing these changes in your group?

2. Would you describe your organization as inter-active or one-way in its communication flow? How can it become more interactive?

3. If you are trying to move forward with change, you must:

- be available to them,

- be accessible to them,

- be in touch with them,

- be focused on them, and

- practice your MBWA. That's management by wandering around, as in getting out regularly among the people (first coined by Tom Peters and Robert Waterman in their classic In Search of Excellence).

4. What formal and informal listening tools do you have in place in your organization? These may in-clude:

- suggestion boxes

- E-mail

- group meetings

- town-hall meetings

- discussions with the president

- roundtable forums

- pizza parties

5. When was the last time you actually did some-thing with what was told to you? Listening implies a response—how have you been responding?

6. Are your coworkers/followers eager to speak with you regarding a new idea or has it been a long time since someone asked you to listen?

7. How are those in your organization acknowledged or rewarded for their suggestions, ideas, concerns, and warnings?

- dismissed

- ignored

- rebuked

- scorned

- praised

- brought in for more discussion

- promoted

- given bonuses

- given raises

- ridiculed

- honored

- given a juicy, exciting project or assignment

- given the leftover assignments that no one wants

24
Learn, Unlearn, and Relearn

> The illiterate of the 21st century
> will not be those who cannot
> read and write, but those who
> cannot learn, unlearn, and relearn.
>
> *Alvin Toffler*

Whether it's Richard James, his wife Betty, or someone else, it's clear that someone has been keeping their eyes and ears open at Poof Products, the current owner of Slinky. The simple five-foot length of coiled wire has done a remarkable job of remaining relevant and vital in its over half-century of existence. One glance at the company's web site (and of course, their Internet site is itself a basic sign of keeping up with the times) reveals a plethora of innovations, updates, and permutations that can offer even the most longtime Slinky freak something to look forward to.

I'm heartened to see that. For no matter how strong its core product, a company needs to stay open and flexible to its life and times. I have no idea whether these new ideas came from within Poof, from without, or both. What matters is that they were implemented by an apparently perceptive leadership.

It's not enough for leaders to listen, as we saw in the last chapter. The organization itself has to possess a culture of listening and learning. How much does your group listen to the outside world and take clues from its environment? Do you have research and development people in place to plan for the next great innovations? Does the organization listen to them?

NEVER TURN YOUR BACK ON THE OCEAN OR THE CURRENTS OF CHANGE.

During a recent visit to northern California, my wife and I found a hotel along the Pacific called the Mendocino Hotel. Mendocino is one of the most beautiful spots on earth—an artsy, New England-style hamlet bordered on one side by the craggiest sights of the Pacific shore, and on the other by northern California's towering redwood forests.

I found myself swept away by its beauty, until I caught sight of the following, sobering statement at the top of a hotel brochure:

"Never turn your back on the ocean."

It turns out that along this stretch of the Pacific, rogue waves can come along when backs are turned and sweep folks out to sea. Many an unsuspecting traveler has been a victim of the rogue wave.

This is priceless advice for organizations as well as travelers. When we take our eyes off our external realities, turning inward to admire the personal reality we have so proudly created, we may be swept away by the swirling waters of change.

So it is with innovation. Creative ideas that come from outside of our group are the result of *outsight*. Outsight is the power to perceive external realities. We become knowledgeable about what is going on by keeping doors open to new ideas and information.

In the words of Ann Bowers, president of the consulting firm Enterprise 2000, "People who get extraordinary things done are always out and about."

In Search of Humility

One of the most important traits shared by learning organizations that are open to change is the quality of *humility*. Arrogance means we think we know all the answers and understand all of our problems and their solutions. The arrogant have no need or room for "outsight" (insight by others). On the other end of the continuum comes humility, which recognizes that we don't have all the answers and in many ways are groping in the dark.

After twenty years of working with organizations, Karl Albrecht has formulated the following axiom:

> The longer you have been in business, the greater the probability you don't really understand what's going on in the minds of your customers. There is a certain arrogance of tenure that blocks many organizational leaders from

innocent-minded inquiry into their customers' attitudes.[1]

That is why ongoing learning must take place. In *Changing the Essence,* Richard Beckhard and Wendy Pritchard observe:

An integral part of the fundamental change strategy must be a conscious decision to *move toward a learning mode where both learning and doing are equally valued.* This is an essential precondition for managing fundamental change effectively and is also a fundamental change in its own right."[2]

How to Combat Institutional Navel Gazing

How can we combat the institutional paralysis of always looking inside? Of living in a bubble that is increasingly disconnected from reality? By staying creative. By turning outward. Let me state anew the Albrecht axiom: "The longer we have been in business, the greater the probability that we don't really understand what's going on in the minds of our customers, our congregation, or our community."

We naturally think just the opposite; that we become experts by virtue of longevity. Yet a common effect of all those years of practice is isolation and conformity to traditions. We end up with the answers to questions people quit asking long ago. We end up looking at ourselves, engaging in a kind of vain navel gazing. This sort of "arrogance of tenure" blocks many organizations from seeing truths that are obvious to outsiders.

He who never walks except where he sees other men's tracks will make no discoveries. Creativity, on the other hand, forces us all to look at old problems through new eyes. It makes us question the status quo and constantly look for improvements and enhancements to our life's work. It is about improving the quality of the work of our hands.

One of the best things we ever did at CBInternational was hire an outside consultant to conduct a complete, organizational audit. What is such an audit? To me, it resembled my last annual physical—the kind you get after you reach mid-life. They put you through *all* the paces—everything possible and conceivable in the world of prodding, poking, testing, analyzing, stressing in order to produce a portrait/profile of your health.

In our case, the audit involved hundreds of hours of interviews with every type of stakeholder from board member to rank and file employee. What emerged was a new snapshot of reality that we could never have self discovered—a true SWOT picture of our strengths, weaknesses, opportunities, and threats. We were now in possession of reality therapy; the results of our physical. We could either choose to use it in improving our future, or do what many leaders unfortunately do with this kind of information: *bury it.*

We chose to listen. We are using our organizational ears to move out with a plan of action. We chose to use the harsh reality of what we learned as the marching orders of our change team.

What's the Point? An environment conducive to change is a learning place. Leaders and followers should share a great sense of common humility, not presuming to know what lies ahead. As with the leaders we dealt with in the last chapter, the group itself has to take on the learning spirit so that it can change effectively. To avoid hardening of the categories, develop the practice of listening constantly to everyone you can—to your whole environment—which can help you figure out the future.

TAKEAWAYS

1. In the quest to become a learning organization, try these exercises:

- *Describe your current state of active/intentional learning. Do you consider yourself a part of a group that listens to external realities? Do you possess outsight? A little or a lot?*

- *Make a list of the people in your organization who seem to be tuned in to the outside world. Who are your realists who help the group learn? These are your allies of change.*

- *Make a list of all the people, experts, consultants, or specialists you could bring in and ask about your type of organization. Who can speak into your group with reality therapy from outside?*

- *Hire a consultant and ask the person to be brutally honest with you about the organization's health and its future. Be sure to hire a* consultant who has a proven track record with organizations you are familiar with. Ask the person for help. Follow his advice.

- When was the last time you attended a seminar, lecture, or class? Consider taking classes at a local college, university, extension program, or via the Internet.

- Continue to read journals, magazines, books, and listen to tapes in your field. And start reading outside your field.

- Start keeping an electronic journal of thoughts, insights, comments from others, and reflections from your readings. Use the lookup feature to collect scattered ideas and thoughts.

- Network often, both within and outside your field. What can you learn from trends on the other side of the globe organizationally and literally?

- When attending tradeshows, be sure to include the seminars in your schedule.

2. In order to evaluate the extent your organization offers skills development and education, answer these questions:

- What skills are you developing? How are you personally and organizationally getting better at something this quarter, this year?

- How much of your organization's budget is allocated for training and education?

25
The Law of the Boomerang Effect

It is difficult to change organizations. It is like tending the gardens. When you relax, the culture goes back to the weeds.

Ichak Adizes

Gravity is Slinky's best friend. Without it there would be no Slinky. But there is another ingredient necessary to make it work. Someone must give it a nudge down the stairs. Left on its own, Slinky is always in a state of rest. It is dormant . . . immobile . . . inert . . . motionless. It is stagnant. To get it off the dime requires a push. To see action requires a shove. And to keep people changing requires the same constant "push."

It is difficult to make changes that last. Everything tends to revert to the old way. People do. Systems do. Habits die hard and new ones are hard to ingrain. People

I work with have told me with sincerity and enthusiasm that they are committed to the new way. But then they frequently turn right around and go back to their offices and preserve the former customs! Even the very "core" people on your team who are the strongest advocates for a new way of doing things are prone to such lapses.

This powerful force of human nature is what I call the *Law of the Boomerang Effect*. The boomerang always wants to come back.

To use another metaphor, it reminds me so much of those wagon ruts engraved in stone on the Oregon trail. Just try to blaze a new path and see what happens.

Returning to What Has Been

The boomerang effect is always there pulling you back to the previous status quo like gravity to earth.

All I have to do is take one look at the rooms of my teenage children and I know that everything goes from a state of order to a state of chaos. If order is the new system under the changes you have tried to implement, then chaos is the old order of things. Anyone who does not believe in the devolution of mankind and the second law of thermodynamics has never raised teens!

In an article titled "The Seven Dynamics of Change," Ken Blanchard observes one key principle to remember: *If you take the pressure off, people will revert back to their old behavior.* For change to be lasting, it must be self-perpetuating. Managers and leaders have to keep the pressure on and make it clear that there is no turning back to the old days.

We looked at John Kotter's eight-stage process to accomplish lasting change in chapter 10. He observes from years of watching groups try and fail at major change that most change initiatives ultimately fail because the final two steps of the change process were ignored. Recall those two steps which are:

7. Consolidating gains and producing more change (by such steps as hiring, promoting, and developing people who can implement the change vision, and reinvigorating the process with new projects, themes).
8. Anchoring new approaches in the culture (by such steps as creating better performance through customer- and productivity-oriented behavior, more and better leadership, and more effective management).

Clearly a long-term change process takes years. Kotter wrote, "Until changes sink down deeply into the culture, which for an entire company can take 3–10 years, new approaches are fragile and subject to regression."[1]

Change is Like . . .

This thing we call *change* is so elusive. It is hard to get a handle on and hard to manage. It is unpredictable and difficult to control. Even the people who say they are committed to it wander back to the comfort of the tried-and-true easy chair of the status quo.

To illustrate more thoroughly the Law of the Boomerang Effect in human nature, consider the following analogies:

CHANGE IS LIKE UNDERGROUND WATER SEEKING ITS PATH OF LEAST RESISTANCE.

The gifted writer and oil field geologist Rick Bass, in his wonderful book *Oil Notes*, described water's unfailing pull toward its previous course in a way that evokes the Boomerang Effect perfectly.

> The water remembers. Paths taken by the earth are not easily reversed by anything, and certainly not by man. It is hard to change the paths, really, of even the slightest of natural things: a relationship, a moth to a light, a dragonfly trying to get to a pond, a dog that chases flies. How are you going to tell an old ocean that has broken through a gas cap to stop remembering that blue sky, and go back down?[2]

Similarly, those hearing calls for change tend to wander back to their previous, well-known and well-traveled course.

CHANGE IS LIKE AN INVISIBLE MONSTER LURKING IN THE HALLS.

We always like to come back to the familiar. The old ways are safe and secure, like our favorite clothes and shoes that fit so well. The old culture in our organization is like an invisible monster that grabs the well intentioned and pulls us back. He is lurking in the shadows by the cubicles and water fountain. Our people will be pulled back to old relationships and reporting structures; they will naturally go where they have always gone for answers.

As the wildly successful book *Who Moved My Cheese?* communicates so well, even when the cheese is gone, mice keep going back to where it used to be. It takes a long time and consistent effort to get people to make new tracks and follow the new structures that have been launched. It seems as though they are constantly being dragged back by the unseen monster of the status quo.

CHANGE IS LIKE TRENCH WARFARE.

We think we have won the war when we have only had small victories in a few skirmishes. The enemy we are trying to defeat—the old way of doing things—isn't dead. In most cases he's just sleeping. Wounded, but eager to come back swinging. He will not give up easily. This is trench warfare!

Sustained victory requires rooting out the old ways in the deep habit patterns of the organization and anchoring the new order in the culture. Part of the new order is to cultivate in the new culture an ongoing openness to change.

CHANGE IS LIKE GARDENING.

If you work at it, the weeds are gone and the flowers bloom. If not, the weeds will overtake the flowers.

Ichak Adizes used this metaphor in his classic book on change, *Corporate Lifecycles*: "The companies that do not continue changing their new cultures, those that say, 'thank you, now let's get back to work', are like untended gardens that eventually go back to weeds. It is difficult to change organizations. It is like tending the gardens.

When you relax the culture goes back to the weeds."[3]

CHANGE IS LIKE SELLING YOUR FAVORITE EASY CHAIR.

If you are trying to change the corporate culture, people will always go back to the old symbols, values, and traditions of the past. It is just cozy there! Please don't get rid of my favorite chair!

Changing Corporate Culture

During my days in postgraduate school, I became fascinated with the concept of corporate culture. In fact, I even entitled my doctoral dissertation, "A Descriptive Model for Discerning Corporate Culture." Sound impressive? How about boring? It did became a useful tool to figure out corporate culture, however, advancing the idea that you cannot change your culture until you understand it for what it is.

An organization's corporate culture is *the way insiders behave based on the values and group traditions they hold.* Never underestimate the power of your group's culture. Ralph Kilmann describes it well:

Culture is different things to different people. For some, it's family, or religion. It's opera or Shakespeare, a few clay pots at a Roman dig. Every textbook offers a definition, but I like a simple one: *culture is the shared values and behavior that knit a community together.* It's the rules of the game; the unseen meaning between the lines in the rulebook that assures unity. All organizations have a culture of their own.[4]

In chapter 20 we first looked at how people resist change. The six coping mechanisms were:

- *hold out* (hope that the past returns)
- *keep out* (hunker in the bunker)
- *move out* (relocate and hide in nostalgic yearnings for the status quo)
- *close out* (toss in the towel and admit defeat)
- *reach out* (change with a direction toward the future)
- *dish out* (oppose the leaders every step of the way!)

Let's consider another way of viewing reactions to change, this time as levels of the Boomerang Effect. When you begin to tamper with the old way of doing things, you'll provoke one of these reactions to aggressive change programs. In some ways, these can be seen as the intensity level of the Boomerang. Which one describes you?

EIGHT LEVELS OF THE BOOMERANG EFFECT

1. *Ritualist.* "Whatever. I am not really here in spirit anyway, just in body, so let them do what they want."
2. *Retreatist.* "I will do what I can to prove that they are wrong with quiet resistance." This is the passive-aggressive employee.

3. *Rebel.* "I will actively do what I can to prove that they are wrong with aggressive sabotage."

4. *Conformer.* The compliant one. "I will do whatever I am told. Never rock the boat."

5. *Complainer.* "Those people in management are nuts! I will let them know it at every turn."

6. *Early adopter.* "I see what they are proposing and it makes sense. I will push the boomerang in the right direction and try to keep it from going back home."

7. *Late bloomers.* Those who eventually come along when they have warmed up to the new ideas and had their minds and hearts convinced. They are from Missouri: "Show me."

8. *Innovator.* Those wonderful people who say, "I can improve what they are talking about and make it even better. I'll help throw the boomerang!"

The goal, of course, is to move to level eight.

Getting the Egypt Out of the People

As in the case of the children of Israel leaving Egypt and heading to the Promised Land, you can take the people out of Egypt but it's hard to take the Egypt out of the people. The Israelites were constantly asking their leaders to return to Egypt.

Whatever the old system is, it always "follows" people and tries to pull them back, just as Pharaoh's army did. In the case of a technological change, the old machines try to pull people back; in the case of strategic change, it is the old strategy that holds onto people; in the case of a reorganized work force, it is the old reporting relation-ships and the old peer groupings; in the case of cultural change, it is the old values, symbols, and ceremonies that exert the pull on people.[5]

Moses knew that the pull of the past had to be broken. He called on God to part the Red Sea and after the people went through, the armies of Pharaoh drowned. Significantly, once on the other side, the people could not readily return; they had to move toward the goal. Similarly, when Cortez landed on the shores of Mexico to settle a new land, he burned all the boats. It was a statement that there was no turning back.

People always want to go back. It is not a condem-nation, just a fact. Reckon with it and don't declare victo-ry too soon. Keep the pressure on and keep shoving the old Slinky.

What's the Point?

Human nature demands that people will go from a state of the new changes back to the old way of doing things. It's the Law of the Boomerang Effect. We have to be fully aware of how strong a pull this is and we have to take actions to break its gravitational force. Change agents are push-ers for life.

TAKEAWAYS

1. Try to articulate a list of characteristics of the old culture you are leaving behind and the new one you would like to have. Remember, culture is the

shared values and behavior that knit a community together.

2. You have to find breaking points with the past—
seas to part or boats to burn. Remove those structures
or policies or people that are pulling you back to the
former way of doing things.

3. Be careful to honor the past—do not denigrate
the past even as you burn your bridges. What they did
back then was right for their time, just not for yours.

4. In the change process one needs a point of reference. A starting point. You don't want to be months
into the project only to find you are back where you
began. Answer these questions about the prevailing
setting:

- How do you do things where you are?

- Who reports to whom?

- How do decisions get made?

- What gets rewarded, praised?

- What gets discouraged, rebuked?

- How fast do things happen?

- What is considered a long time?

5. We tend to do and think in ways that are easiest
or comfortable or convenient—personal ruts. What
are yours?

6. There is a need to put up roadblock and detour
signs of your own making, not the ones that automatically go up opposing change. Where will you set
them up?

7. How will you go about building new habits to re-place the old ones?

PHASE SIX

Align Your Team As You Stay the Course of Change

1. ACCEPT

2. AIM

3. ANTICIPATE

4. ATTACK!

5. ADJUST

6. ALIGN

Here is a quick question for you: If you are asked, "Why are you pushing change all the time?" what is your answer? There could be many correct answers, but one I often use is "alignment." We mentioned early on that the goal of change is to bring all the members of a group into alignment. In these last five chapters we cycle back to the quest for alignment as your ultimate goal. Alignment is everyone singing from the same sheet of music. It is about everyone knowing and pursuing the group's mission *with equal passion.*

Success is a long-term proposition. Never give up. And don't forget: Trust and encouragement must be in the mix in order for change efforts to succeed.

26
Take the Long View of Success

I find the great thing in this world is not so much where we stand, as in what direction we are moving; to reach the port of heaven, we must sail sometimes with the wind and sometimes against it—but we must sail, and not drift, nor lie at anchor.

Oliver Wendell Holmes

Despite its obvious cuteness, the Slinky was no overnight success. Richard James was forced to take the "long view" of success. He searched for several years to find steel wire that would behave exactly the way he'd seen it. In the meantime, Betty found just the right name. Believing in their vision, the couple started making Slinkys with five hundred dollars of borrowed money. Eventually, one snowy night in a Philadelphia department store, the first four hundred Slinkys flew off the shelves in ninety minutes.

Few people remember how easy it would have been for the Jameses to set aside their idea as just another whimsical, nonsensical idea that gets batted around the dinner table and just as quickly forgotten. How many grand ideas have you and I given up on that could have been the Next Big Thing?

Do obstacles get you down when you're trying to get something done? The inspiring book *Chicken Soup for the Soul* asks you to consider the following:

- After Fred Astaire's first screen test, a 1933 memo from the MGM testing director said: "Can't act. Slightly bald. Can dance a little." Astaire kept that memo over the fireplace in his Beverly Hills home.
- An expert said of famous football coach Vince Lombardi: "He possesses minimal football knowledge. Lacks motivation."
- Louisa May Alcott, the author of Little Women, was advised by her family to find work as a servant or seamstress.
- Walt Disney was fired by a newspaper for lacking ideas. He also went bankrupt several times before he built Disneyland.
- Richard Bach endured rejection of his 10,000-word story about a soaring seagull from eighteen publishers before Macmillan finally published it in 1970. By 1975 Jonathan Livingston Seagull had sold more than seven million copies in the United States.[1]

And according to *Chicken Soup's* Jack Canfield and Mark Victor Hansen, "Beethoven handled the violin awkwardly and preferred playing his own compositions instead of improving his technique. His teacher called him hopeless as a composer."[2]

Keep on Pushing

And you think your ideas have been shot down? My advice to you: Keep trying and keep pushing. Don't give up. Be the Beethoven or Fred Astaire of your vision. Don't let people rob you of it. No matter how much cold water they pour onto your ideas (and ideals), keep on pushing.

Many change efforts fail because people give up too soon or because the people in charge are not aware of how complex the change process is.

Like the Jameses, take the long view. Heed the warning of Richard Beckhard and Wendy Pritchard:

> An increasing number of organizations around the world are engaged in massive change efforts, which are designed to improve their competitive position, maintain their present ownership and financial structure, and insure the future. Many of these efforts will either fail or be short lived because the leadership is unaware or does not pay attention to the complexity of the processes involved in such changes.[3]

Seven *T*'s of Successful Change

Several years ago I came up with my own personal list of seven signposts to follow for being a successful change agent. This is taking the long view. I have tried to follow my own advice in the radical things I have promoted in my own backyard.

1. *Trust* God and *Trust* Yourself

If you have been given a vision by God of what you think He wants you to accomplish, don't give it up. Men and women have done amazing things in this world inspired by their Creator.

Trust God *and* trust yourself. Believe in your abilities. Self-confidence is an absolute prerequisite to fighting the battles of change. Acknowledge and embrace your God-given talents and abilities, as well as those skills you've developed over the years.

2. *Trend* Watching

Leaders are not paid by the hour; they are paid to watch the future as it is coming at us. This presupposes that we do *not* believe that we have arrived and have all the answers.

"If it works, it's obsolete." That's what the futurists are telling us. Leadership is about the future, and the worst thing a leader can do is fear the future. Since our present methods are already obsolete, we must constantly refine, improve, listen, and learn. Others may fear, but those who lead as change agents must boldly face the future

3. *Timing*

The greatest ideas can die on the bedroom floor and on the boardroom floor if the timing is not right. Timing is everything. Those of you who are married know this is true. I was asked to travel to Brazil one summer on an important assignment. I knew that I had to try to find the perfect time in the spring to share this with Donna, because I don't usually travel on business when the kids are out of school. That's the time I try to give to my family. But this was such a strategic opportunity that I waited for just the right moment—when I really had a lot of love in the love bank, when she was thinking that I am the greatest husband anyone could ever want. Then, when she was just in the right mood, I sprang it on her . . . and she said, "Go for it!"

People in my office have learned to check with my assistant in order to gauge my temperature before coming in, especially if they want to spring some big, new idea on me. "Hey, how's he feeling today. Is he up, is he down, are things OK? Which way is the wind blowing today?" Recently, a fellow asked me if he could produce a $10,000 video for a very important project. His request came after some bad financial news, and of course I said *no*. His timing could not have been worse.

4. *Trial* and Error

Whether you are working in Paris, France, or Paris, Texas, you should be a pioneer. No matter what your line of endeavor, we need pioneers. These are people who get on the wagon train not knowing what lies ahead . . . only that they are up for the journey and for whatever comes their way. A pioneer is someone who looks for new solutions to old problems. The person takes risks with the unknown, which may mean trial and error along the way.

Here's what Kouzes and Posner say in their book *The Leadership Challenge*:

> Leaders are pioneers. They are people who venture into unexplored territory. They guide us to new and often unfamiliar destinations. People who take the lead are the foot soldiers in the campaigns for change . . . the unique reason for having leaders—their differentiating function—is to move us forward. Leaders get us going someplace.[4]

I am a pioneer and I push pioneering. I am so committed to pioneering that we included it in our organization's mission statement, which reads: "In vital partnership with churches at home and abroad, the mission of CBInternational is to be a pioneering force in fulfilling Christ's commission to the final frontiers of the harvest."

Remember, pioneers have to be able to try, and they will make mistakes. I believe in the 80/20 rule: 80 percent of the decisions are going to be good, 20 percent are going to fall on the floor. But that's OK. We have to allow ourselves, as well as our employees, to make mistakes. We all make mistakes.

5. *Talking* to Everyone with Both Ears Open

If you want to be a change agent, you need to talk. You need to talk to everyone with both ears open. You've probably heard that "God gave us one mouth and two ears because we should listen twice as much as we talk." As we saw in the early chapters on listening and being a learning organization, "listen" is the most important word in the leader's vocabulary. You will never be a change agent if you don't listen, and if you don't listen, you will be possessed with your own ideas. You'll think you have all the answers and that you have arrived. The greatest innovations, the greatest progress in your work will come from those on the peripheral edge, not the core of leadership. Maybe you are one of those edge people!

The great revolutions of history were initiated by radicals on the fringes. Revolution rarely comes from the establishment or from the institutional core. Look for mavericks and encourage pioneers in your midst. The only way a leader is going to harvest those ideas is to listen. *Listen* and talk to everyone.

At all costs, avoid "the big surprises." One thing the folks in three generations—the Baby Boomers and Generations X and Y—agree on is that people and organizations have to be open and transparent. Nothing turns followers off more than ivory-tower announcements. "It has been decided." Have you ever heard that? Those are death words. People want to be in the process which requires talking. So change should involve talking and listening *before, during, and after* the change takes place.

6. *Tact* and Diplomacy

A change agent needs good old-fashioned tact and diplomacy. Change agents must possess excellent social skills. One of the first writers on change was Machiavelli. Remember what he said in the 1500s about trying to change things:

> There is no more delicate matter to take in hand, nor more dangerous to conduct, nor more doubtful of

success, than to step up as a leader in the introduction of changes. For he who innovates will have for his enemies all those who are well off under the existing order of things, and only lukewarm supporters in those who might be better off under the new."5

Don't be guilty of doing really stupid things in the name of change, such as:

- Making grand announcements from behind closed doors. Nothing is more damaging than a spirit of secrecy. Today's workforce demands an open system and access to decision making.
- Promoting leadership that no one respects. There is no tact or diplomacy there.
- Firing or demoting truly valuable players.
- Failing to keep the board of directors and key stakeholders informed about major decisions.

7. Tenacity

Never give up. This is such an important issue that I will save this for the final chapter, "Never Give Up Your Dream!"

Remember, don't give up on your dream.

One day I was jogging down a city street in a Chicago suburb when I went past an old, old house. In the middle of the yard was a marble stone with a brass plaque on it that looked like a gravestone. I thought, *Is someone buried in this front yard?* Well, curiosity got the best of me, so I took a little circuit into the yard to read the plaque. Here's what it said:

> ## "ON THIS SPOT IN 1897 NOTHING HAPPENED."

I looked up at the house thinking someone was probably looking out and laughing at me. As I went off, I thought to myself that this silly stone really was speaking to me. "May it not be said of me that under my leadership, nothing happened. He played it safe." The only way anything is going to happen is for you and I to be change agents.

What's the Point?

When committed to being a change agent, be sure to take the long view. It is not easy to bring about change. Many will oppose you. Watch your behavior and do all you can to make things work for you and not against you by following the seven T's for successful change: Trust, trends, timing, trial and error, talking with both ears open, tact, and tenacity.

TAKEAWAYS

1. Go through the list of the seven T's of successful change and rate yourself. Which of the seven do you consider yourself good at? Where do you tend to fail?

2. Make a list of projects or ideas you have given up on. Why did you give up? Which ones might be revivable? What can you learn from this chapter about where you went wrong in the long view?

3. Try these suggestions for several of the seven T's of change:

- *Trust. When the bad reviews start coming in, trust yourself; have your reasons at hand for starting and completing what you have started. Strength of one's convictions—having a good sense of what one believes and values, and knowing (and documenting) where one wants to go or be makes it easier to resist being persuaded to give up.*

- *Trends and timing. Be sure to do your homework; lay a good foundation before moving forward with your change plans. Who else do you need to talk with? Are there political or regulatory issues pending to check into a little further? Is your change or new idea already considered old hat and you're going to show up just late enough to look silly?*

- *Trial and Error. In any industry or organization, there has to be a different new way of accomplishing the goals and values you desire. How can you be a pioneer, charting a fresh path for your organization?*

- *Tact. It might be time to reread and put into practice principles from* How To Win Friends and Influence People *by Andrew Carnegie.*

27

Encouragement: The Oil of the Change Process

Encouragement is oxygen to the soul.

George Adams

Put yourself in the shoes of one Richard James, circa 1943. You're a trained engineer, engaged in the development of military instruments for one of the world's great superpowers. Your brains and position have earned you a measure of security and respect. Not a bad place in life.

And now, based on thirty seconds of bemusement one day as you dropped one of your materials and watched it "walk" across the floor, you're going to abandon your whole career, your stable income, promising future and all, in favor . . . of what? Of starting a from-scratch toy company with a single product consisting of something most folks already have gathering dust in their garages.

Some would say Richard needed some good shock treatment to disabuse him of his farfetched aspirations.

I say, however, that more than psychiatric help, more than capital, more than retail distribution, more than trained help, he desperately needed one thing: *encouragement*.

Thank God his wife was at his side, or Richard would not have maintained the faith he placed in his idea. In the early days of the enterprise, Betty James constantly encouraged her husband as he launched into the great unknown. We don't know precisely how often, and in what context, but Betty was certainly a constant source of encouragement to Richard, especially in those early-morning dark hours of doubt.

Without her exhortations that his moving coil was a winner, that Richard's single moment of amusement had revealed a hidden treasure, we certainly would not have the Slinky today.

If trust is the glue (and it is . . . see chapter 29), then encouragement and affirmation are the oil that makes the change machine keep running.

Encouragement to Overcome Doubt and Discouragement

Several years ago I pulled the rug out from under our employees in our international headquarters. After fifty years of solid and predictable stability in suburban Chicago, enjoying the steadfast conservative climate of the Midwest, I announced that we were selling our buildings and properties and moving west—to Colorado. The leadership team had concluded that it would take an external change of scenery to bring about deep internal change at headquarters. I worked through the "Circles of Ownership" (see page 152), yet there was a point when the major change needed to be announced to the rank and file.

We were going to be pioneers, forging a new day for our organizational culture as we embraced the progressive spirit of the West.

Needless to say, the decision hit people hard. Although we offered to take along all full-time employees, half of them decided not to make the move. The decision produced doubt, discouragement, and even anger.

Among the smarter things we did in those days, perhaps without even knowing it, was to hire a full-time relocation coordinator. His task was not only to coordinate the logistics of moving a large office and twenty-five families across the country. He was also assigned a task I consider just as important—to be counselor and encourager for the troops. He was available to meet with everyone, to process the decisions ahead of them and to make things happen that would encourage them.

For some it was the tall challenge of retooling to find new employment, while others needed early retirement benefits. He was the "go-to guy" to hold hands and become the heart of the organization during this turbulent transition.

Be Intentional in Encouraging

This person's presence made a huge difference in how well the organization weathered the trauma of upheaval. While morale certainly took a hit, it was shored up by the knowledge that staff members had somewhere, and someone, to go to with their issues. He was a tangible sign that leadership acknowledged the difficulty of the situation and remained committed to taking action in order to alleviate it.

Some might have considered the "encouragement" and emotional aspects of the coordinator's job as somehow "soft" and less substantial than other tasks, like lining up office space or planning the move itself. But without the encouragement we directed to our staff, the organization making the move would have been substantially diminished from the one entrusted to me.

This example demonstrates how important it is to be intentional about offering encouragement. It's not enough to just say a few words on the subject in a staff meeting, encouraging management to be "supportive" and offer a soft shoulder. The actual encouragement that will trickle down from such a suggestion is usually minimal. No, leadership must find intentional and concrete measures not only to convey, but actually *give* support to employees who need it. This will require some creativity and sustained brainstorming, but it is well worth the cost of time and dollars.

Supporting Your Employees: How Important Is It?

At times of massive upheavals, organizations need leadership and management to provide facilitation and support for people to process their fears and doubts.

"Encouragement is oxygen to the soul," remarked George Adams many years ago. Some things never change. Giving positive feedback for a job well done has always and will always be an essential part of leading well. Encouragement is one of the strongest allies we leaders have in our coalitions of influence.

Jesus Christ used it liberally in his leadership: "His master replied, 'Well done, good and faithful servant! You have been faithful with a few things; I will put you in charge of many things. Come and share your master's happiness!'"[1]

Leadership is about supplying oxygen to our followers. And I have never met a leader who did not need encouragement along the way.

I like the way Tom Peters, of *In Search of Excellence* fame, stated the need for regular encouragement:

> We wildly underestimate the power of the tiniest personal touch. And of all personal touches, I find the short, handwritten "nice job" note to have the highest impact. (It even seems to beat a call—something about the tangibility.)
>
> A former boss (who's gone on to a highly successful career) religiously took about 15 minutes (max) at the end of each day, at 5:30 P.M., 6:30 P.M., whenever, to jot a half-dozen paragraph-long notes to people who'd given him time during the day or who'd made a provocative remark at some meeting. I remember him saying that he was dumbfounded by the number of recipients who *subsequently thanked him for thanking them.*[2]

Along the road to effective change, be sure to develop the daily habit of letting people know you are pleased with them and their progress. *Become known as a person who gives out more positives than negatives*, whose trademark is letting people know when a job is well done. One commodity in life that most people can't get enough of is the compliment. The human ego is never so intact that its owner can't find a hole in which to plug a little praise. But remember that compliments by their very nature are highly biodegradable and tend to dissolve hours or days after we receive them—which is why we can always use another.[3]

When do people need the most encouragement during the processes of change? Throughout the course of change implementation. According to William Bridges's previously referenced booklet, *Getting Them Through the Wilderness*, the psychological reorientation process of change occurs in three stages:

THREE STAGES OF TRANSITION DURING TIMES OF CHANGE

1. ***It begins with an ending.*** People have to let go of the old reality and their old identity. An actual grieving process takes place.

2. ***The Neutral Zone.*** A time between the old and the new where people are "neither hot nor cold." They have not emotionally embraced the New World, yet they still miss the old. People go "dormant" as old behaviors and attitudes die out.

3. ***Beginning over again.*** A new energy, a new sense of purpose, a new outlook, and a new image of themselves starts to emerge/take hold.

SOURCE: William Bridges, *Getting Them Through the Wilderness* (Mill Valley, Calif.: William Bridges & Associates, 1987), 2.

How do we encourage people in all of these phases? First, by recognizing that they all exist. We cannot expect people to *just change* and get a grip on the new order. It takes time. The heart must learn to follow the head. And the head must be dealt with. Likewise, the head will not be ignored, either.

A History Lesson in Encouragement

It is in the first two stages of transition that people need the most encouragement. History is filled with well-worn examples of how the tiniest bit of encouragement can make or break a landmark development whose success lies in the balance.

For instance, Robert Fulton was utterly discouraged with his invention of the steamboat. The public had scoffed at him and said it would never work. Fulton was about to give in to this verdict when a man boarded his boat and asked if he could take him to New York with it. Fulton said he would try—for six dollars. That man became the first person in history to pay for a trip on a steamboat. This act of encouragement so buoyed Fulton that four years later, when he met this first passenger again, he told him, "The vivid emotions caused by your paying me that first passage money will always be remembered. That, sir, seemed the turning point in my destiny—the dividing line between light and darkness—the first actual recognition of my usefulness from my fellowmen."[4]

Henry Ford said, "The ability to encourage others is one of life's finest assets." He knew, for he had been the target of severe criticism and ridicule when he invented the gasoline engine for the automobile. Most mechanical engineers were convinced electric carriages were the cars of the future. Thomas Edison heard his plan, however, and with one sentence of encouragement he changed history. He said to Ford, "Young man, you have a self-contained unit carrying its own fuel. Keep at it!" That was all Ford needed to motivate him to press on and perfect his engine.[5]

What's the Point?

Change is often discouraging to people. Massive change can be disheartening. People need to have regular encouragement along the journey: assurance that things are going to be OK, that the future is not gloomy but bright. Change agents need to have a positive attitude and give forth encouragement liberally, especially in the early stages of a new change journey, as many are in a process of grief.

TAKEAWAYS

1. What has been the most disruptive change in your organization's recent history? Who are the people still suffering from its aftereffects?

2. Identify tangible, concrete ways in which you can encourage these individuals in their challenges. Make a list of ways in which you can make encouragement a vital, integral part of your personal relations toward others.

3. Now try these suggestions:

- *List ten ways you have been encouraged in your organization.*

- *List ten ways you can be an encouragement to and for others.*

- *Sometimes encouragement comes from the personal relationships of your life—an intentional direction you have chosen. Who or what are these encouragers? If there is now no one or nothing, who or what can fill that need?*

- *Sometimes encouragement comes serendipitously, out of the blue. Describe such a time. How can you do that for another person?*

28
Paradigm Pliancy: The Ongoing Quest for Alignment

If you're not an agent of change, you're at best the steward of something that is going to erode.

Stephen Friedman

What is the number one trait of a Slinky that makes it work just as well for kids in 2004 as it did in 1954? How about flexibility? It will do whatever you want it to do because it has a built-in, fundamental flexibility that gives it its enduring value.

In fact, its flexibility is so pronounced that it also represents its most glaring weakness—the ease with which it can be twisted out of all usefulness by an ignorant toddler or mischievous older sibling. If you've owned a Slinky and used it for any period of time, then you've spent your patience unraveling those coils and restoring them to their former pliant gracefulness. Just to put your mind at ease, a Slinky can be stretched twenty-five feet without doing serious damage.

And that is the trait that must characterize all organizations of the twenty-first century: *paradigm pliancy.* Stretchiness. Flexibility. Paradigm pliancy is the only strategy in times of rapid and turbulent change.

I was watching CNN news and was blown away by a Conoco commercial. That's Conoco, the petroleum and gas station company that I think of as old, big, and set in its ways. I don't know why, but I just assume anyone that has been around as long as it has (my whole life at least) must be set in its ways.

Not really. Conoco's corporate power slogan is: "Think Big. Move Fast." Wow. I am impressed. Here is one company that gets it.

"BIG AND FAST" DOESN'T HAVE TO BE AN OXYMORON.

Big and *fast* usually contradict each other. And "old" evokes images of organizational molasses. But companies everywhere are learning that no matter how big they are, or how old they are . . . they have to be fast. That is what paradigm pliancy is all about.

In fact, corporate pliancy can help companies make frequent shifts from centralized to decentralized structures that, while criticized by many, are actually the lifeblood of many a large corporation. Consider Hewlett-Packard. The early 1970s found the computer maker decentralized into many small divisions. When the personal computer revolution came along, HP found itself with three divisions working on the same product, none of them compatible with the other. So the company centralized all of its computer divisions. Predictably, that system became a bureaucratic nightmare that drove out innovation and talent. In 1990, management switched back to a decentralized structure that fostered creativity but was poorly coordinated. Then, in 1994, they switched again. And in 2000, it once again switched back to a centralized structure.

If you work at HP, you might be dizzy at all the changes. But in fact, analysts believe that such swings have helped the company stay alive this long. If nothing else, they show that they're one flexible company. In recent news the company is doing better than ever after its controversial merger with Compaq.

Could it be that one reason for the creativity at HP/Compaq these days has been the great leadership of their CEO, Carly Fiorina? Since she joined HP in 1999, Fiorina has led HP's reinvention as a company that makes the Internet work for businesses and consumers. Under her leadership, HP has returned to its roots of innovation and inventiveness. Prior to joining HP, Fiorina spent nearly twenty years at AT&T and Lucent Technologies, where she held a number of senior leadership positions. At Lucent, she expanded the company's international business and spearheaded the planning and execution of its initial public offering and subsequent spin-off from AT&T.

ARE YOUR RULES MORE IMPORTANT THAN PEOPLE?

The web site www.betterworkplacenow.com asks this question to great benefit. The day you sacrifice real-life breathing people in order to maintain the sanctity of your institutionalized guidelines, you're in major trouble. They suggest the following remedies:

- Address the immediate situation in a flexible way— and recommend changes to the policies so flexibility is easier to achieve in the future.

- Have a dialogue on this topic of organizational flexibility, focusing on rules and policies that seem to be causing the most heartburn. "Apply the mission test: Do the rules contribute to the greater mission of the organization, or are they actually making it more difficult for people to carry out the mission? This is guaranteed to be a robust conversation. Be ready to act on the answers."[1]

- "Avoid the 'rule creation reflex,' which can afflict well-intentioned managers who face difficult situations." For example, a manager learns that an employee is using work time to browse pornographic web sites. Consider these two responses and their impact. "Unfortunate Response #1: Browsers are removed from the computers of virtually all employees. Unfortunate Response #2: Employees who are allowed to keep their browsers are issued a list of permissible web sites, along with the requirement that Internet research should be kept to a maximum of thirty minutes per day. Result #1: The company seals off a massive pipeline of information, much of which can serve the business. Result #2: Employees complain about 'corporate' and begin finding ways to sneak their web searches." That's "rule creation reflex" in action.[2]

DO YOU THINK YOU KNOW WHO YOU ARE?

During the Persian Gulf War in 1991, the story circulated of three British soldiers lost in the desert, stumbling around, separated from their troops. They were lost, hungry, and searching for help when they literally bumped into a four-star U.S. American general. Excitedly, they blurted out, "Do you know where we are?"

The general stiffened. Upset at their lack of protocol and rituals of respect, he looked down at them and demanded, "Do you know who I am?"

One of the English soldiers elbowed his buddy and mumbled, "Now we are in deep trouble. We don't know where we are, and he doesn't know who he is."

Being Ready to Reinvent

Today's pliant organizations know what they don't know. And they're quite sure that what they're becoming is not what they used to be.

We cannot be what we used to be and we are constantly reinventing ourselves for the future.

The Swiss watchmakers rejected the idea of the all-digital, battery-operated clock because in their opinion, "It had nothing inside that they were good at making." No paradigm pliancy in their cubicles.

PONDERING THE NEW PARADIGM

The things to remember about new paradigms are:

- New paradigms show up before they are needed or wanted.
- Who comes up with the new paradigms? Outsiders!
- The person most likely to change your paradigm is an outsider.
- You don't have to create a new paradigm shift to benefit from its effects.
- You see best what you are supposed to see.
- Old paradigms will make it difficult to see new paradigms.
- Begin the search for the new paradigm while the old paradigm is working successfully.
- It is fatal to project the future as a simple extension of the past.
- A new paradigm means that everyone goes back to zero.
- When the horse is dead, it is time to dismount.

Here is the vital paradigm question: *"What is impossible to do in your business, but if it could be done, would fundamentally change it?"*[3]

The Quest Continues

To refer back once more to Richard Beckhard and Wendy Pritchard in *Changing the Essence,* "Organizations can be sure about one thing regarding the future: the environment will be increasingly uncertain. Predicting the future will be both difficult and challenging."[4] Beckhard and Pritchard argue the thriving organization of the future will show about a dozen key behavioral traits.

THE THRIVING ORGANIZATION OF THE FUTURE

- A superior ability to send signals in the environment
- A strong sense of purpose
- The ability to manage toward visions
- Widely shared knowledge of where the organization is going
- An open culture with open communications
- A commitment to being a learning organization with policies and practices to support the stance
- High respect for individual contributions
- High respect for team and group efforts
- High tolerance for different styles
- High tolerance for uncertainty
- Explicit and continuing recognition of innovative ideas and actions
- High correlation between corporate or group visions and unit goals and strategies
- Good alignment between business goals and plans and the organization's capacity to perform

SOURCE: Richard Beckhard and Wendy Pritchard, *Changing the Essence* (San Francisco, Jossey-Bass, 1992), 94–95.

Take a look at the chart, "The Thriving Organization of the Future." Do you notice how many of these bullets have to do with Paradigm Pliancy? Never give up the quest!

What's the Point? Organizations have to learn to be flexible and stay that way. Whatever created your success in the past will cause you to fail in the future if you adhere rigidly to it. Your fundamental business may stay the same, but how you deliver your service or what your product is will change constantly. If it works, it really is becoming obsolete.

TAKEAWAYS

1. What has been your greatest success as an organization? Make a list of your strengths.

2. Now think about how things are changing in your field. Where do you need to exhibit paradigm pliancy? Is it a new product? A whole new way of servicing people? Are there competitors out there that are drawing people away from you? What are they doing that you need to learn?

3. Jerry Garcia, the lead singer of the Grateful Dead, once was reported to have said, "We don't want to be the best at what we do. We want to be known as the only ones who do what we do." With that in mind,

> *• List the ways you personally or organizationally are trying to be like someone else.*

- *List the ways you personally or organizationally are trying to uniquely be yourself, reflecting your own set of values, beliefs, and goals.*

- *List some ways you can start becoming a reinvention of yourself, uniquely becoming the only one who does what you do.*

4. *Concerning trends past and present,*

- *List ten or more trends that helped establish your organization in its industry.*

- *List ten or more current or future trends that are not yet having an impact on how your organization behaves.*

- *To better accomplish your goals, what do current trends suggest or mandate that your organization start doing in a different manner?*

29

Trust:
The Glue That Keeps
the Team Together

Trust is the emotional glue that binds followers and leaders together.
Warren Bennis and Burt Nanus

I've heard combat soldiers talk about the remarkable trust that develops among them under fire, but I never saw that quality illustrated as vividly as when I saw the epic war movie *We Were Soldiers*. Lt. Col. Hal Moore, played by Mel Gibson, led his troops into one of the bloodiest battles of the Vietnam War. I found the film's imagery of trust between leader and soldier pervasive and deeply moving.

Part of the reason is that the trust was made concrete—it's far more than just impassioned speeches and lip service. As he promised, Hal Moore was the first soldier to set his foot on the ground from the helicopters as they walked into the jaws of death. His was the last foot to leave the ground when they were done. Many lives were lost between those two footsteps, yet the commander built up a mountain of trust with his men by stepping first into the jaws of death.

Likewise, when we take people into the great unknown, we have to be willing to go first and get dirty in the process.

Greg has been working with me for over a decade. No one is as dependable, enthusiastic, devoted, or dedicated to the task as Greg is. I enjoy him and have appreciated our years of mutual respect. But in a major rollout of new structural changes in our organization, I "lost" Greg—for a season. I lost that which is most precious in the bond between leader and follower: his trust. In Greg's view, I became guilty of a long list of infractions which fall into a category I call "trustbusters":

- Breaking unspoken agreements
- Not keeping promises
- Not involving people in the process
- Lying
- Deceiving
- Making people-pleasing statements
- Keeping people in the dark

My intentions were honorable and I in no way engaged in deceit or lies. But Greg's perception was reality to him and others among his close associates. Trust was busted and the change process came to a screeching halt.

WATCH OUT FOR TRUSTBUSTERS.

Without the trust of those around you, it is only a matter of time before you're gone. A change agent must develop and sustain trust between leaders and followers. It is nonnegotiable. In their book *Leaders*, Warren Bennis and Burt Nanus write, "Trust is the emotional glue that binds followers and leaders together. The accumulation of trust is a measure of the legitimacy of leadership."[1]

Though I had been accumulating trust with Greg for over a decade, it evaporated in a matter of days. It can happen that quickly when you don't keep an eagle eye out for trustbusters—whether actual or perceived. I am happy to report that Greg and I are back on track after a great deal of mutual soul-searching and soul-baring. But it took several giant steps backward for me into the rebuilding-trust process before we could move forward again toward the changes that I knew had to be implemented.

Along these lines, think what a tall order the new leader of Enron received. When the new CEO took over bankrupt Enron, he went as far as to give every employee a daily voicemail to let him or her know what was going on. This tangible commitment began to rebuild trust where there was none. That company faces the monumental task of rebuilding trust. That is why I doubly admire the Herculean efforts of the new leadership.

The Right to Know

What are some of the common trustbusters that derail legitimate change efforts? Here is my list of the big ones that seem obvious to me. I am sure you can think of others. And remember, you don't have to actually be guilty of committing these; by even tolerating the impression that you are, you'll dig yourself a deep hole. Once again, perception is reality in organizational life.

COMMON TRUSTBUSTERS

- Plans hatched in secret
- Lack of openness and honesty
- Planning processes conducted in a closed system without stakeholder feedback
- Denial of the real problems
- Lying and deceit
- Half-truths
- Breakdown of integrity
- Selfishness and self-serving decision making
- Broken promises

If you scan this list, you will notice that several of them have to do with the flow of information. Nothing kills trust faster than withholding vital information that affects the lives of real people. Today's workforce demands authenticity and transparency in matters of change affecting the whole group.

"The right to know is basic," wrote Max DePree in his excellent book *Leadership Is an Art.* "Moreover, it is better to err on the side of sharing too much information than risk leaving someone in the dark. Information is power, but it is pointless power if hoarded. Power must be shared for an organization or a relationship to work."2

Trust Saves Lives, Changes Them, and Changes the World

There's a paradoxical dynamic at work in the world today involving trust. The more our world becomes big and bad and technologically formidable, the more low-tech and intangible our greatest priorities become. For instance, our global stock exchanges represent one of the most advanced and intimidating networks of our modern age. Yet behind all the technology and global financial might, they stand and fall, tremble and shake at the feet of an invisible emotion called trust. Trust in economies. Trust in governments. Trust in currencies. Trust in earnings reports. Trust in executives. Without that wispy little emotion, none of it stands.

And it has always been so. In wartime, lives depend on it—and in peacetime as well.

The renowned theologian and novelist Frederick Buechner wrote that he once reached a time in his ministry where he seemed to believe most of the right things, yet his inner life was mired so deep in despair that he decided to commit suicide. He drove out into the Vermont countryside on a lonely road and prepared to take his life. He had an impulse to cry out to God one more time, and he did. He implored, "God, if you're real then give me some kind of sign that I should go on. And please tell me what it is that I need to do."

Buechner looked up and saw a car coming down the road. He decided to wait until the car went by before he did the deed. And as the car got closer he noticed that the car had vanity plates on it. The tag had one word: *TRUST*. God answered his prayer.[3] Buechner took that word to heart, and began to put it into action. First, by standing up and going home. Then through a deliberate effort to make trust a hallmark of his spiritual life. His whole life soon turned completely around.

Charles Blondin was the greatest tightwire walker in the world at the turn of the twentieth century—the Evel Knievel stuntman of his day. He pushed the envelope, always looking to do something that no one else had ever done before. He came up with the idea to walk a tightwire stretched from the United States to Canada above Niagara Falls.

Now picture Niagara Falls for a second. Millions of gallons of water roaring over that precipice create a tremendous updraft, so that wire must be pulled tight, anchored with guy wires on both sides.

Thousands gathered on each side as he headed out with his pole. And he made it to the Canadian side. The crowds cheered and the light bulbs flashed. Then he turned around and walked back to the American side and the people went crazy, shouting his name as one.

He stood on an elevated stand and said, "How many of you here today believe that I could walk back across to Canada with a man on my shoulders?"

And everybody said, "We know you can!"

And he said, "May I have a volunteer?" Not one hand went up. They all believed he could, but could not muster the courage to put their trust on the line. So Blondin turned to his manager and asked, "Do you believe I can do this?"

His manager said, "Yes!"

"Are you willing to get onto my shoulders?"

"Yes!" So the manager climbed onto his shoulders, and they headed out across the void for Canada.

Then one of the guy wires snapped. The wire began to sway.

Blondin said to his manager, with all the bravado gone from his voice, "Unless you do exactly what I say, unless you become one with me and do exactly what I tell you, we are both going to die. If the wire sways to the right and your gut tells you to lean left but you feel me leaning right, you've got to go with me."[4]

Second by agonizing second the two men inched along, allowing their trust to meld them into a single balancing pivot. The manager subordinated every instinct he had to his client's words.

And they made it.

Trust really is the emotional glue that holds the team together through all attempts at change. If the trust is gone, all bets are off. Without a conscious effort to build trust and maintain trust all your efforts will fail.

What's the Point? Trust is a nonnegotiable in the world of change. Kill trust and there is no hope for progress until you get it back. Change usually breeds doubt and lack of trust among the people in an organization. Without a conscious effort to build trust and maintain trust, all your efforts will fail.

TAKEAWAYS

1. Have you been in a situation where you lost faith in members of your group/organization? Perhaps you have given up on the leaders. List the trustbusters that they committed.

2. Have you done things that have broken trust from others? What can you do to win back their trust?

3. Information flow and keeping people in the loop are vital to building and maintaining trust; trust breaks down through insufficient and inadequate spreading of information.

- Who do you intentionally keep in the loop? Who has slipped through the cracks and is being left outside the loop?

- List the manifold ways you will intentionally communicate throughout your organization the change both in question and in process.

4. How will you monitor levels of trust within your organization?

5. Who do you have as an ally to be on the lookout for trustbusters and broken-trust relationships?

6. Who do you need to do some trust-mending work with before continuing the change process?

3 0
Never Give Up
Your Dream!

**If one advances confidently in the direction
of his dreams, and endeavors to live the life
which he has imagined, he will meet with a
success unexpected in common hours.**
Henry David Thoreau

You've already read plenty in this book about the wild
dream of one Richard James, and his vision of launching
a successful toy company based on a single, errant spring.
So perhaps I should not belabor your imagination with
one more appeal to consider how unlikely and farfetched
his dream was, or how steadfast his and wife Betty's tenacity, or how well-deserved their success.

No, perhaps I'll skip that in this, our final chapter. Instead I'll hearken to one of the many other hundreds of
such examples. In fact, it's hard to find a truly memorable
success story that does not involve an unshakable

commitment to fostering change through a new enterprise, and an unwavering, even insane faith in the dream of its eventual triumph.

When Fred Smith, founder, chairman, president, and CEO of Federal Express, first came up with his idea for a new kind of shipping company, he was a student at Yale. Another warm body occupying a desk. His business paper that first proposed a radical new way of shipping packages overnight received a *C* grade! Now, I don't have possession of that paper, so I cannot tell you if the mediocre grade was due to poor spelling and grammar, formatting, or just unconventional thinking. I like to imagine, though, that a self-important business prof read the words and found the ideas they embodied ridiculous.

A national airborne network! Hah! Next-day delivery! Hah! Taking on the U.S. Postal Service! Hah!

And of course, today FedEx is a company with twenty-one billion dollars in annual revenue, delivering in 210 countries of the world. And no one dares mention to this business prof the *C* he gave to young Fred Smith.

NOTHING IS MORE IMPORTANT FOR SUCCESSFUL CHANGE THAN STICK-TO-IT-NESS.

How did Mr. Smith feel when he saw that *C* besmirching a research paper he'd clearly found exciting? We cannot say for sure. Whatever discouragement he experienced, whatever letdown he felt, Mr. Smith obviously did not give up on his dream because of the small setback of a *C!*

To the tenacious belong the spoils—the spoils of success that come from effective change. There is no more important ingredient for long-range success in implementing change in your organization than stick-to-it-ness. Genius won't do it. Scheming won't cut it. Money can't buy it. Pedigree is worthless.

It can be very lonely to step forward as an agent of change. Consider the long, lonely journey of Robert Manry, copy editor turned dreamer.

On June 1, 1965, a thirteen-and-one-half-foot boat slipped quietly out of the marina at Falmouth, Massachusetts. Its destination? England. It would be the smallest craft ever to cross the Atlantic Ocean. Its name? *Tinkerbelle*. Its pilot? Robert Manry, copy editor for the *Cleveland Plain Dealer*, inexperienced sailor, amateur adventurer, and all-around neophyte. Manry had decided that ten years at the desk was enough boredom for a while. So he took a leave of absence to fulfill his secret dream.

Manry was afraid—not of the ocean, but of all those people who would try to talk him out of the trip. So he didn't share his goal with many; just some relatives and especially his wife Virginia, his greatest source of support.

The trip was anything but pleasant. He spent harrowing nights of sleeplessness trying to cross shipping lanes and avoiding supertankers. Weeks at sea caused his food to become tasteless. Loneliness, that age-old monster of the deep, led to terrifying hallucinations. His rudder broke three times. Storms swept him overboard, and without the rope he had knotted around his waist, he would never have been able to pull himself back on board. Finally, after seventy-eight days alone at sea, he spotted land ahead and sailed into Falmouth, England.

During those nights at the tiller, Manry had fantasized about what he would do once he arrived. He expected simply to check into a hotel, eat dinner alone, then check the next morning to see if perhaps the Associated Press might be interested in his story.

Was he in for a surprise!

Word of his approach had spread far and wide. To his amazement, three hundred vessels with horns blasting escorted *Tinkerbelle* into port. And *forty thousand people* stood screaming and cheering him to shore.

Robert Manry, the copy editor turned dreamer, became an overnight hero. His story has been told around the world. But Robert couldn't have done it alone. Standing on the dock was an even greater hero—Virginia. Refusing to be rigid and closed-minded back when Robert's dream was taking shape, she encouraged him, willing him to take risks, allowing him the freedom to pursue his dream. Their willingness to embrace change led to another change altogether: an entry in the *Guinness Book of World Records*. One with Manry's name on it.

The future belongs to those who are willing to risk all in a process of change. It starts with a gnawing feeling that things are just not working right. You observe the many symptoms I described early on that betray a need for change. Once you decide that things are not what they should be and you want things to change, you have to push hard and keep on pushing. Never give up! Go for broke.

How can we summarize all we have learned along our journey of coming to grips with change? Note the "Ten Tips For Change" on the next page.

TEN TIPS FOR CHANGE

1. Stay fluid and light on your feet.
2. Think vision.
3. Break free from the padlocks of tradition.
4. Make change your ally, not an enemy.
5. Always strive toward greater alignment.
6. Find like-minded change agents.
7. Do not let the detractors and adversaries dictate your agenda.
8. Remember that the pace of change constantly speeds up.
9. Be a positive person of encouragement.
10. Take the Slinky out of the box and go for it! Have a Slinky bash and see what happens!

WOULD YOU LIKE A LITTLE COFFEE BEAN INSPIRATION?

Do you ever feel that you are alone in trying to bring about significant change in your organization? Have you sensed the loneliness of being misunderstood because you are the only one pulling the alarm lever? Do you alone seem to feel that all is not good aboard your ship? A lone voice crying in the organizational wilderness of outmoded traditions and worn-out methods?

Well, you are *not* alone. There are others. And there is help. I have spent a large slice of my career working in older institutions in need of major turnaround. Why a maverick like me gets stuck in these situations only God knows. He seems to call me to be a change agent against impossible odds. Maybe you feel the same way.

I assure you that *you can succeed.* You can make a difference. My exhortations are:

> *Don't give up.*
> *Don't sacrifice your ideals.*
> *Don't be afraid to show passion.*

Why passion? Because . . .

- People respond to passion.
- People follow passion.
- People are pumped by passion.
- People need to see your passion.

I am not sure how many hours and dollars I spent at Starbucks during the birthing of this book, but there were many. Countless lattes went toward inspiring these pages! So perhaps the best way to draw things to a conclusion is to evoke the inspiration of that change agent who revolutionized the way America, and now the world, enjoys the fruit of the coffee bush, Howard Schultz.

I introduced Schultz, who against incredible odds built the Starbucks empire, in chapter 7. I will repeat his challenge here:

- Care more than others think wise.
- Risk more than others think safe.
- Dream more than others think practical.
- Expect more than others think possible.

NOTES

CHAPTER 1: KEEP YOUR COILS LIGHT

1. Based on a study by the Computer Industry Almanac: "Internet Users Will Top 1 Billion in 2005," press release of Computer Industry Almanac, Inc., 21 March 2002; as cited in www.c-i-a.com. Click "Press Releases." Accessed on 3 June 2003.
2. Anthony Perkins, "The Wireless Heaven Up North," *Red Herring,* June 2002, 16.

CHAPTER 2: RESISTANCE IS FUTILE

1. Corinthians 9:22. Paul explained that to make the message of salvation appealing, "to the weak I became weak, to win the weak. I have become all things to all men so that by all possible means I might win some."
2. Also known as Generation Y and, to some, the Mosaic Generation.
3. The Scriptures call upon us to call upon God. See, for example, Psalm 50:15, Jeremiah 29:12, Philippians 4:6, and 1 Peter 3:12.
4. James M. Kouzes and Barry Z. Posner, *The Leadership Challenge* (San Francisco: Jossey-Bass, 1987), 32.

CHAPTER 3: WITH THE SLIGHTEST NUDGE, YOU CAN CHANGE THINGS

1. Hans Finzel, *Empowered Leaders* (Nashville: Word, 1998), 148–49.

CHAPTER 4: CHANGE FOR CHANGE'S SAKE

1. Compiled from history on the Slinky web site at www.pooftoys.com under "History." Accessed on 3 June 2003.

CHAPTER 5: A LOVE-HATE RELATIONSHIP WITH CHANGE

1. Robert Reich, "Your Job is Change," *Fast Company*, October 2000, 143.

CHAPTER 6: GOT VISION?

1. Richard Beckhard and Wendy Pritchard, *Changing the Essence* (San Francisco: Jossey-Bass, 1992), 35.
2. Karl Albrecht, *The Northbound Train* (New York: AMACOM, 1994), 93.

3. Joel Barker, *Future Edge* (New York: Morrow, 1992), 28.
4. This definition of vision is by the author.
5. Warren Bennis and Burt Nanus, *Leaders: The Strategies for Taking Charge* (New York: Harper & Row, 1985), 89.

CHAPTER 7: PLAYING TAKES A DREAMER

1. Peter Drucker, *Managing for Results* (New York: Harper & Row, 1964), 206.
2. We are created in the image of God, He being the ultimate creator (Genesis 1:27, Isaiah 45:18). All of us therefore have built into our nature the ability to be creative. See also James 1:17, which indicates "every good and perfect gift" comes from God.
3. Hans Finzel, *The Top Ten Mistakes Leaders Make* (Colorado Springs: Cook Communications, 2000), 71.

CHAPTER 8: FOLLOW THAT BOUNCING CHANGE!

1. Ray Jutkins, *Power Direct Marketing,* 2nd ed. (Lincolnwood, Ill.: NTC Business Books, 2000), n.p.; as cited at http:/www.rayjutkins.com/pdm/pdm10-03.html. Accessed on 12 August 2003.
2. John Seely Brown, "Storytelling: Scientist's Perspective: John Seely Brown," on the Internet at http://www.creatingthe21stcentury.org/JSB2-pace-change.html. Accessed on 12 August 2003.
3. Ibid.
4. Many are surprised to learn a relationship with God is possible and even required. Yet the Scriptures say just that. For instance, see Matthew 11:28–30; John 6:35–37; 10:10; and 1 John 5:11–12.
5. The accuracy and inspiration of the Scriptures have stood the test of time. Among the verses showing the power of the Bible to direct our lives are: Jeremiah 23:29; John 5:39; 2 Timothy 3:16; and Hebrews 4:12.
6. Luke 6:48–49.
7. Julie Bick, "Running a Business Microsoft Style," *United Hemispheres,* September 1997, 44.
8. Ibid.

CHAPTER 9: BECOME A FUTURIST

1. Joel Barker, *Future Edge* (New York: Morrow, 1992), 8.

CHAPTER 10: IT'S ALL ABOUT ALIGNMENT

1. John P. Kotter, *The Force for Change* (New York: Free Press, 1990), 49.
2. Burt Nanus, *Visionary Leadership* (San Francisco: Jossey-Bass, 1992), 56–57.
3. "Management Guru Lifts Up Humanity," *USA Today,* 27 October 1997, 8B.

PHASE THREE: ANTICIPATE YOUR ADVERSARIES AND ALLIES

1. Niccolo Machiavelli, *The Prince,* trans. Henry C. Mansfield Jr. (Chicago: Univ. of Chicago, 1985), 23.

CHAPTER 11: CREATE A SENSE OF URGENCY

1. John Kotter, *John Kotter on What Leaders Really Do* (Boston: Harvard Business School Press,1999), 36.

2. James Belasco, *Teaching the Elephant to Dance* (New York: Penguin, 1990), 17–18.

CHAPTER 12: BUILD CONSENSUS FROM THE INSIDE OUT

1. Harvey McKay, "Prolific Author, 76, Serves as Sage of Effective Leaders," *Denver Post*, 1 April 2001, 5k.

CHAPTER 14: THE NEXT BIG THING

1. Adapted from Everet Rodges, *The Diffusion of Innovations*, 3rd ed. (New York: Free Press, 1997), n.p.; cited in *Netfax*, Leadership Network, no. 53, 2 September 1996.
2. Jim Collins makes a big point about getting the right people on the bus and the wrong people off the bus in *Good to Great* (San Francisco: HarperCollins, 2001).

PHASE FOUR: ADVANCE THE PLAN WITH COURAGE AND TENACITY

1. As quoted in John Maxwell, *Leadership 101* (Nashville: Nelson, 2002), 152.

CHAPTER 16: LAUNCH WITH COURAGE

1. On the Internet at www.highlanderweb.co.uk/wallacethe truth.html. Click "Who was William Wallace? Part II." Accessed on 12 August 2003.
2. "William Wallace ('Braveheart')," cited on the Internet at www.lawbuzz.com/justice/braveheart/hero.htm. Accessed on 29 May 2003.
3. Ibid.
4. Theodore Roosevelt, "Citizenship in a Republic," as cited on the Internet at www.theodoreroosevelt.org/research/speeches.htm. Accessed on 12 August 2003.
5. As cited in Warren Bennis and Burt Nanus, *Leaders: The Strategies for Taking Charge* (New York: Harper & Row, 1985), 43.
6. As quoted at www.calvin-coolidge.org/pages/history/research/quotations/quotesp.html. Accessed on 12 August 2003.
7. Warren Bennis and Patricia Ward Biederman, *Organizing Genius* (San Francisco: Perseus, 1998), 204.
8. This poem also appears on various Internet web sites under the titles of "To Laugh," "To Risk," or no title at all, and no author is attributed. To the author's knowledge, the poem is anonymous.

CHAPTER 17: COMMUNICATE, COMMUNICATE, COMMUNICATE!

1. Click "History" to hear the song (accessed on 11 August 2003).
2. John P. Kotter, *Leading Change* (Boston: Harvard Business School, 1996), 94.
3. Patrick Lencioni, *Obsessions of an Extraordinary Executive* (San Francisco: Jossey-Bass, 2000), 142.
4. Ibid.

CHAPTER 18: THINK 1-3-5

1. "It's not how many ideas you have, it's how you make them happen." Accenture advertisement in *Hemisphere* magazine, 2002, n.p.

CHAPTER 19: THINK LEAPS, NOT TWEAKS

1. *John Kotter on What Leaders Really Do*, John P. Kotter, ed. (Boston: Harvard Business School, 1999), 10.
2. James R. Healey, "It's a Car. No It's a Truck," *USA Today*, 18 October 1999, money section.
3. James M. Kouzes and Barry Z. Posner, *The Leadership Challenge* (San Francisco: Jossey-Bass, 1987), 56.

CHAPTER 20: BE SURE TO ISSUE FLAK JACKETS

1. Leonard Sweet, *Post-modern Pilgrims* (Nashville: Broadman & Holman, 2000), xiv.
2. Burt Nanus, *Visionary Leadership* (San Francisco: Jossey-Bass, 1992), 52.
3. James 1:19.
4. James 1:2–4.

CHAPTER 22: READ THE SEASONS

1. Kevin Freiberg, Jackie Freiberg, and Tom Peters, *Nuts* (New York: Bantam, Doubleday, Dell, 1998), 60–61.
2. Ibid., 77, 85–86.
3. Adapted from Joel Barker, *Future Edge* (New York: Morrow, 1992), 15–17.
4. Ibid., 17.

CHAPTER 23: LISTENING LEADERS

1. Warren Bennis and Burt Nanus, *Leaders: The Strategies for Taking Charge,* (New York, New York: Harper and Row, 1985), 96.
2. Leonard Sweet, *Post-modern Pilgrims* (Nashville: Broadman & Holman, 2000), 58.
3. Ibid., 61.

CHAPTER 24: LEARN, UNLEARN, AND RELEARN

1. Karl Albrecht, *The Northbound Train* (New York: AMACOM, 1994), 138.
2. *Changing the Essence,* Richard Beckhard and Wendy Pritchard (San Francisco, Jossey-Bass, 1992), 4.

CHAPTER 25: THE LAW OF THE BOOMERANG EFFECT

1. John P. Kotter, *Leading Change* (Boston: Harvard Business School, 1996), 13.
2. Rick Bass, *Oil Notes* (Dallas: Southern Methodist Univ., 1995), 112.
3. Ichak Adizes, *Corporate Lifecycles* (New York: Prentice Hall, 1990), 276.
4. Ralph Kilmann, *Managing Beyond the Quick Fix* (San Francisco: Jossey-Bass, 1989), 92.
5. William Bridges, *Getting Them Through the Wilderness* (Mill Valley, Calif.: William Bridges & Associates, 1987), 79.

CHAPTER 26: TAKE THE LONG VIEW OF SUCCESS

1. *Chicken Soup for the Soul,* Jack Canfield and Mark Victor Hansen, comps. (Deerfield Beach, Fla.: Health Communications, 1995), 228–30.
2. Ibid., 228–29.

3. Richard Beckhard and Wendy Pritchard, *Changing the Essence* (San Francisco: Jossey-Bass, 1992,) 92.

4. James M. Kouzes and Barry Z. Posner, *The Leadership Challenge* (San Francisco: Jossey-Bass, 1987), 32.

5. Quoted earlier in the introduction to phase three, page 135.

CHAPTER 27: ENCOURAGEMENT: THE OIL OF THE CHANGE PROCESS

1. Matthew 25:21.

2. Thomas Peters, "Management Excellence," *The Business Journal*, 9 September 1991, 24.

3. The Scriptures say our words should offer life and encouragement to those we meet; see Proverbs 18:21 and I Thessalonians 5:11, for example.

4. Robert H. Thurston, *Robert Fulton: His Life and its Results* (New York: Dodd, Mead, 1891), n.p. On the Internet at www.history.rochester.edu/steam/thurston/fulton. Accessed on 3 June 2003.

5. As quoted on the Internet at www.Edison-Ford-Estate.com/bios.asp. Accessed on 13 August 2003.

CHAPTER 28: PARADIGM PLIANCY: THE ONGOING QUEST FOR ALIGNMENT

1. See http://www.betterworkplacenow.com and access "Insights and Inspiration." Accessed on 3 June 2003.

2. Tom Terez discusses "rule creation reflex" in his web site article, "Creating a Flexible Workplace." I have quoted his examples. See http://www.betterworkplacenow.com and access "Insights and Inspiration." Accessed on 3 June 2003.

3. This question was first posed by Joel Barker in *Future Edge* (New York: Morrow, 1992), 147.

4. Richard Beckhard and Wendy Pritchard, *Changing the Essence* (San Francisco: Jossey-Bass, 1992), 94.

CHAPTER 29: TRUST: THE GLUE THAT KEEPS THE TEAM TOGETHER

1. Warren Bennis and Burt Nanus, *Leaders* (New York: Harper and Row, 1985), 153.

2. Max DePree, *Leadership is an Art* (New York: Dell, 1989), 104, 105.

3. Timothy K. Jones, "Frederick Buechner's Sacred Journey," *Christianity Today*, 8 October 1990, 51.

4. Ron Rand, *Won by One* (Ventura, Calif.: Gospel Light, 1988), n.p. As quoted on the Internet at http://ionanet.com/apron/1998/62498.htm.Accessed on 13 August 2003.

GOLD HUSH

MYSTERY HISTORY
– BOOK TWO –

By Sonny Barber

Prospect Harbor, Maine, the setting for this story, is located in Hancock County on the Schoodic Peninsula. The only portion of Acadia National Park situated on the US mainland is on the peninsula.

The Prospect Harbor Lighthouse, located on Prospect Harbor Point, is on land that is part of a US Naval Communications Center. The lighthouse was established in 1850 and shut down from 1859 to 1870 but has operated continuously since reopening. It is on the National Register of Historic Places.

In the present-day story setting, names, characters, businesses, places, events, and incidents are products of the author's imagination and used in a fictitious manner. Any resemblance to actual persons, living or dead, or actual events is purely coincidental.

Cover design by AuthorSupport.com

ISBN: 1499623836
ISBN 13: 9781499623833
Library of Congress Control Number: 2014909606
CreateSpace Independent Publishing Platform
North Charleston, South Carolina

To my daughters, Heather and Andrea, who inspired my characters, and to Jane Petty and all the other great teachers who inspired me to write.

CHAPTER ONE

April 15, 1865, off the coast of Maine

A zigzagging bolt of lightning lit up the sky and painted the surface of the water with a shimmering layer of silver. Squinting through the wind-driven rain that pelted and stung his face, the young man caught a glimpse of the abandoned lighthouse. He pulled hard on the oars of the small boat. His mind raced. Why did he leave the ship at dusk with the storm coming? He could have taken his chances with the Yankees. That was not an option. He would rather risk the weather and rough seas than endure the chains and solitude of a prison cell…or worse. But was drowning in the cold, dark sea any better? And what of his prize, the two heavy wooden barrels in the middle of the boat, wobbling and bumping with each pounding wave?

He shook his head to clear his mind and tightened the thin ropes holding the tottering containers. Gripping the oars, he gritted his teeth and winced. Open blisters on the palms of his soft hands throbbed from the salty seawater. The lightning flashed again followed by an ear-piercing clap of thunder. The man recoiled, slid back off the seat, and lost his grip on one oar, grabbing it before it slipped away.

Larger waves struck the frail craft. One of the barrels came loose and fell against the side of the boat. The rail dipped below the water. The cold liquid rushed in. Scrambling to keep the second barrel from coming loose, the man fell on one knee. The wooden container broke away from its binding and crashed against the first. More water poured in. The man strained to push the barrels back to the center of the boat, but the craft had taken on too much water. It was no use. The water

rose, covering his feet and then his legs. Ten seconds later it reached his chest. He clung to his leather suitcase, gazing down as the boat disappeared beneath him.

The waves broke over his head. He gagged and coughed. Something bumped him from behind. Reaching out, he grasped a half-submerged barrel and let go of the water-soaked suitcase. A flash of lightning illuminated the second barrel. He swam over and put his other arm around it. Another flash lit up the coal-black night sky. The shore was no more than thirty feet away.

Suspended between the two barrels, he kicked hard in the frigid water, propelling him slowly toward land. He felt one barrel sink lower and let go, holding on to the remaining one until it, too, vanished beneath him. With his last bit of strength, he swam toward the shore. His hand hit a rock and touched cold metal—a link in a large chain. The man dragged himself along the metal lifeline to its end at the peak of the rock, resting on land.

Lying on the rain-soaked ground, he aimed his face away from the downpour. He mustered his last bit of strength, stood, and stumbled in the darkness to the lightkeeper's house. The young man's hands shook, his body racked with chills. He opened the door and groped along the cold, rough-plastered wall in the darkness. More lightning revealed a fireplace. He ran his fingers along the wall until he touched the mantle and discovered a box of matches. He struck one and held up the flickering weak light. In a nearby bin were five small logs and some twigs. Tossing the kindling and wood into the fireplace, he lit the pile and lay in front of the hot, golden flames. Within a few minutes, the heat penetrated his wet clothes. Wrapping his arms around his chest, he drew his legs up and closed his eyes.

• • •

A loud squeaking jolted the young man from his paralyzing sleep. His face gray with fatigue, he rolled sideways and sat upright. Sunlight poured in through the open doorway and silhouetted a tall man

dressed in a light gray frock coat and wearing a straw top hat and elegant boots.

"Who are you and what are you doing here?" the tall man asked, his right hand hidden beneath his coat.

The young man stood and shielded his eyes from the glare. "My name is...Cyrus...Cyrus Macauly. I...I escaped...Yes. I escaped from a Confederate ship last evening. It overtook our schooner, and I was taken prisoner."

The tall man scanned the room and then stared at Macauly. "I'm Jonathan Wheatlye. You say you jumped ship?"

What should he tell Wheatlye? Groggy and exhausted, Macauly closed his eyes tight and wiped crusty, dried salt from around his forehead. Raking his hands down the front of his tattered coat, he attempted to make himself presentable to this man who obviously had wealth. He ran his thumbs behind the lapels, starched stiff by the now dried seawater, and stood erect. "I tossed a barrel...yes, that's what happened. I tossed a barrel over the side of the ship during the storm and floated in."

"My daughter happened to see a light over here last night during the storm. The lighthouse hasn't operated for several years. Considering the weather, you were fortunate to find the lightkeeper's house in the dark. And you're certainly luckier than President Lincoln."

Macauly again wiped his face with his hands and jerked his head back. "What? Mr. Lincoln? I don't understand."

"He was shot two days ago. He died yesterday morning."

Macauly staggered a few steps backward and grabbed the mantle.

"It's tragic," Wheatlye said. "But the good news is that Richmond has fallen. Lee has surrendered. The war is over."

"Of course...yes, Mr. Lincoln, a tragedy. And Richmond...Lee...the war." He pivoted his head left and right and turned back to Wheatlye. "This is Prospect Harbor, isn't it?"

"It is, indeed, Mr. Macauly. Welcome to Prospect Harbor, Maine"

CHAPTER TWO

Present day, Prospect Harbor

"**W**hat *is* that?" Kay Telfair sandwiched her head between two pillows.

Her friend Anna covered her eyes with her forearm. "It's called morning."

Intense sunlight flooded the vacation house at five-thirty on this August morning. The sun's greeting was most direct in the girls' east-facing room with the expansive glass and a view of the harbor and the lighthouse.

"Make it go away," thirteen-year-old Kay said. "I'm not ready to get up. Why is the sun up so early? Doesn't come up till after six back in Jersey."

Anna rolled to one side and pulled the sheet up over her eyes, leaving her jet-black hair exposed. "It's a time-zone thing."

"Time zone? It's the same time in New Jersey."

"Forget it," Anna said, her voice muffled by the bed covers. "It's too early to explain it."

Kay threw the pillows aside. The gurgling and hissing of the coffeemaker echoed from the kitchen. "Mom's up."

Bobbie Telfair stared at the coffeemaker. The black liquid dripped down into the carafe. "Hurry up. Why are you so slow?"

"Who are you talking to?"

Her mom spun around and grabbed her chest. "I didn't hear you come in the kitchen."

Wearing a tank top and shorts, Kay plopped down at the counter and rubbed her eyes. "Didn't mean to scare you."

"Mmmm, fresh coffee," Anna pulled up a stool beside Kay. "Good morning, Mrs. Telfair."

"Good morning, Anna. You're both up early. Couldn't sleep?"

Kay stretched her arms and fluffed her hair. "The sun was too bright."

Her mom tapped the side of the coffeemaker to hurry the last few drops. She poured two cups for her daughter and Anna. "What are your plans for the day?"

Kay shrugged. "I don't have any yet."

"You could go to the library for me. I forgot my e-reader. Last night I read a three-month-old magazine. I was so tired it didn't matter. I fell asleep in no time. That drive from Jersey did me in."

"The library may not be open on Sunday," Anna said.

Bobbie touched her finger to her head. "I forgot. Today is Sunday. We can go tomorrow."

Kay opened the fridge. "We'll take a bike ride after breakfast and check out the hours they're open."

"I'm going to stay here and relax on the porch," her mom said. "It's going to be a beautiful day. I wish your dad were here."

Anna rested her mug on a coaster. "He couldn't get even a week off for vacation?"

"He started the new job in June, and others in his office had priority on vacations this summer. He also had to do his two weeks of active duty with the navy in July. He didn't want to take more time off being so new with the company. Next year, Jim wants to do his active duty in Rhode Island at the Navy War College in June. We want to rent a house there for the month."

"In Newport, right?" Kay asked.

"We'll see. Let's focus on the next four weeks here in Maine," Bobbie said. "Your dad would enjoy the quiet. I'm glad he's at least coming up for your birthday next weekend."

"We could all use some quiet after the summer we've had," Anna said. "Don't you agree, Kay?"

Kay's mind flashed back to the events of the first few weeks in June: her family moving from Florida to New Jersey, finding the 240-year-old letter at the park, the run-in with the FBI, and her near plummet into the Delaware River from the Washington Crossing Bridge.

"Kay, are you all right?" her mom asked.

"Yeah. I'm fine. Why?"

Bobbie tilted her head at her daughter. "You had a stressed look on your face."

"I was thinking."

Anna leaned on the counter. "Thinking about what happened in June?"

"Maybe." Kay topped off her coffee mug. "Let's discuss what we're going to do today."

"Whatever we do, let's make sure it's relaxing," Anna said. "I've had enough excitement for one summer."

Kay tightened her lips and shook her head. "Don't worry. I'm avoiding any activity that involves excitement. I've learned my lesson."

Anna glanced at Kay's mom and gave a huge eye roll.

" *What?*" Kay raised her right hand. "I promise. No crazy stuff while we're here."

Pouring herself another cup of coffee, Bobbie smiled, winked at Anna, and gave her daughter a quick hug. "We believe you, dear."

CHAPTER THREE

The young male driver slowed and casually waved, his hand held only a few inches out the window of his truck.

"That's something we don't see much back home," Anna said, riding behind Kay.

"Maybe it's a friendly place, or people around here don't see girls on bikes riding through town that much."

"Could be both." Anna twisted her head around to view the back of the rusty, blue pickup with a basketball-sized dent on the right rear fender. She snapped her head back to the front and steered into the gravel parking area at the library. Squeezing the brake levers, she skidded to a stop past Kay. "I didn't see you turn into the parking lot."

"That's because you were staring at the guy in the pickup."

"He waved at us. I just wanted to see who it was."

Kay hiked the front tire of her bike up over the walkway at the entrance to the library. She lifted her sunglasses and squinted at the sign. "The library doesn't open till nine tomorrow. Let's ride through the village."

The girls pedaled up and down the gentle rises in the road. Wild flowers along the side signaled the waning days of the Maine summer: the delicate pale blue of chicory, the clustered flowers of the tansy looking like large yellow buttons, and the bright white of Queen Anne's lace spreading like a remnant of an elegant wedding dress.

With each buzzing rotation of the bike chain along the colorful roadway, the stress of Kay's adventures earlier in the summer faded.

The sun rose higher, and the wispy, early morning fog lifted up and away.

"The lighthouse looks like it's floating on an island." Kay said, pulling off on the shoulder. "That's so beautiful. Isn't it, Anna?"

No answer.

"Anna?"

Kay caught up with Anna fifty feet ahead, and the two rode into the parking lot at the town dock.

Anna slowed and pointed. "There's the truck of the guy that waved at us." She stopped a few feet from the bed of the pickup. "Where's the driver?"

"Forget him. Let's ride a few more minutes then go home and get some lunch."

Anna removed her helmet, straddled the bike, and reached for her water bottle. "I need to rest a minute."

"Nice day for a bike ride," a male voice said.

Anna gulped down her mouthful of water. "What? A nice day... yeah, it is." Balancing her helmet on the handlebars, she put the cap on her bottle and bumped the helmet. It fell forward, bounced off the tire, and hit the ground.

The young boy picked up the helmet and gave it to her.

Blushing, Anna took the helmet. "Thanks."

"I saw you two riding near the library. Haven't seen you here before."

"We got here yesterday. I'm Anna, and this is my friend, Kay."

"I'm Matt Hubbard. I live here in Prospect Harbor."

"We're from New Jersey," Anna said.

Kay jumped in. "I moved there in June—from Florida."

"Are you here on vacation?"

Kay removed her helmet, parked her sunglasses on top of her head, and shook her light brown, fog-frizzed hair. "Yes, we're here for the rest of the month. What is there to do? We've never been to Maine."

Matt waved his hand. "Besides enjoying the great scenery, I guess there's lobster fishing."

Kay slid forward off the seat and straddled her bike. "Do *you* catch lobsters?"

"We, that is, my family, we have a commercial lobster license."

Anna asked, "That's hard work, isn't it?"

"It is, but it helps keep me in shape for ice hockey in the winter." Matt stood six feet tall, and his tight T-shirt showed that he worked out—or worked at a strenuous job.

Kay inched her bike closer to him. She was only a few inches shorter than Matt but three inches taller than Anna. Taller than most of the boys in her eighth-grade class, Kay often intimidated them. They called her "wonder woman." That name embarrassed her at first until she stared down some of the name-callers and won their respect.

"Why aren't you fishing?" Kay asked, fixating on Matt's polished-marble blue eyes. His wind-blown, dark-brown hair reminded her of a boy she liked in seventh grade. Unfortunately, the boy was so shy he couldn't talk to her without his face turning beet red.

"In the summer, lobster fishermen aren't allowed to haul traps on Sunday. It's a state law." Matt alternated his gaze between Kay and Anna. "On the days we do fish, I help my dad in the summer. The rest of the year, I haul traps the days I'm not in school. I've done it a couple of times by myself when my dad had to work."

Anna leaned on the handlebars. "Do you go to college?"

"*College?* I'll be a junior in high school in the fall." With a straight face, Matt asked, "Where do *you* go to college?"

Anna blushed.

Kay's eyes widened. "College? You think we're *college* girls?"

Brushing back his thick hair, Matt put on his ball cap and fought back a grin. "You look like college girls to me."

"We do?" Anna asked.

Kay poked Anna with her finger. "He's kidding." She shook her head and put on her familiar devilish smile. "We're not in college. We're both seniors next year."

Matt's eyes bugged. "I...well...that's...you know—"

Kay grinned. "Now *I'm* kidding. We're freshmen. My birthday's Saturday. I'll be fourteen. Anna's fourteen next month."

Anna touched the truck fender and raised her eyebrows. "Is it legal for you to drive?"

"I was sixteen in June."

"I didn't know you could drive at that age," she said.

"In Maine, you can get an intermediate license at sixteen. I can't get an unrestricted one till next year."

"What's the difference?"

"It means I can't give you a ride unless I have a person with me who has an unrestricted license."

"We can't get one until we're seventeen," Kay said, gazing across the harbor at the lighthouse. She turned to Matt. "What do you do for fun around here other than lobster fishing and sightseeing?"

"If you go to Bar Harbor, there's a lot of tourist stuff to do—shops and restaurants. But around here, there's fishing and boating. And I do some scuba diving."

Anna shook her shoulders. "Isn't the water cold?"

"Very."

She rested her foot on the bike pedal. "And what do you see down there?"

"There's a lot to see—fish, lobsters, all kinds of sea life. I like to dive around piers and wrecks. I look for old bottles and things that I can sell to the antique shops. Sometimes I do hull cleaning for owners who don't want to pull their boats out of the water."

Anna grimaced. "That sounds dangerous."

"Not dangerous at all. The hull cleaning takes me ten feet down. Most of the other diving I do is forty feet or less."

"You do this by yourself?" Anna asked.

"My dad and I dive together. You never dive without a buddy."

Kay put on her helmet. "We should get moving. Nice meeting you, Matt."

Reaching down to put her water bottle in the holder, Anna dropped her helmet. It landed at Matt's feet. He dusted it off and handed it to her.

"Thanks," Anna said, her face again turning red. She wiggled the helmet onto her head and removed the bunched-up hair from beneath. "Maybe we'll see you around."

"I hope so," he said. "Do you have a cell phone?"

Anna nodded.

"May I see it?"

"My phone? Sure, I guess." She unlocked the phone and held it out.

Matt took it, typed something, and handed it back. "In case you ladies need some help while you're here."

"Anna, are you coming?" Gripping the handlebars, Kay smiled at Matt, threw her hand up in a quick wave, and stood on the pedals.

Anna pushed off. "See ya."

The two girls rode for several minutes, with Kay out front. She slowed and fell back even with Anna.

Anna said, "Let's don't mention Matt to your mom yet. Maybe when we know more about him, we can tell her."

"Do you actually think he'd want to hang with two high school freshmen?"

Anna pulled out the cell phone. She waved it at Kay, put on a wide grin, and pulled ahead, pedaling hard.

Kay shook her head. "What-ev-er."

CHAPTER FOUR

"I can't believe we're going to the library on our vacation." Kay followed her mom and Anna through the doorway.

"You could've stayed at the house," Bobbie said.

Kay shrugged.

Bobbie walked toward the librarian's desk and called back to her daughter. "Pick out a book—maybe a mystery. You like mysteries and figuring out the endings."

"I'm going to search the catalog," Anna said, sitting down at one of two computers.

Kay huffed and sat next to Anna. She tapped the keyboard and stood. "I think I'll wander around." Stopping at a table, she spent five minutes flipping through a news magazine. She scanned the room and walked to an area with books marked for library use only. Kay peered through a glass enclosure at two books. "I knew Alcott wrote *Little Women*. I love that book. But what's *Good Wives*?" She walked over to the librarian.

"Could I see the books in the display, please?"

The librarian took her gaze from her computer screen and peered over her large dark-rimmed glasses. "Are you a fan of Alcott?" She rose from her chair and led the way to the display.

"I read *Little Women* this past year, but I never read *Good Wives*."

"Most readers of Alcott aren't aware that there were two books." The librarian lifted the glass. "*Little Women* was the first book. It was so popular Alcott wrote a second book called *Good Wives*. It was just as successful. Both books were made into a single volume in 1880."

The woman waved her hand across the display. "The first two books were published in 1868 and 1869, three years after the Civil War. This was an interesting time in our country. Have you studied the War Between The States?"

"Some," Kay said. "It was mostly about freeing the slaves. Right?"

"Yes, the war settled the argument about whether the states had a right to keep or not keep slavery. But after the war, there was a lot of discussion about the rights of individuals. For example, up until the war, only white men could vote."

"No women could vote?"

"No women and no slaves. There was a period called Reconstruction that lasted for more than ten years after the war. During that time Congress passed the Fifteenth Amendment to the US Constitution. It gave the right to vote to all men, black and white. The change didn't give women the right to vote, but the war did raise the issue of universal suffrage."

"What's that?" Kay asked.

"Universal suffrage means everyone having the right to vote on who represents them in government."

"Everybody can vote now, right?"

"All US citizens and those who aren't felons can vote. But women have only had the right to vote since 1920 when the Nineteenth Amendment was passed."

Kay touched the glass. "We were told in school that the book talked about new roles for women—that they were becoming more independent."

"Alcott's books in a way did start women thinking more about their roles in this country and their civil rights." The librarian slid the books from beneath the glass and placed each on a padded cradle. She touched the cover of one of the books. "These volumes are rare, and many are quite valuable. Some are worth thousands of dollars. This one is not that valuable, but it's important to us here in Prospect Harbor. The ancestors of Cyrus Macauly gave it to the library years ago. He was a prominent businessman who married the daughter of one of the families who settled the area." The librarian lifted the cover

of *Little Women.* "Here's an inscription to Macauly's wife. 'My dearest Elizabeth. My life had not begun until I met you. Happy fifth anniversary, September 24, 1871. Your loving husband, Cyrus.'"

"That's nice. They must have had a happy life together."

"I suppose—for a short while anyway. He died in 1879." The librarian pointed to a three-ring binder with the title "Cyrus Macauly, 1839-1879" on the spine. "This is a collection of information on him and his family. He led an interesting life here in Prospect Harbor. How he found his way here is quite remarkable. You're welcome to look at this, too."

Kay ran her finger along the edge of the *Little Women* cover.

"Be gentle with them. To be honest, I doubt anyone has opened them in many, many years. I'm here if you need me."

Kay opened the binder filled with copies of newspaper clippings and other papers housed in plastic sleeves. Pausing on an obituary from the *Bangor Daily Whig and Courier,* she sat in a nearby chair and read in a low voice. "'Mr. Cyrus H. Macauly, owner and proprietor of Wheatlye Dry Goods and Marine Stores, died at the age of forty at his home in Prospect Harbor, Maine, on December 12, 1879. Mr. Macauly is survived by his wife, Elizabeth Ann Wheatlye Macauly, and two children, Artemus and Elizabeth.

"'Mr. Macauly was an orphan, having left the orphanage in Maryland to join the merchant marine prior to the secessionist movement and the forming of the Confederate States. He arrived in Prospect Harbor under unusual circumstances. Having been held prisoner aboard a Confederate ship, he escaped when the ship attempted to get fresh water in Prospect Harbor. He was found hiding in the lightkeeper's house by the late Jonathan Wheatlye, who later would become his father-in-law. Wheatlye was a prominent—'"

"Kay, did you have any books you wanted to check out? I gave the librarian my credit card number since we aren't residents. Anna has a few that she picked out."

"No, I didn't find anything I liked. I'll come back another day." Kay closed the binder and walked with her mom to the door. "Thanks for letting me look at the books," she said to the librarian.

"Mom, did you know that *Little Women* was two volumes when it first came out? The library has a copy that's over 140 years old."

"No. I wasn't aware of that."

"And the version I read for school wasn't the original. Some ancestors of this guy named Cyrus Macauly donated these *Little Women* books here in the library. Macauly was a prisoner or something and jumped off a Confederate ship and came to Prospect Harbor."

"You're into this, aren't you?"

"I think it's interesting. I guess learning more about George Washington crossing the Delaware made me appreciate American history more."

Anna lowered her head and squinted at Kay.

"What? I *do* like history. Maybe Prospect Harbor won't seem so dull if we know more about the place."

Anna walked out the door ahead of Kay, shaking her head and chuckling.

"What's so funny?" Kay asked.

"Prospect Harbor dull? With Kay Telfair here? I doubt that."

CHAPTER FIVE

"**W**hat're you doing?" Anna rolled over in the twin bed on the other side of the room.

Kay stretched across her bed and closed the window. "The lobster boats are so loud. Why do they have to leave so early?" She slid out of bed and reached for the door handle. "That's so annoying. I'm awake now. I can't sleep."

"Neither can I. And it's only six-thirty."

"I think Mom's up, too."

The two girls shuffled into the kitchen.

Anna grabbed a glass from the cabinet and filled it with water.

"Boy, those boats are loud," Kay said. "And they do this every morning."

"Except Sunday," Anna said. "Remember what M..." Anna coughed. "Never mind."

Kay shook her head. "Remember what?"

Anna pursed her lips and waved her hands.

Kay nodded, remembering it was Matt Hubbard who told them about no fishing on Sunday. And they weren't going to talk about Matt—yet.

Bobbie put her arm over her daughter's shoulder and gave her a squeeze. "Another beautiful day in Prospect Harbor. Isn't this great."

"I'll take your word for it. It's so early. Ugh."

Anna stuck a straw in her water glass. "We should go to the library and get your mom some more books."

"Thank you, Anna. That's very thoughtful." Bobbie closed the refrigerator door and put the carton of half-and-half on the counter. "I'm almost done with the books I checked out Monday. I'm enjoying the quiet time to read. You girls know what I like to read. Pick out one or two books."

"We can do that, Mrs. Telfair, and I'd like to find something else to read myself. I didn't like one of the books I checked out. Maybe we'll spend the morning and afternoon there and get something to eat at the deli down the street."

Kay said to Anna, "I don't think it will take that long to—"

"I don't like to rush. I need to take my time, *OK*?" Anna glared at Kay, eyes bulging and lips drawn tight.

Kay drew back, holding both hands up. "What-ev-er."

"Don't use that word, please," her mom said. "It sounds rude."

Kay's mom took her coffee and headed toward the porch. "You girls go to the library, and I'll run to the market in Winter Harbor."

Kay stood next to Anna at the kitchen sink and whispered, "What are we going to do at the library for the whole day?"

Anna leaned in. "We're not going to the library all day. I texted Matt last night after you went to sleep. He's going to meet us at the dock where we talked Sunday, and we're going to bike over to Acadia Park."

"You texted him?"

Anna broke into a weak smile. "Yes. What's wrong with that? He said he'd make lunch for us, too."

"I thought he worked on his dad's boat."

"Not today. He'll meet us at ten-thirty. We'll go to the library after."

"We should tell my mom where we're going."

"Let's tell her we may do some more touring of the area after the library. If it all works out, maybe we can invite Matt to the house."

"We only met him a few days ago," Kay said.

"What? You don't think it's a good idea?"

"If you get the chance, invite him. I don't care."

CHAPTER SIX

"He's here," Anna called out.

Kay rolled up beside Matt's bicycle next to the truck. Anna stopped on the other side of him.

The air compressor vibrated and hissed. Matt checked the pressure in his front tire and gazed up at Anna. "Are you ready for a ride through the park?"

"Yeah, we're looking forward to it."

Matt stood, put the compressor in his truck, and brought out a bag. "Lunch: homemade lobster rolls, some chips, and sodas. There're a couple of places in the park where we can stop and eat."

"Wow," Kay said. "Lobster rolls. Did your mom make them?"

"I made the rolls," Matt said, stuffing the items in his backpack.

Kay leaned forward, resting on the handlebars. "Your mom is lucky to have someone who can catch lobsters *and* cook them."

Matt zipped the backpack and faced the girls. "My mom died two years ago. It's only my dad and me. We take turns cooking."

Kay groaned inside. "I'm sorry. I didn't know."

"Please, don't feel bad. You couldn't know. I *did* use her recipe for the rolls. She taught me and my dad how to make them." He chuckled. "I think she thought we would starve after she was gone."

Anna adjusted her sunglasses. "I'm sure you miss her a lot. I don't know what I would do if I didn't have my mom."

"I think about her every day. But it's been worse for my dad." Matt jumped on his bike and put on a big smile. "Enough about me. It's a beautiful day, and we've got a great ride ahead of us. Let's get going."

Several hills challenged the cyclists on the road to the park entrance. Matt led, with Anna behind, and Kay bringing up the rear. On an uphill section, Kay maneuvered between Matt and Anna and pulled alongside Matt.

Anna regained her position with a daring surge on a downhill run.

The maneuver caused Kay to brake hard and fall behind, grumbling. "How juvenile."

After the incident, Kay fell far behind three times, forcing the two up front to slow so she could catch them.

With the park entrance a hundred yards away, Kay forced a fourth slowdown. Riding up beside Matt and stopping, she glanced at Anna and said to Matt, "Thanks for waiting. Sorry I couldn't keep up back there."

"Not a problem. The ride through the park has only a few small hills. We'll stop and have lunch, and that'll give us all a rest. Do you think you're ready to go?"

Kay bared her teeth at Anna and showed a broad smile to Matt. "I'm ready. Let's go."

Shaking her head, Anna squinted at Kay.

Kay gave her the fake smile and pushed off.

Under blue skies and white puffy clouds, the group cruised the road running along the rocky shoreline.

Anna caressed the brake levers and came to a slow halt, her companions stopping beside her. She pointed across the bay. "What's that mountain over there?"

"That's Cadillac Mountain on Mount Desert Island," Matt said. "It's fifteen hundred feet high. It's the highest point on the East Coast."

Kay giggled. "You sound like a regular tour guide.

Matt blushed. "We had to learn this stuff in school. I guess living in the area the information kind of sticks with you."

No one spoke for the next ten minutes of the ride till Matt pointed to large rocks near the road and under some trees. "Do you want to take a break and have some lunch?"

Kay slowed. "Sure."

Anna pedaled on.

Matt rode off the paved surface and leaned his bike against a gnarled pine tree.

Kay stopped and straddled her bike.

Anna veered toward the shoulder of the road and made a wide turn. She snatched the brake levers. Her bike bumped hard three times as the back tire locked up.

Kay called out. "Anna, what happened?"

Anna waved and walked her bike back to where they were. "I have a flat. I ran over some rocks a little too fast."

Matt fingered the cut in the tire and shook his head. "My patch kit and bicycle pump won't help this."

"What're we going to do?" Anna stooped to look at the tire.

Kay put her hands on her hips. "We can't walk back. It'll take hours."

"I could ride back and get my truck, but I can't give you a ride because of my license."

"I guess you'll have to call your mom." Anna winced. "I'm sorry. I—"

"What d'ya say let's have lunch," Matt said. "Then we'll figure out what to do." He opened the package of lobster rolls. "Grab a seat—or a rock—and enjoy."

Kay took a bite of the roll, stared at Anna's flat tire, and made a slight headshake. How would she explain to her mom why she had to come to the park and pick them up? She hoped Matt had a better plan, one that didn't involve her mom.

CHAPTER SEVEN

Reclining on a piece of mottled gray granite the size of a small car, Kay aimed her head toward the sun and closed her eyes. She forgot for the moment Anna's busted tire, enjoying the glorious August day in Maine. A light breeze came off the water. She wrapped her arms around herself and ran her fingers over the forming goose bumps on her arms.

Anna helped Matt pack the empty water bottles, plastic containers, and trash into his backpack.

"You two should grab a rock and relax," Kay said. She raised her head and squinted at the van approaching on the one-way road. "That looks like my mom's."

Anna jerked her head around. "What did you say?"

"That van looks like...it *is* my mom." Kay sat up and slid off the rock.

Bobbie pulled up to the teens' picnic area, lowered the passenger window, and removed her sunglasses.

Kay walked over to the van. "Mom, what are you doing here?"

"I beg your pardon, young lady, but the question is what are you and Anna doing here? You told me you were going to the library and then to the deli for lunch. What's going on?"

"The library didn't open till one, and I did say we wanted to do some more touring of the area." Kay caught a quick glimpse of Anna.

"But you said nothing about going to Acadia Park. This is quite a ways from the house."

Anna arched her shoulders, her hands under her chin, and mouthed the words, "I'm sorry."

Kay waved her off. "Matt asked us if we wanted to ride through the park with him. How did you know we were here?"

"I *didn't* know you were here. I was coming back from the market in Winter Harbor and decided to take the drive through the park. I drove by the entrance on the way to the store, and that gave me the idea to take a quick tour on my way home." Bobbie tilted her head to see around Kay. "And who is Matt?"

The girls' biking companion walked over to the driver's window. "Hi. I'm Matt Hubbard. I met Anna and Kay on Sunday, and I asked them if they wanted to bike through the park."

Bobbie frowned at the girls, focused her attention on Matt, and put her hand out the window. "I'm Bobbie Telfair, Kay's mom."

"We stopped and had some lunch." Matt shook her hand. "Anna cut her tire. It's flat. Could you give the girls a lift?"

"How are you getting back?" Anna asked.

"I can bike to my truck. It's at the dock in town."

"You drive?" Bobbie asked.

"Yes, ma'am. I was sixteen in June. But I have a restricted license. I can't give the girls a ride unless I have someone in the truck who has a regular license."

Bobbie glared at Kay and shook her head. "We can get three bikes on the rack," she said. "And you can ride with us."

Matt loaded the bikes and climbed in the van. Kay sat in the front seat and Matt in the back with Anna. An uncomfortable silence filled the van during the ride. Opening the console to get a mint, Kay stole a quick glimpse in the back. Anna stared out the side window. Matt swiped at his phone screen.

"That's it—over there." Matt pointed at his truck.

He unloaded his bike and Anna's and placed them in the truck bed. "I have an extra tire, Anna. I'll put it on and drop your bike off later today." He shuffled over to the driver's side.

"Thanks for repairing Anna's tire," Kay's mom said. "I'm not sure how or where we would get it fixed."

"I'm glad to do it. Thanks for the ride." He threw a wave at Kay across the van and touched Anna on the arm. "Sorry our tour was cut short, ladies. I'll see you later."

Anna leaned out the window. "Bye, Matt."

"Thanks for the lobster roll," Kay said.

Opening the door of his truck, Matt waved and started the engine.

Bobbie wheeled the van out onto Main Street. "Fill me in girls. What's going on?"

CHAPTER EIGHT

"**A**nd that's all there is to it," Kay said, ending her explanation the moment her mom made the right turn into the driveway. She caught a glimpse of Anna in the backseat and waited for her mom's response.

"Would you and Anna please bring in the grocery bags when you get the bike off the rack?" Her mom closed the van door and walked to the house.

The girls sat, neither looking at the other. Kay yanked the door handle and hopped out. "Help me with my bike, please."

With Kay holding the back of the bike, Anna grabbed the front tire. "What do you think she's going to do to us?"

"I don't know."

"Whatever happens thanks for not telling your mom this was my idea."

"It wouldn't have made much difference. I could have said no. But, to be honest, I wanted to go as much as you."

"Do you think your mom's going to ground us?"

"I'm not sure. This has not been my best summer for keeping out of trouble."

Kay stood in the kitchen doorway and grunted, shifting a grocery bag from one arm to the other. "Mom, where do you want us to put the bags?"

"Put them on the counter, please, and you two go out to the porch. I want to have a talk."

Following Anna onto the porch, Kay sighed, anticipating her mom's lecture. She'd been there before.

Her mom came through the doorway and sat in a chair. She tapped her left index finger on her cheek and slid it around to touch her chin.

The color drained from Anna's face. "It's all my fault. I was the one who—"

Kay jumped in. "It was both our fault. I—"

"Stop, please." Bobbie stood, put her hand on Kay's shoulder, and reached over and touched Anna. "My only concern is for your safety. I want you to enjoy this vacation. Anna, I'm responsible for you, too. Your mom and dad are depending on me to keep you safe while you're with us."

Anna lowered her head. "I know. I'm sorry."

"I must admit I was more than a little upset, knowing what the both of you..." Bobbie took a deep breath. "What *we all* went through this summer. You must tell me where you're going, how long you expect to be gone, and also who you'll be with."

"I know we should have told you about Matt," Kay said.

"That would have been the thing to do. He seems like a responsible person, and I don't object to you riding bikes with him or doing other activities. But I need to know in advance. If your plans change, call me. You both have cell phones, and reception is not bad."

Anna's color returned.

Kay exhaled as if she'd reached the end of a breath-holding contest.

"I promise. *We* promise," Anna said.

"Yes, we promise." Kay went over to her mom and gave her a hug. Looking over her mom's shoulder, she motioned to Anna.

Anna moved next to Kay's mom, giving her a long embrace.

Bobbie blushed and stepped back from the group hug. She grasped each girl's hand. "Let's sit, and you tell me more about Mr. Matt Hubbard."

CHAPTER NINE

"It looks like a blue truck," Kay's mom said, peering out the kitchen window.

Anna and Kay jumped up and scurried out the front door.

Matt unloaded Anna's bike and walked it over to the garage door. "I thought I would drop this off in case you wanted to do some riding tomorrow."

Anna inched closer to him. "Thanks. I appreciate you doing this for me—and so fast."

"You're welcome. My pleasure."

Anna stood behind Matt, motioning to Kay's mom with a scooping motion of her hand to her mouth.

Kay gritted her teeth and tilted her head back.

Her mom turned to Matt. "Can you stay for dinner?"

Matt looked at Anna and Kay.

Anna beamed.

Kay wanted him to stay, but Anna was making a big deal. What was with her?

"If it's not too much trouble," Matt said.

Bobbie motioned him into the house. "It's no trouble at all."

"Thanks. I need to call my dad and let him know. I was cooking tonight, but he can survive without me."

• • •

Kay's slight annoyance at her mom inviting Matt for dinner vanished when she sat next to him at the table.

Her mom returned from the kitchen with the iced-tea pitcher. "How long have you lived in Prospect Harbor?"

"All my life. My great-great-great-great-great-grandfather on my mom's side of the family—I think that's right, five greats—he was one of the original settlers in the area. He was born in the early 1800s in Massachusetts before Maine became a state."

Kay chuckled. "More of that tour guide stuff?"

Bobbie stopped in the middle of pouring Matt a glass of iced tea. "Tour guide?"

"The girls were kidding me because I was pointing out things on our bike ride in the park."

Anna held out her glass and cracked a smile. "He's very knowledgeable."

"We should hire him as our personal guide," Kay said with a grin.

"That's enough, you two." Bobbie shook her head at the girls and said to Matt, "Your family has quite a history here."

"My five-greats grandfather was Jonathan Wheatlye. He settled here and opened a store. He sold supplies to the fishermen and their families." In a softer voice, Matt continued. "My mom was a history teacher at the school here in Prospect Harbor. I guess that's why she was into genealogy. She loved doing the research. She liked visiting libraries and old cemeteries."

"The girls tell me you and your dad have a lobster boat."

"Yes, ma'am. My parents bought it a few years ago when lobster prices were good. We fished on weekends and Dad's days off. The boat is not a thirty-eight-footer like most. It's a twenty-eight with twin outboards. We have a little over a hundred traps."

Kay's mom sipped her iced tea and set her glass down. "What does your dad do?"

"He worked at Northern Atlantic Forest Products, but they had a layoff last year. He has a degree in forestry management but works part-time for a lumberyard in Bangor. We fish when he's not working."

Listening to Matt, Kay's mind wandered. Something he said earlier prompted her to run through her brain's data storage. Wheatlye. That name was in the obituary for Cyrus Macauly.

Matt centered his glass on a coaster. "What brings you to Prospect Harbor for a vacation? It's not exactly the hot tourist location. Bar Harbor usually is the big attraction."

"My husband and I like Maine, and we were hoping to stay at the Prospect Harbor lightkeeper's house. But we couldn't get a reservation."

"That's run by the navy," Matt said. "That means Kay's dad must've been in the military."

"He's in the Navy Reserve. He's a commander. You can only stay a short time at the lightkeeper's house. We would've had to rent another place anyway, and we thought Prospect Harbor would be nice. We could do with some peace and quiet, especially after all the excitement we had this summer."

"What kind of excitement?"

"It's nothing," Kay said, staring down at her plate. "Pretty boring."

"It was a little exciting," Anna said. "We kind of got in trouble with the FBI and—"

"We didn't get in trouble with the FBI." Kay laid her fork on her plate and glared at Anna. "We helped them solve a case."

For the next ten minutes, Kay told the story with Anna jumping in.

"That's definitely exciting. No wonder you're looking for a laid-back vacation here in our little village."

Bobbie nodded. "Amen."

Matt checked his watch. "I need to get going. I told Dad I'd be home by dark. Thank you for dinner and the conversation. My dad and I don't talk much in the evening."

"It was a pleasure having a male in our midst," Bobbie said. "Speaking of males in our midst, we're celebrating Kay's fourteenth birthday Saturday evening. We'd like you and your dad to come. Kay's dad's flying up for the weekend."

The girls turned toward each other, jaws dropping and eyes bugging.

"Thanks. I'm sure my dad will want to come if his work schedule doesn't stop him. He sometimes works evenings."

The girls walked Matt to his truck and returned to the porch. Bobbie lounged on the chaise with her book. Anna sat at the table and typed on her phone.

Pulling a wicker chair close to her mom, Kay sat and drew her legs up, wrapping her arms around them. She stared into the darkness, listening. A light wind rustled the leaves on the trees and lazy waves slapped the rocky shore. The beam from the lighthouse made its predictable rotation, its brilliant flash piercing the star-strewn sky over tranquil Prospect Harbor.

CHAPTER TEN

The wind and rain chased the trio from the van to the library entrance. Stepping through the doorway first, Kay wiped her feet and shook her windbreaker. "The weather changed in a hurry from yesterday."

The librarian, seated at her computer, peered over the counter and smiled. "Mark Twain said, 'If you don't like the weather in New England now, just wait a few minutes.'" She tapped a couple of keys and stood. "Welcome back, ladies. If you need help, please don't hesitate to ask."

"Thanks," Kay said, standing closest to the librarian. She left the others, walked to the shelf with the binder, and flipped through the pages to the obituary on Cyrus Macauly.

Reading the document twice, she came back to the page with the Wheatlye family tree. She ran her finger across the page and spoke in a low voice. "There's Jonathan Wheatlye, who was Matt's five-greats grandfather. It says here he married Elizabeth Victoria Andrews. And they had a daughter named Elizabeth Mary. She married Cyrus Macauly in 1866."

Kay read the note next to Macauly's name. "He died on December 12, 1879. It's sad that they were only married a short time."

Closing the binder, Kay stared at the books under the glass display.

"Are you still interested in Alcott's books?" the librarian asked.

Kay spun around. "What? Yes, I am. May I see them again?"

The librarian lifted the books onto the cradles. "Here we are. I'll leave you to your browsing."

Kay opened the first book and turned the pages, one at a time, then selecting larger sections to read. She closed the book and fanned pages in the second volume. Two pages fell open, and Kay spotted a page that was not part of the book. She lifted out the sheet. At the top were the words, "My dearest Elizabeth." It was a letter written on paper smaller than the book pages and dated December 9, 1879.

Reaching for the binder, Kay scanned the obituary. "This is strange. This letter was written three days before Macauly died."

Kay jumped to the bottom of the page. The words ended in the middle of a sentence, but the letter didn't continue on the back. Was this it? Where was the rest of it?

She fanned a few more pages. Two separated, showing another page of the letter. At the bottom of that page, the words also ended in the middle of a sentence. Opening more of the book, she found three more pages of the letter. The fifth page ended with, "God bless you, my dear Elizabeth. Your loving husband, Cyrus."

Kay sat, read the letter, and stacked the pages in front of her. "Wow," she whispered, re-reading one of the pages. Did Matt know this? Should she tell him? If he didn't know, it could be a shock to him and his family.

Looking around the room, Kay pondered her predicament. The librarian opened a file folder and typed on the computer. Anna sat at a table reading magazines. In a large leather chair in the corner near the door, her mom pored over a book.

Placing the five pages of the letter inside the binder with the obituary, Kay went to the copier. She took out three one-dollar bills from her pocket. She thrust the first one into the slot, placed a sheet on the glass and pressed the button. The machine hummed, paper shot out into the tray, and coins clanked into the change cup. Kay reached into the cup, slid out the quarters, and looked around the room. She copied the letter, the obituary, and the family tree and placed the pages of the original letter back in the volume of *Good Wives*.

What should she do with the copies? What if Anna or her mom saw them? If Kay told them it was a letter she found, her mom and Anna

might bring up another letter that got her in trouble—the letter from the park in New Jersey.

Walking over to the shelves, Kay found an illustrated history of Maine—a book large enough to hide the copies. She returned to the table with the binder, dispersed the sheets among the pages of the big book, and walked to the desk to check out.

"It looks as if you're going to learn something of the history of Maine while you're here," the librarian said.

"Yes, ma'am." Kay gave only a trace of a smile—a nervous smile. "I think it's an interesting place." Interesting place? That was lame. Kay didn't know what else to say. She wasn't going to read the book. It was only a way to get her copies of the letter out of the library.

Instead of scanning the bar code, the librarian lifted the cover and opened a few pages. "This is a beautiful book. Artists and photographers from Maine took the photos and drew the illustrations."

Kay's heart pounded.

The librarian hands lingered over the book and turned to another page. "This article was written by a historian who grew up here in town."

Closing her eyes, Kay prayed that the woman would not find the copies. There was nothing illegal about what she'd done, but it would be so embarrassing

The librarian closed the book. The bar code scanner beeped. "I think you'll enjoy this." She handed the book to Kay. "I put this on your mother's account."

Kay walked toward Anna, who sat reading a magazine. Making copies of the letter eased Kay's conscience only a little. But memories of her earlier summer adventure and the letter from the Park at Washington Crossing flooded her mind. What might happen with this one? A chill swept over her.

"Are you all right?" Anna rose from her seat. "You're so pale. Do you need to sit for a minute?"

"No, I'll be fine. Maybe I didn't eat enough breakfast."

Her mom walked up beside her. "You have no color in your face."

"I'm fine. Can we go, please?"

"That's quite a book you have there." Anna chuckled. "You should know a lot about Maine by the time you finish reading it—or looking at the pictures."

Kay stared down at the book in her hands. "What?" She gave Anna the fake smile. A corner of one of the copies stuck out from the book. She folded the corner over and held the book close. "For your information, there're some interesting things inside." Interesting, yes, but not about Maine—about their new friend, Matt Hubbard.

CHAPTER ELEVEN

"**W**hat are you doing?" Kay said, standing in the doorway, holding a towel and hairbrush. "That's personal."

Anna jumped off the bed and handed the copies of the letter to Kay. "You left the book lying on your bed, and I saw these papers sticking out. I was curious. I wasn't trying to be nosy. I was—"

"Forget it." Kay plopped down on her bed. "I'm sorry I raised my voice at you. It's that this is another letter that could get me in trouble."

"What do you mean, another letter? You mean like the one you found at the Park?"

"Yes, like that one."

"Where did you find this?"

"In a book in the library. I made a copy."

"You found this letter in a book in the library. I don't understand. How can it get you in trouble?"

"Not exactly trouble, but it could change our friendship with Matt if I show it to him."

Anna sat on the edge of the bed next to Kay. "How?"

"The guy who wrote this letter is Matt's four-greats grandfather. His father-in-law was Jonathan Wheatlye. Remember, Matt told us when he had dinner with us." Kay gave the copy of the obituary to Anna. "Read this."

Anna ran her finger down the document, pausing to read passages. "It says here Cyrus Macauly was a prisoner aboard a Confederate ship during the Civil War. He jumped off that ship here in Prospect Harbor."

"How much of Macauly's letter did you read?" Kay asked.

"Not a lot. I did read some of the last page. At the end it sounded like he was dying."

Kay held up the copies. "Correct. Macauly wrote this to his wife a few days before he died. Listen to this. 'My dearest Elizabeth, I know I won't be with you much longer. Every day was a joy being with you. I've been happy from the first moment I met you when your father took me into his home. I have never forgotten that kindness and will cherish your love and devotion always.

"'I was born William Hunter Fields in Fairfax, Virginia, in 1839. My mother died when I was born. I was sent to live with an aunt and uncle until they fell on hard times and placed me in an orphanage.

"'When I was fifteen, I joined the United States Navy. Because of my aptitude for seamanship and my willingness to learn, I was appointed to the Naval Academy. When I was twenty-two years old, the war started, and I remained at the academy until graduation. It was then I joined the navy of the Confederate States of America.

"'I survived several battles serving aboard the *CSS Virginia* and then was assigned to the war department in Richmond.

"'I came to Prospect Harbor under some nefarious circumstances.'"

Kay picked up the next page and continued.

"'In April 1865, I was in Richmond at the time of its evacuation. I became privy to information concerning the transfer of the Confederate treasure out of the city for safekeeping.

"'During the last few months of the war, I befriended a black-market speculator named Artemus White. I knew the end of the war was near.

"'I devised a plan to take some of the treasure and leave with it from Richmond with the aid of Artemus. He provided me with an assumed name, Cyrus Macauly, and identification. He devised a plan for me to travel to Norfolk and sail north on a ship, which carried black-market goods to both sides in the war. North of Boston, a Union warship followed us. I knew if we were overtaken and boarded, I would be imprisoned and the treasure confiscated. The ship's captain recommended

that I leave the ship and hide in the Prospect Harbor lightkeeper's house, which had not been in use since before the war.'"

Kay laid the pages she'd read on the bed and held the last two. "I need some water. My mouth is dry."

Anna handed her the bottle from her nightstand.

Kay swallowed and wiped her mouth. "'The captain of the ship assured me, or mostly assured me, that he would later return and pick me up. He told me to row to the lighthouse. As I left the ship, a spring squall approached. The boat sank no more than twenty-five yards from the lighthouse. I swam for the shore, but I was exhausted. I found a large chain that stretched into the water and used it to pull myself onto dry land.

"'With me were two barrels containing gold ingots and coins. I gave the ship's captain some of the gold as an incentive to return for me. The bullion was marked with the CSA, and some of the coins were from Mexico. I estimated the weight of the barrels to be fifty pounds each. The barrels floated for a time, but they, too, went to the bottom not far from shore. I planned to hire someone to retrieve the gold and then I would sell it in Europe. That day never came. The money I would use to ensure you and our children a secure future. I will leave you soon. I hope you will forgive my weakness in not being able to reveal these facts to you in person. I am placing this letter in your cherished volumes that I know you will read some day again after I have left this earth for a better place. Your loving husband, Cyrus.'"

"So, Macauly's real name is Fields," Anna said. "But how does that affect Matt?"

Kay unfolded the copy of the Wheatlye-Macauly family tree. "His ancestors who had the Macauly name should have been Fields. This includes his mom." She showed Anna the paper and pointed at Matt's mom's name. "Her maiden name was Macauly."

"Do you think this will upset Matt if he finds out?"

Kay gathered up the pages of the letter. "Maybe. I'm not sure." She lowered her head and laid the papers back on top of the book. "Matt does seem to be proud of his heritage."

Anna grabbed the sheet with the family tree and held it up. "Jonathan Wheatlye is still his five-greats, and *his* background is real."

"True," Kay said. "But—"

"But what? It could be a shock to Matt. I don't think we should say anything."

Kay pulled her feet up onto the bed and lay on her side, her left arm supporting her head. "Of course, I could ask him how much he knows about his other great-grandparents. He might know some of this. If he doesn't know, he may appreciate me giving him the information. We can talk to him at my birthday party—if he comes."

"I still don't think it's a good idea to tell him. I don't want to make him mad at me...at *us*." Anna's phone vibrated. "It's a text from Matt. He wants to know if we want to go for a boat ride tomorrow."

Kay stared at the letter. Maybe she'll have a chance to ask Matt more about his family. Without looking up, she said, "Sure. Why not? Let's do it."

CHAPTER TWELVE

"**A**pologies for the last-minute invitation, but my dad and I couldn't go lobster fishing today. He got called in to work. I thought we could take a ride and show you Prospect Harbor from the water." Matt said to Kay, "I'm sorry your mom couldn't come."

"Mom gets nauseous on boats. This only started a year ago. She said she would relax and read."

"I like the name of your boat," Anna said. "*Maria.*"

Kay stepped back to read the name on the side. "*Maria*—that is a nice name. Who's it named after?"

Matt didn't respond. Helping the girls down from the dock, he started the motors and turned to face Kay. "The boat. She's named for my mom."

Kay winced. She knew his mom's name was Maria from reading Matt's family tree. Why didn't she think before opening her mouth?

"Anna, if you'll untie the stern line, and, Kay, if you'll get the bow line, we'll get underway."

Dropping the line, Anna walked up next to Matt. "That's a great way to remember your mom."

Matt spun the wheel and rounded a channel marker. "Hold on, crew." He maneuvered around a lobster buoy. The boat rocked. "Anyone feel the need for a life jacket?"

Anna swiveled her head around and stared wide-eyed at the skipper. "Why? Are we sinking?"

Matt laughed. "No, we're not sinking. I wanted to make sure you're comfortable being out on the water. Can you swim?"

"I can do well enough to get by. I'm not great."

"And you, Kay?"

"I'm a decent swimmer. I started swim lessons when I was five."

"Wow, that's young."

"My school in Tallahassee had a swim team, and my mom thought it would be good for me to take lessons. When I was older, I joined the team."

"So, you've been competing for a while?"

"For the past nine years."

"You obviously don't need a life jacket."

"I also took scuba lessons and got certified as a junior open-water diver when I was thirteen. When I turn fifteen, I want to get full certification."

"You didn't tell me you were a diver when I mentioned I was one."

"It was our first meeting, and I didn't want to sound like I was bragging after you told us you were a diver. I hate it when people do that."

The *Maria* bounced and rolled, crossing the wake of another boat. Anna held on to the seat back and stood next to Kay. "It's not bragging. I think it's pretty daring for you to be a scuba diver. I could never do that."

Matt leaned back, holding on to the wheel. "Sure, you could."

"No, I'll never do that. Breathing underwater isn't natural."

Matt smiled. "We don't need scuba today, so let's enjoy the ride." He pushed the throttles ahead. The cruise around the inner harbor brought the three teenagers to a point off the lighthouse.

"Can you get closer?" Kay asked.

Matt eased the motors in gear. "Yeah, but we have to watch for the rocks."

"This is a beautiful spot. Do you have any binoculars?"

Matt unlocked the compartment beneath the steering wheel and handed Kay a weather-beaten, black case. "Try these."

"How close can you get to the shore?" Kay panned from left to right and back again.

"The depth finder shows we're at thirty feet. Anna, look for lobster buoys. I don't want to get any lines wrapped up in the props."

Anna leaned over the bow rail. "The water is so clear I can almost see to the bottom."

"Sometimes we have great visibility. At other times, not so good."

The boat moved closer to the rocky shore. Anna continued her vigil. "Looks good so far. There's a buoy on the right."

"I see it," Matt said.

Kay stopped panning and adjusted the focus. It was there—the rock with the chain. The one Macauly said he used to pull himself on land. This was where the boat and the barrels had sunk.

Kay handed the glasses to Matt. "That's good. Thanks." She glanced at Anna.

Shaking her head, Anna pushed herself back in the seat.

"Interesting." Matt adjusted the binoculars. "That's an unusual buoy."

Kay strained to see what he was looking at. "You know every one of them?"

He laughed, lowering the binoculars and handing them to Kay. "I have a good memory, but not like a terabyte hard drive. There're three million lobster buoys in Maine's waters. It's unusual because there's only one in this area, and it has some strange markings on it."

Kay adjusted the focus and locked on the floating object. "What does it mean?"

Matt pushed on the throttles. "I have no idea."

In the still air, the water shimmered like a liquid mirror, the only breeze coming from the boat's movement.

Kay sniffed. "I love the smell of the ocean."

"Except for low tide." Anna pinched her nose.

"Yeah, that smell can curl your nose," Matt said.

Kay sat back, closed her eyes, and listened. The engines' undulating drone and the gentle slap of the water against the hull made Kay's eyes heavy. She drifted off to sleep.

The *Maria* bumped the dock, and Matt tossed a line around a cleat.

"Kay jumped up and rubbed her eyes. Grabbing a handrail, she shuffled closer to Matt. "At dinner the other night, you said your were related to—"

"We didn't talk about your girlfriends," Anna said, stepping between Matt and Kay.

"What? My relatives?" Matt looked at Kay and pivoted toward Anna. "Dating? Girls?" He blushed. "I dated a few girls last year—girls in my class. I'm not going with anyone. There was a girl in my freshman class that I liked. But my mom got sick and things didn't work out. Lately, I've been too busy with school or helping my dad with lobster fishing."

Kay glared at Anna.

Matt checked the lines and climbed up on the dock. He walked the girls to his truck to retrieve their bikes.

"Thanks for the ride." Anna extended her hand.

He drew her close and gave her a light hug.

Blushing, Anna pulled back.

Matt then extended his hand to Kay and did the same. She, too, blushed.

"What were you asking about my relatives?"

"It was nothing. Forget it." Kay cleared her throat. "I love being out on the water. Thanks for giving us the tour."

Matt stepped toward his truck. "Thank you both for a great morning. I haven't had this much fun in a long time."

Biking back to the rental house, Anna slowed several times, but Kay never pulled up alongside. Kay didn't want to discuss Matt's hugs or her attempt to discuss his ancestors. The hugs were a pleasant surprise, but if she told Matt about her discovery it might not be so pleasant for him. And it would definitely upset Anna. Kay had to let it go. She had to, she must...but she couldn't.

CHAPTER THIRTEEN

Bobbie drove out onto Main Street. Kay waved.

Anna tugged on Kay's arm. "You didn't want to go to the airport to pick up your dad?"

"She told me I didn't have to go. And I didn't want to spend three or four hours on the road and waiting for dad's plane."

"I can understand that, but what are we going to do?"

"We'll make my birthday cake. But I also want to do some research online."

"Research what?" Anna asked. "More information on Matt's ancestors?"

"Maybe." Kay stepped inside the house ahead of Anna.

Anna walked up behind her in the dining room. "On the boat, you were going to ask Matt about his ancestors, weren't you? I thought we agreed it wouldn't be good to bring up the subject with him."

"I didn't agree to that. And, yes, I was going to bring it up till you cut me off. All I wanted to know was if he had heard of anyone doubting Macauly's story."

Anna sighed. "I understand your need to find out things—I think. But why do you need more information? Isn't the letter enough?"

Kay sat at the dining room table and slid the computer in front of her. "If I do bring up the subject—and I'm not saying I will—I don't want to ask him until I'm absolutely sure Macauly's story is true. My dad has a subscription to a website for researching your ancestors. Plus, I want to check out the other parts of Macauly's letter."

Anna shook her head. "I should start calling you Detective Telfair."

"Very funny. I'm only interested in knowing if what Macauly says in his letter is true. If it is, maybe I'll ask Matt if he knows any more about his family history. Or maybe I won't ask him. It depends."

"Depends on what?"

"I don't know—lots of things." Kay opened the laptop and adjusted the screen angle.

Anna sighed and went to the porch. "I'm going to read my book."

Kay spread the copies of the letter and the obituary on the table. She opened the browser window and spoke quietly. "Macauly said the lighthouse wasn't being used, and that's why he hid there."

Kay typed in the search window and clicked on an item. "It says here that Congress decided to shut down the Prospect Harbor lighthouse in 1859." She read further. "'A new lens apparatus was installed in the lantern room, and the light was once again exhibited for the benefit of mariners on the night of May 15, 1870.'"

"The lighthouse part is true, but what about the rest of his story?" Kay read aloud from the copy of the obituary. "'He was a crewmember aboard a US merchant ship in late 1864 when his ship was attacked and taken by the Confederate Navy ship *Chameleon*.'" Searching for fifteen minutes, Kay said in a low voice, "Macauly couldn't have been on that ship at the time he said he was there."

She unfolded Macauly's letter. "He says he was born in Fairfax, Virginia, and was a lieutenant in the Confederate Navy. It says he served on the CSS *Virginia*."

Kay went to the genealogy website. Within ten minutes, she found what she was looking for—William H. Fields and a notation next to his name. "He did join the navy at fifteen. It's true." She slouched back in the chair.

"What's true?" Anna asked, walking in from the porch.

Kay quickly jerked around ninety degrees. "Nothing. I'm thinking out loud."

"By the way, I'm sorry for teasing you," Anna said. "But you do obsess over some things, *Detective Telfair*."

"I'll admit I have a strong interest in some things—"

"Strong interest?" Anna raised her eyebrows and lowered her head at Kay. "I'll say you do."

Kay faked a frown and held it for a few seconds until she giggled. "Do not."

"Do too."

"Do not."

"Do too."

"Do not—OK maybe a little." Kay chuckled and then laughed out loud.

"All you need is a police badge, an overcoat, and a notepad." Anna laughed. "You could have your own TV show, *Kay Telfair, Teen Detective.*"

Kay slid off the chair, laughing and pointing at her friend. "And there's my assistant, Police Sergeant Anna Gardino."

Anna held her sides, laughing harder. "Stop, Kay, don't say anything else. I'm dying here. I'm laughing so hard I think I broke a rib."

Anna gasped for air, holding back the laughter.

Kay wiped the tears, and returned to the computer. "Where was I before I was so rudely interrupted by my assistant, *Police Sergeant Gardino.*"

Anna burst out laughing and walked away. "Kay, stop, please."

Without shifting her focus away from the screen, Kay winked. "Whatever you say—*Sarge.*"

From the bedroom came the muffled laughter of Kay's friend—her best friend.

CHAPTER FOURTEEN

"**G**reat lobster roll, Derek." Kay's dad finished the last bite. "Kay and Anna told me to expect a real treat."

"I'm glad you liked them," Derek said. "It's my wife's recipe. Matt did most of the work."

Jim leaned forward and placed his glass on the table. "I'm sorry about your wife."

"Thanks…we, Matt and me, we miss her a lot. She was a terrific woman."

"From what I've heard from Bobbie and the girls your son is pretty special, too. It's obvious he got some great guidance from you and your wife."

"Matt's grown up fast these past two years. He's been a great emotional support to me and helped in a lot of other ways. We bought the lobster boat a few years ago, and Matt can work it by himself if I'm not available. We aren't able to pull traps as much as we would like since my work schedule is so erratic."

"How *is* the lobster business?" Jim asked.

"Some years good; others not so good. I hope we can do OK this year. Maria's medical expenses and me losing my job put us in a bind. But Matt has stepped up, and we hope we'll finish the season in good shape." Derek smiled at his son. "I want him to go to college. Maybe U-Maine where Maria and I went."

Matt blushed and shifted in his chair, catching a glimpse of Kay.

Kay waved at her mom and mouthed the word "cake."

Her mom stood. "Why don't I put the coffee on, and we can light the candles. Kay, would you get the ice cream from the freezer?"

"I'm stuffed," Kay's dad said. "First, lobster rolls and, now, cake and ice cream?"

●　●　●

"If everyone's finished, let's open some gifts." Kay's mom reached into a large bag. "These are from your grandparents." She handed Kay two envelopes.

Kay opened them, read the cards, and held up checks for a hundred dollars each. "Wow," she said. "This will get me that pair of shoes I wanted."

Her mom gave Kay another envelope. "This one is from Anna."

"That's from me and my mom and dad…and Buddy, too. He wanted to give you a video game, but I told him you'd rather go shopping."

"Thanks. I guess your little brother's not such a pain after all." Kay gave Anna a light embrace.

Anna shook her head. "No, he's still a pain. I love him, but he's a pain."

Bobbie handed her husband a package and kept another for herself. "They say that, in life, timing is everything." She handed the package to Kay. "This is from your dad and me."

Kay tore open the box. "A watch." She held it up. "It's beautiful."

"It's a lady's watch," her mom said, putting her arm across Kay's shoulder. "An elegant watch for an elegant young lady."

Kay blushed and gave her mom and dad a hug. "Thanks."

Her dad held out another package. "Wait, there's more. This is to show you the *depths* of our feelings for you."

Kay ripped part of the paper from the box and read the information. "A computer? The box is so small."

Pulling back more of the paper, her dad pointed to an area on the box. "A *dive* computer."

"I have one of those." Matt drew closer to Kay. She handed him the box. "Makes diving a lot easier. You don't have to do manual calculations."

Kay again moved from one parent to the other, giving hugs.

"You have one more gift to open." Her mom pointed to the package Matt and his dad had brought.

Blushing, Kay's hands shook. She fumbled with the ribbon and paper and opened the rectangular box.

"A book," Kay said in a flat tone.

Matt reached out and opened the cover while Kay held the book. "It's about lighthouses in New England. It has the Prospect Harbor lighthouse in here." He chuckled. "You can be your *own* tour guide with this."

"Thanks very much, Matt." She grinned and winked. "Maybe, but you're the best tour guide around here."

"Tour guide?" Kay's dad reached out for the book.

"Matt? A tour guide?" Derek squinted at his son.

Matt blushed and closed the cover. "I was pointing out some things about Maine when Kay, Anna, and I went on our bike ride. They called me their tour guide."

"I know you want to look at this," Kay said, handing the book to her dad. "You all go out on the porch and chat. Anna and I will clear the table."

Jim grabbed his wife's arm, nudged her from the chair, and chuckled. "Come on Matt, Derek. Let's go before the girls change their minds."

"I feel guilty," Kay's mom said. "You baked your own cake for your birthday party, and now you're cleaning up."

"I'll help." Matt walked over to the dining room table and picked up plates and glasses. He grinned at Kay. "You mean the birthday girl had to bake her own cake?"

"I like to bake. My mom and my grandmothers taught me. Anna and I made the cake this afternoon. Anna likes to bake, too."

Matt stacked dishes and handed them to Kay.

Kay stooped at the dishwasher. "Is the lobster roll a recipe your mom made up or is it an old family recipe?"

"My mom said it was from her great-great grandmother, who came from Canada."

Kay wanted an opening to discuss Matt's Macauly ancestors. "That's interesting. So the recipe didn't come from the Wheatlye side of the family?"

"Nope. The Wheatlyes weren't into lobster fishing. They ran the store that sold supplies to the fishermen."

Anna shook her head at Kay.

Matt wasn't volunteering any information that would help Kay decide whether to share with him what she'd found. She tried again. "I noticed the initials M-M-H painted on the cooler you brought." She opened it and put Matt's plastic containers inside. "What's your middle name?"

"Benjamin."

"Nice name," Kay said.

Matt put down the pan he had washed and dried. "That's not my cooler. It was my mom's. She used it to take food to the church dinners or to make lunches for me and my dad when we were fishing. She went by Maria Macauly Hubbard. Her middle name was Frances."

Kay glanced at Anna, who gritted her teeth and glared.

Kay was getting nowhere with Matt to find out if he knew about Fields. The teens worked in silence for the next three minutes.

"Would you like to try our ride again through the park?" Kay asked.

"Sure. We can't pull traps tomorrow. It's Sunday."

"Let me ask my mom and dad if we can go." Kay walked toward the porch and stopped at the doorway.

"I'm happy Matt's made friends with Kay and Anna," Derek said. "Ever since Maria passed away, he's been keeping me company a lot—more than he should. I think he was worried about me. Believe it or not, he's always been a little shy around girls. But he said he enjoys being with Kay and Anna. I've noticed he's been more upbeat the last few weeks."

"I can tell the girls enjoy being with him," Bobbie said. "I was afraid they'd be bored up here. As you heard, Matt has become their local tour guide."

"He's a great kid, and I'm glad they met." Derek checked his watch. "We'd better get moving. I have to be at work at seven. Thanks

for inviting us to Kay's party. Matt and I don't go out much these days. Work and all."

"I understand that situation," Jim said. "I have to leave Monday to fly back to New Jersey."

Kay eased back into the kitchen.

"What did they say?" Anna asked.

"I didn't ask. I'll do it later."

The Hubbard men stepped out onto the front porch and down the stairs. The girls walked a few steps down behind Matt.

"See you tomorrow, ladies."

"Bye, Matt," Kay said.

Anna waved, whirled around, and hurried inside.

"You're seeing Matt again tomorrow?" Kay's mom asked.

"If it's OK with you and Dad. We thought we'd try our bike ride again in the park. Can we?"

"OK by me," her dad said. "Your mom and I can have lunch in Winter Harbor."

Kay ran to catch up to Anna. "What's the problem?"

"You're going to tell him about the letter, aren't you?"

"I don't know. I still haven't decided. Let's see how the bike ride goes tomorrow."

"If you do, this could be the end of our friendship with him."

Kay huffed and went to the bedroom. She picked up the copies of Macauly's letter. Shaking her head, she tossed the papers on the nightstand and fell across the bed. Anna's words lingered in her mind. What should she do?

CHAPTER FIFTEEN

"I saw you put the copies in your backpack," Anna whispered to Kay. "Please don't say anything to him."

Kay shrugged and walked over to help Matt take her bike off the rack.

"It was very nice meeting you, Mr. Telfair," Matt said, standing at the van door. "I'll follow the girls home in my truck when we finish the ride."

Kay leaned in through the van window and kissed her mom. "Thanks, Dad. You and mom have a great lunch."

The trio biked through the park, stopping every few minutes to walk down to the rocky shore.

At one stop, Matt said, "I hope you're ready for some more tour-guide stuff. You're in part of Acadia National Park. The largest section is on Mount Desert Island. That's where Bar Harbor is located."

Kay pushed her sunglasses up on her head. "Where's that?"

Matt pointed across the bay. "Over there. Bar Harbor is on an island. Most people don't realize that when they visit."

Kay and Anna each did a small eye roll.

"That's it. No more tour guide," Matt said, faking a frown. He winked. "For a while anyway. Let's head for the picnic area and rest-rooms. The tour guide needs a snack."

At the picnic area, the teens sat at a table—the girls on one side, Matt on the other.

Kay spread the bags of pretzels and snack mix. "You said your mom was into genealogy. How much do you know about the Macauly side of your family?"

Anna frowned at Kay. "Don't you think that's a bit personal?"

Kay blushed. "Sorry, Matt, I was—"

"No, no. I'm not offended. But I am curious. Why are you interested in my family?"

Kay's heart beat faster. She took a drink of water. "Well...I...I was in the library, and the librarian showed me these books by Alcott."

"You mean the *Little Women* books donated by my great grandfather? My mom told me about those, but I've never seen them. Most guys don't read *Little Women*."

Relieved that Matt was aware of the books, Kay had the opening to tell him about the letter.

"Yes, those books. The librarian let me look at them. She also showed me the binder with the obituary for Cyrus Macauly, and I saw the name Jonathan Wheatlye. You told us about him when you had dinner with us. He was your five greats grandfather."

"My mom gave that material to the library. I remember her saying something about my four greats grandfather jumping off a ship and landing here in Prospect Harbor."

"Right. Cyrus Macauly," Kay said, her mouth as dry as cotton. She took another swig from her water bottle.

"I thought it was pretty boring stuff," Matt said.

Anna tugged at a bag of snacks. It ripped open, launching crackers across the table.

Kay jumped. She helped Anna scoop up the loose snacks and continued her explanation. "When I went through the *Little Women* books, I found a letter sandwiched between the pages of the second book. It was written by Macauly."

"A letter? In the book? You mean not part of it?"

Anna slid off the bench seat and stood. "I need to go to the restroom. Do you need to go, Kay?"

"No, I'm good."

"Are you sure you don't need to go?"

"No, Anna. I don't."

"Then I'll wait." Anna sat at the end of the bench, looking away from the conversation.

"Are you sure you can wait?" Kay asked. "Maybe you *should* go."

Matt raised one eyebrow and half smiled at the conversation between his bike companions. He glanced first at Anna and then at Kay. "If either of you need to go to the restroom, I'll sit here and wait."

Kay shook her head and leaned on the table. "Back to Cyrus Macauly. He wrote the letter to his wife a few days before he died."

"What's in the letter?"

"Do you know the whole story of Macauly escaping from a Confederate ship during the Civil War?"

"I don't remember all the details."

Kay reached into her backpack and pulled out the copies of the obituary. She handed the paper to Matt and caught a quick glimpse of Anna's scowl.

Matt shuffled through the papers, stopping to read passages.

Kay popped her knuckles—a habit her mom warned her about many times—and bit her lip.

Anna jumped up. "I'm going to the restroom."

Kay waved her off and shook her head. "Finally."

"I remember my mom was doing some more research on her family. She said there were some things in the obituary that didn't make sense."

Kay unfolded the copy of the letter and handed it to Matt. "I think your mom was correct. There *was* something wrong with Macauly's story."

For the next five minutes, Matt read and reread the letter. "Looks like it's the Fields family name instead of Macauly." He said nothing for the next ten seconds, a frown building on his face. "Why did you show me the letter?"

Stunned, Kay hadn't expected this question. She assumed he would be disappointed at finding out that his ancestor Macauly was a fraud. This question she couldn't answer without hurting his feelings. Why did she always have to be right? Why couldn't she let it go?

"I...well, I saw the letter, and I—"

"Do you mind if I keep these copies?"

"No. No. Sure, keep them. Do you want to show them to your dad?"

"I don't think so. It'll remind him how much mom loved genealogy and looking into her family history, which seems to be a lie at this point."

Kay fought back tears. How could she have been so stupid?

"Let's get moving." Matt hopped up and walked to his bike.

Anna returned and whispered to Kay, "You told him, didn't you?"

Kay picked up her backpack and stuffed the remaining snacks inside.

"You're crying," Anna said. "What did he say?"

Kay shook her head, zipped the backpack, and mounted her bike.

Matt set a fast pace, slowing several times when he saw the girls lagging behind but always staying ahead of them.

Arriving at the park exit, Matt placed his bike in the bed of his truck. Kay and Anna continued pedaling past. Matt waited several minutes before pulling out onto the highway and following them.

Before they reached the parking lot at the dock, Matt passed the girls and stopped.

The girls pulled up beside his truck.

"We can make it to the house from here," Anna said. "Thanks for following us."

Kay's voice cracked. "Thanks, Matt."

"No problem," he said. He jerked the truck into gear and drove away.

Anna pushed off ahead of Kay.

Struggling to get her foot on the pedal, Kay pointed her bike toward the vacation house. She lifted her sunglasses and wiped the small tears streaking down her face. What had she done? Matt would never speak to her again.

CHAPTER SIXTEEN

"I need to lie down." Kay laid her bike helmet on the dining table. Bobbie put her hand to Kay's forehead. "What's the matter? Are you ill?"

"I think I need to rest." Kay pulled away and went to the bedroom. Anna followed her.

Kay lay on the bed, her face buried in the pillow. "I messed up. I never should have mentioned the letter."

"I'm sure he's not upset. Maybe he needs time to think about what he read. That's all."

"It's not *what* he read. He asked me why I showed him the letter. I feel like a jerk. I didn't know what to say. I wasn't trying to make him feel bad."

"Then *why did* you tell him?"

"I don't know. Maybe I wanted the pieces to fit."

"Pieces? Pieces of what?"

"You know, puzzles."

"What puzzles? Kay, you're confusing me."

Kay rolled over. "When I see something or hear something that doesn't make sense or isn't true, I have to find out the truth. I need to make all the pieces of the puzzle fit. Understand?"

"I think so. It's the detective in you."

Kay daubed at her tears with a tissue and fell back on the bed. "Go ahead, say it."

"Say what?"

"That you told me so."

Anna sat next to her friend. "I won't say that." She took Kay's hand. "OK, I will say it—I told you so. But all you did was tell someone the truth. Maybe Matt didn't understand what you were trying to do. You didn't do anything wrong."

"Yes, I did. I hurt someone." Kay's tears dribbled onto her pillow.

"Kay, stop. If your mom hears you crying, you'll have to explain all this to her and your dad. And he's leaving tomorrow. You don't want him to leave feeling sad for you."

Kay blew her nose and wiped her eyes.

"Kay, do you have a cold?" Her mom stood in the bedroom doorway.

Startled, Kay sat up and swung her feet off the side of the bed.

"We think it's allergies, Mrs. Telfair. There were lots of flowers blooming in the park."

"I wonder if there is mountain laurel in the woods here," Bobbie said. "Kay had a reaction to that on a visit to Pennsylvania a few years ago. It was everywhere at our friend's house."

"That must be it," Anna said.

"I'll be all right."

Her dad stuck his head in the door. "Who's going to be all right?"

"Kay's allergies are bothering her," her mom said, sitting beside her daughter.

"Get better," her dad said. "We're going to the Lobster Pot for dinner. My last night here with you."

Kay sniffed. "Give me a little while. I'm sure I'll recover."

Her mom ushered her dad out and took a step back into the room. "Rest for a while."

Kay gave Anna a hug. "Thanks for helping me out. I'm sorry I'm such a jerk."

"You're welcome, and you're not a jerk." Anna put her hands on Kay's shoulders and chuckled. "Well, most of the time, you're not."

Kay chuckled between sniffs and pushed her friend back with her index finger. "You're right. I am a jerk sometimes." She grinned at Anna. "And so are you."

"Am not."

"Are too."

Anna laughed. "Am not."

Kay gave a weak smile. "Thanks for supporting me. I know you think what I did was awful."

"Stop beating yourself up. I'm sure Matt will come around."

Kay flopped back on the bed and pulled the pillow under her head. "In a hundred years."

"I'll leave you alone. Do you want me to close the door?"

"Yes, please. I need to lie here for a few minutes." The door clicked shut. Kay grabbed a tissue from the nightstand, rolled over, and faced the wall. "I can't believe I told him. What was I thinking?"

CHAPTER SEVENTEEN

Kay's dad drove out of the restaurant parking lot. "I'm glad you're allergies got better. Those lobster rolls were delicious."

"The lobster rolls were good but not as good as Matt's," Kay's mom said. "What do you think, girls?"

"I think Matt's are better," Anna said.

"What do you think, Kay?" her dad asked.

Kay maintained her blank stare out the window. Anna poked her with her finger. "Don't you think Matt's were better?"

"What? Yeah, absolutely."

"I guess that settles it," Kay's dad said.

Kay caught a glimpse of her dad in the rearview mirror. He smiled at her.

Kay gave a weak smile.

"Everything all right, dear?" he asked.

Before Kay could answer, Anna jerked, reaching into her pocket. "It's a text from Matt."

Her voice weak and trembling, Kay whispered, "What does he say?"

Anna leaned close. "He says to tell you he's glad you gave him the letter."

Kay closed her eyes and leaned back against the headrest.

"He says he wants to talk on Tuesday. He's fishing tomorrow. What should I tell him?"

"Say sure, we can talk."

Anna lowered her voice. "You don't sound excited."

"I'm not un-excited, if that's a word." Kay gazed out the window of the van. Inside she cheered. Matt didn't hate her.

CHAPTER EIGHTEEN

"**D**id I hear my name?" Anna approached the counter and reached for the coffeepot. She poured a cup and sat with her phone.

"We wondered if you were going to sleep till noon," Kay said.

"What time is it?" Anna squinted at her phone. "It's only...oh my gosh. It's 10:20."

Kay tapped Anna on the shoulder. "Did you hear from Matt?"

"He texted me but didn't say what he wanted to do. I'm checking messages and my e-mail." Anna fingered the screen with a swipe in one direction and then back. "Here it is. He sent an e-mail and another text late last night. I guess he wanted to make sure I got his message. He wants to meet at the library at one. That's when it opens."

Bobbie raised her eyebrows. "At the library?"

"That's what he says."

"That's strange. Why the library? I thought you three might be off on some adventure."

Kay had an inkling of why Matt wanted to meet there, and it made her nervous. She glanced at Anna, looking for help.

Anna put down her phone. "On our ride through the park, we talked about his ancestors who lived in the area. Maybe he wants to do some research or something."

Kay's eyes widened. She gritted her teeth. Why didn't Anna tell her mom everything—the letter, her revealing Matt's ancestor's real identity?

Bobbie opened the dishwasher and placed her cup inside. With the door half open and still bending over, she tilted her head toward the girls. "Not to make too much of this, but why would he want to meet you at the library to do research? He could do that on his own."

Kay jumped in, thinking she should risk revealing some information. "I saw a book at the library donated by his great-grandfather. Remember."

"I think so," her mom said.

"The librarian showed it to me. It was that two-volume set of books of *Little Women* and *Good Wives*. Matt knew about the books, but he'd never seen them. My guess is he wants us to meet him there since I mentioned it to him. Maybe he feels weird looking at *Little Women* by himself. Most guys wouldn't read the book." With pursed lips, Kay stopped rambling and glowered at Anna.

"It's also an excuse to be with us," Anna said. "What guy wouldn't want to be with the two best-looking girls in Prospect Harbor. Make that two of the *three* best-looking girls."

Bobbie smiled. "Why, thank you, Anna."

CHAPTER NINETEEN

Kay wasn't sure how to handle this. In his text message Matt said he wasn't angry, but the situation could be awkward. Kay hadn't spoken to him since she showed him the letter.

The two leaned their bikes against the building. Kay hesitated and let Anna enter first.

Anna called out in a loud whisper. "He's over here."

The girls moved to either side of Matt.

Kay felt the blood pulsating in her neck.

"I asked the librarian to show me the books. She laid them out only a minute before you walked in. Where did you find the letter?"

Kay moved in closer and stood in front of the second volume. Her hand trembled. She reached for the book. "The pages of the letter aren't in one place. And you have to look carefully because the letter paper is smaller than the book pages."

Kay flipped through the volume, trying to remember where she placed the letter after making copies. With a gentle tug from her index finger and thumb, she removed the first page of Macauly's letter. "Here's one."

"By the way, thanks for telling me about the letter."

Kay's heart rate slowed. The saliva returned to her mouth. She kept her gaze on the book and said softly, "You're welcome." She found the other pages and handed them to Matt.

"Let's go over there." Matt gestured toward a small table with four chairs near the magazine rack. He sat, caught a glimpse of the librarian over his shoulder, and spread the pages on the table. Kay and

Anna stood by his side. "I found my mom's copy of her family tree that started with Jonathan Wheatlye. I also found some of her notes where she had done some research on Cyrus Macauly. She must've had some doubts about his story."

"After I did a little digging, so did I." Kay pulled out the chair and sat next to Matt. "This letter fascinated me from the start. Then I read the obituary, and there were so many things between the two that didn't make sense." "I was afraid I had made you angry by showing you the letter."

"I'm sorry I made you feel that way. I was surprised to find out my ancestors were fake." He fumbled with the pages. "It also reminded me of my mom and how much she loved doing research on her family."

Anna sat, slid a page of the letter in front of her, and ran her fingers down it. "The letter mentions gold."

Matt reached for the page and held it up. "That's what caught my attention."

"I never checked to see if the Confederate treasure part was true," Kay said. "If Macauly made up a story about how he came to be in Prospect Harbor, how do we know his story about the gold is true?"

Matt waved his hand toward the computers. "Let's find out."

Kay hopped up and went to one of two keyboards on a nearby desk. She typed in "Civil War" in the search box.

"Hmmm. That's a lot of search returns," Anna said, looking over Kay's shoulder. "Don't you think you should narrow it?"

"I will, but look at this one. 'Quick Facts About the Civil War.' Maybe there's something here that will help us."

"I think we're studying that in history next year," Matt said. "I remember some of it from middle school."

"I don't remember much at all," Anna said.

Kay clicked on the link. Matt and Anna leaned in and followed along as Kay read in a low voice. "'The Civil War, also known as The War Between the States, lasted from 1861 to 1865. It was fought between the United States of America and the Confederate States of America. The CSA was a collection of eleven southern states that left the Union in 1860 and 1861 and formed their own country in order to protect the institution of slavery.

"'The first battle of the Civil War occurred when Southern troops bombarded Fort Sumter, South Carolina in April 1861.

"'Abraham Lincoln was the President of the United States during the Civil War. On January 1, 1863, he issued the Emancipation Proclamation, which freed the slaves in the southern states and laid the groundwork for slaves to eventually be freed across the country. On April 14, 1865, John Wilkes Booth, a southern sympathizer, assassinated President Lincoln.

"'The issues of slavery and central power divided the United States, setting the stage for the conflict between the north and the south. Many people believed that slavery was immoral and wrong. Southerners felt threatened by people who wanted to abolish slavery—called "abolitionists"—and claimed that the common government had no power to end slavery against the wishes of the states. Eventually, southerners became convinced that the common government would attempt to abolish slavery nationwide.'"

"Here's something about Gettysburg," Matt said, moving closer to the computer screen. "My mom, my dad, and I went there. It's a huge battlefield. Listen to this. 'The bloodiest battle of the Civil War was the Battle of Gettysburg, Pennsylvania. In an effort to gather fresh supplies and intimidate the United States, Confederate General Robert E. Lee launched a daring invasion of the North in the summer of 1863. Union General George G. Meade's army defeated Lee's army in a three-day battle near Gettysburg, Pennsylvania, that left nearly 52,000 men killed, wounded, or missing in action. Many historians mark the Battle of Gettysburg as the turning point in the Civil War when the Confederacy began to lose. After the battle, President Lincoln delivered the Gettysburg Address, which expressed firm commitment to preserving the Union and became one of the most famous speeches in American history.'" Matt looked up. "Did you know that somebody else gave a speech before President Lincoln and talked for two hours? Then Lincoln summed up what he wanted to say in ten sentences."

"Boy, you really are a tour guide," Anna said.

Matt shrugged. "I remembered that from the visit, and I wrote a paper on it for school."

Kay jumped in. "Here's some more interesting stuff." She adjusted the screen. "'More than 620,000 men died in the Civil War, more than the totals of all the other wars in which Americans fought.

"'After the war was over, the Constitution was amended to free the slaves, to assure equal protection under the law for American citizens, and to grant black men the right to vote.'"

"My dad says you should vote in every election," Matt said. "He says that if we don't vote, we really don't have a right to complain about the government or laws that we think aren't fair."

"That makes sense," Kay said. "My grandfather, who's from Georgia, told me that the state made the voting age eighteen in 1943 during World War II. It was the only state to make the voting age eighteen until the 1960's. He said the reason they did that was that the people figured if you were old enough to go to war, you were old enough to vote. Back then men were drafted into the army and navy at eighteen. Today, people volunteer—men and women. My dad volunteered for the navy after he graduated college."

Anna chuckled. "Matt's the *tour guide*, and you're the *historian*."

"I like history, and I remember a lot of the things my grandparents told me," Kay said.

"If you say so," Anna said.

"Your grandparents never told you stories?" Kay asked.

"Of course they did, but—"

"OK, you two. No bickering. Let's get back to the gold."

Kay typed "Confederate treasury," waited, and scrolled through the results. Matt and Anna peered over her shoulder.

"Try that one." Matt pointed to an entry.

Kay read. "'No longer defended, the leaders of the Confederacy evacuated Richmond in mid April 1865 and took with them the last of the treasure of the dying country. Captain William H. Parker, superintendent of the Confederate States Naval Academy, was an eyewitness to the journey of the treasure. He wrote a letter to the *Richmond Dispatch* after the war that helps explain why some continue to speculate on the fate of the treasure.'"

Anna read ahead of Kay. "Click on the link to Captain Parker's letter."

Kay clicked, and the letter popped up. Matt read: "'Accordingly, at six o'clock, I was at the depot with all my officers and men...'" He scanned the page. "This says Parker was put in charge of a train that had the Confederate treasure on it, and some of it belonged to banks in Richmond."

Keeping her voice low, Kay read another passage from the letter. "'The senior officer of the treasury present was a cashier, and he informed me, to the best of my recollection, that there was five hundred thousand dollars in gold, silver, and bullion. We did not unpack the treasure from the cars at Danville. Some, I believe, was taken for the use of the government, but the main portion of the money remained with me.

"'The treasure was delivered to General Duke in South Carolina, intact so far as I know, though some of it was taken at Danville by authority.

"'And here ends my personal knowledge of the Confederate treasure. In my opinion, a good deal of the money was never accounted for.'"

Matt stood back from the computer. "Did you hear what he said? Never accounted for."

Kay spun in her chair and faced Matt and Anna. "Looks like Macauly could have stolen some of the gold. He *was* in the Confederate Navy, and the gold was given to Captain Parker, who was in charge of the Confederate Naval Academy. I believe Macauly's story. And think about this. He was dying. Why would he tell the truth about some things and lie about others in the letter. He was confessing everything."

"I believe him, too," Anna said. "But if the gold *is* underwater, I'll bet it's washed away or rusted."

"I doubt that it's washed away, and gold doesn't rust—not like iron," Matt said. "It's only in thirty feet of water—more or less—according to what Macauly wrote." He picked up a page. "And here he says he crawled out of the water using a chain attached to a rock."

Kay said, "I saw that chain when you took us on that first cruise around the harbor."

"That's why you wanted the binoculars."

Kay blushed. "Yes, I wanted to see if what Macauly said was true."

Matt ran his finger down a page of the letter. "Macauly said the boat sank somewhere off that point where you saw the chain. The gold should be somewhere near there." He hesitated and laid the letter on the table, looking first at Anna and then at Kay. "I don't know how your parents are planning on helping you with college, but my dad doesn't have the money, and I'm two years away from going. My mom's medical bills almost wiped us out."

Kay raised her eyebrows and angled her head toward Matt. "You want to go after the gold?"

"Underwater?" Anna asked.

"We could do it. The depth is not a problem. The water's chilly, but we have dry suits."

" *We* have dry suits?" Kay asked. "I assume you mean you and your dad."

"Well, yes, my dad and I each have one, but we have a lady's size that my mom used."

Kay's voice rose. "Who's going to wear that?" She had in mind what would be his answer.

Matt raised his shoulders and tilted his head toward Kay.

Kay touched her chest with her finger. "Are you saying the ladies dry suit is for me?"

"I'm sure it'll fit you."

"I've never used a dry suit. But how do you know I'll do it?"

Anna jumped in. "I have some questions, please. What's a dry suit? And how much is the gold worth?"

"A dry suit is warmer than a wet suit," Matt said. "It keeps the water away from your skin. For the gold, I did a rough calculation. Macauly says there were a hundred pounds, so I figure that's close to two and a half million dollars."

Kay swung her head in a dizzying arc. "Back to the diving part. You want me to dive with you?"

"I need a buddy. Never dive alone. Remember the rule."

"I remember the rule. But couldn't someone else be your buddy? Maybe your dad?"

"I don't want to involve him yet. Bringing up the letter might remind him of my mom. If we find the gold, we'll all be rich. I can pay for college, and we can give up lobster fishing."

Cold, dark water. Dry suits. Getting her mom's permission. Kay's mind raced. "I don't know. Are you sure we can do this?"

"It's a shallow dive, and I have an underwater metal detector. With the dry suits, we can stay down thirty to forty minutes and maybe longer. We'll dive at slack tide. I have all the gear you need—tanks, regulator, weights, mask, and fins."

"When do you want to do this?"

"As soon as we can. Tomorrow?"

"I'm not sure my mom will let me go diving with you."

Kay stared at the pages of Macauly's letter spread on the table. The memory of the Washington Crossing letter adventure popped into her head. What was it about these letters? Why couldn't she leave well enough alone?

CHAPTER TWENTY

"**A**re you sure you want to go lobster fishing?" Kay's mom stuck a piece of paper between the pages to mark her place in her book. "You didn't care much for fishing when we went out on our boat in Florida."

"I didn't like trolling. It was boring. As long as we were catching fish, I thought it was fun."

"Didn't Matt say they hauled the traps by hand?" her mom asked. "That's hard work."

"There'll be two of us to help him," Anna said. "Besides, he told us we wouldn't check all the traps today."

"I hope you two know what you're getting into." Kay's mom squinted. "Is that your swim-team suit you're wearing underneath?"

Kay cringed. She needed her one-piece suit to wear under the dry suit. "I want to be prepared. We may get wet hauling the traps. Matt also said it would be warm if there's no breeze, and I thought this would be cooler than a shirt. And maybe I'll go swimming."

"Are you wearing *your* suit, Anna?" Kay's mom asked.

"No, I didn't think I would need it."

Kay tilted her head and frowned. She needed Anna's support.

"I probably should wear my suit, too. The water's freezing, and I can't stand swimming in cold water. But maybe I'll try snorkeling for a few minutes."

"If this is what you want to do, girls. Enjoy, but don't forget the sunscreen." Bobbie laughed. "And don't get bitten by a lobster."

"Ha, ha. Very funny, Mom." Bitten by a lobster? If only that were the worst that could happen.

CHAPTER TWENTY-ONE

Why was she doing this? She hadn't told her mom the truth. It wasn't lobster fishing but hunting for gold—underwater.

"Come on. Let's get going." Matt grabbed Kay's backpack. "It'll be slack high tide in thirty minutes. Visibility should be the best by then."

Climbing down the ladder at the dock, Kay eyes widened when she saw the scuba tanks and gear bags. No turning back now.

"I see you came prepared for our underwater adventure," Matt said.

"Oh, this." Kay fingered the right shoulder of the suit. "I brought it from New Jersey. I didn't know if there was a beach here where I could swim. When I read what the water temperature was, I decided I wouldn't go swimming unless I could find a heated pool."

"The water is chilly, but the dry suit will help a lot. Do you have your suit, Anna?"

"I did wear it, but the water's too cold, and I don't like swimming that much anyway."

Kay spread her arms wide and angled her face toward the sun, trying to calm her nerves. "She's a lay-on-the-beach kind of girl."

Anna stuck out her tongue. "Am not."

"Are too."

"Whoa, ladies. No fighting aboard ship. I want harmony on my crew."

"Aye, aye, captain." Anna stiffened her body and touched her hand to her temple in a salute. She glanced at Kay.

Kay whispered, "Are, too."

Matt laughed, shook his head, and started the engines. "Untie the lines, mates, and let's shove off."

Ten minutes later, the *Maria* idled thirty yards from the shore at the lighthouse.

With one hand steadying the binoculars, she pointed with the other. "There's the rock with the iron rod and chain."

Matt maneuvered closer. "Let's drop anchor here. On our dive, we can work our way up and around the point for fifty yards. Then we'll return to the anchor line. We can make two sweeps up and back before we get too cold."

"That makes sense to me," Kay said. "But what do I know?"

"I know what *I* know." Anna shook her head. "You're both crazy."

"We're not crazy," Matt said. "We know what we're doing."

Kay was glad Matt was confident about this venture. She was terrified.

Ripples on the water slapped the hull of the *Maria* at anchor. The heat from the late summer sun helped fight the chill of the light sea breeze.

"How nice is this," Anna said, reclining in the bow.

Matt took out the gear from the large mesh bags. "Here, Kay, here's your dry suit."

Turning her back to Matt, Kay took off her jeans and shirt and put her legs into the neoprene suit. Her hands shook. "Anna, can you help me get into this?"

The two fought with the friction of the dry suit until Kay was covered.

"This thing is warm." Kay tugged at the tight rubber collar around her neck. "I'm sweating."

"It's warm in the sun. It'll be more comfortable when we get in the water."

With all her gear on, Kay sat on the boat rail. Anna helped her put on her fins, and Matt spun the air valve on her tank.

Putting on the last of his gear, Matt shuffled to the rail and sat next to Kay. "All set?"

"Yeah. Let's get going. This suit is hot."

"Anna, when we're in the water, hand me the metal detector." He tapped Kay on the arm. "I'll go first. I'll let you know when to come in."

Sitting on the rail, Matt held the regulator in his mouth, pressed his mask against his face, and splashed backward into the water. Twenty seconds later, he took the regulator out of his mouth and said, "Come on in."

Kay pushed on the fingers on each glove one more time and fell back, fins jutting into the air. She hit the water, submerged three feet, and popped to the surface.

With Matt holding the metal detector, the two divers swam to the anchor line. Kay held a tight grip on Matt's arm and descended into the cold waters of Prospect Harbor.

CHAPTER TWENTY-TWO

The visibility better than she had imagined, Kay steadied herself on the sandy bottom, scanning all around. Her heart beat fast. She checked her depth gauge—thirty-three feet.

Matt pointed ahead of them and gave his dive buddy the OK sign, his thumb and index finger making an oval and the other fingers extended.

Kay returned the sign. The tension in her muscles let go and her breathing slowed to near normal.

Hovering a foot above the sea floor, Matt moved forward and swung the metal detector in a lazy arc. His fins kicked up a thin cloud of silt behind him.

Kay kept close to his side to make sure her dive buddy saw her with each sweep of the device to his right.

Ten minutes into the dive, the detector squealed. Matt stopped, motioned to Kay, and pointed at the spot. He pulled out his knife and poked at the sand.

Kay moved closer, waving away the cloud of silt that floated up from Matt's digging. Her eyes grew big. Gold?

Scraping crusty sand off the object, Matt held up a six-inch-long rusty bolt. He showed it to Kay, shrugged, and tossed it aside.

Five minutes later, Matt faced her, making a swirling motion with his hand. He swung the detector around to start a new sweep. Kay pivoted and followed her dive buddy. At the end of his first sweep, he dropped the detector and did a self-embrace to ask Kay if she was cold. She shook her head. On this return path, Matt moved over onto the rocky areas and floated above the rough surface. Kay followed. Soft

coral and anemones clung to the rocks. Small fish darted in and out of the crevices. Kay spotted a small red crab and paused to watch it skitter back in a hole. She struck the bottom with her knee and stopped, standing on the rocks. She added air to her buoyancy jacket and dry suit and lifted off the bottom. Focusing on her buoyancy problem, she didn't notice Matt moving away from her. She swung around, first left then right. Her heart raced. She cleared her mask, but she still couldn't see him. She had to stay calm. A stream of her bubbles boiled past her face. Which direction should she go? A school of small, slender fish darted between her legs. She felt a tug on her arm and spun around.

With his arms raised, Matt mumbled words that sounded somewhat like "You left me."

Kay shook her head. She understood the garbled words.

Matt took the regulator from his mouth and put on a Cheshire cat grin.

Pulling her regulator from her mouth, Kay said, "Not funny." It sounded like "nof fubby."

Matt touched the area over his heart in an apology gesture and questioned her with the OK hand sign. She nodded but couldn't hide the panic, her eyes as big as clamshells.

Matt pointed his finger up.

Kay shook her head indicating she didn't need to surface, pointed to his detector, and motioned him to keep going.

Ten minutes passed. Matt rested the device on the sand. Kay touched him and motioned that she could help. He waved her off.

The two searched the bottom for five more minutes. Kay shivered. Matt had to be getting cold, too—and tired.

He tugged on Kay's arm and, again, pointed to the surface. She held up fingers—five more minutes.

Matt continued sweeping the bottom. The detector made a loud squeal. He jerked around and waved the device back and forth over a small area. The noise louder, he moved in closer to the rocks and probed with his hand. Kay swam closer and helped him pull away the larger stones. Matt brought out a small flashlight and shined it in the crevice. Something reflected the light back.

CHAPTER TWENTY-THREE

"**D**id you find the gold," Anna said, her hands shaking. Matt reached into the pocket of his buoyancy jacket. "One small piece of it. We found it just before we surfaced." He laid the coin on the console. "There're some towels in that dry bag. Let's get out of these suits."

Anna helped Kay peel off her dry suit and put a towel around Kay's shoulders. " Did you get cold?"

"Near the end of the dive I got chilled, but this feels nice." Kay lay back on the bench seat and aimed her face toward the sun. "I've never been diving in water this cold."

Matt took the coin and rubbed it hard with his towel. The greenish film removed, the coin glistened.

Anna put her face close to it. "Can you make out the writing?"

Matt squinted. "Looks like 'Republica Mexicana' on one side. On the other side it says 'La Libertad En La L' something 'Y.' The date on it is 1860."

Anna held out her hand. "Can I see it? This could be Macauly's gold."

"It could be," he said. "His letter said that some of the treasure was in Mexican gold coins."

Anna held up the shiny object. "Can you go get the rest of it now?"

"Not today." Matt draped a towel over his shoulders.

"You've got all the gear, and we're here." Anna threw her hands in the air. "Why not?"

Kay sat up. "What did you say?"

Matt took the coin from Anna and put it in his backpack. "She asked why we can't dive again today. There are a few reasons. The tide is changing, and the current would be too fast. We also need to refill the tanks. And my dive computer says to be safe we need some time on the surface before we could make another dive. We did hit forty feet a few times."

"I guess those are good reasons," Anna said.

"Those are good enough reasons for me." Kay lay back on the bench and covered her eyes. "I'm exhausted."

"Are you going to tell your dad you found the coin?" Anna asked.

"Not yet. This may be the only gold we find. I'd rather search some more. If we find a few more pieces, maybe I'll tell him."

Kay jerked herself upright again. " *We? Again?*"

"You don't want to be my dive buddy?"

"Well…I…your dive buddy? Sure, I suppose I can do this again. I'll have to ask my mom this time."

"She didn't know you were diving with me?" Matt asked.

"I didn't think she would approve. You being sixteen and…well… what do we tell her? I shouldn't lie to her. I made that mistake earlier in the summer. I told her we were going to help you catch lobsters today. We didn't exactly do that."

"But we will. I'll go over to where we have some traps, and we'll pull a few. You can take some lobsters home with you. How's that?"

Anna raised her index finger. "I have an idea. Why don't you come over, and we'll have a lobster dinner. I'm sure Kay's mom would love to have someone else cook. Then we can bring up the diving thing."

"I can do that. I'll steam some lobsters and make some coleslaw."

"Kay, do you think your mom would mind?" Anna asked.

Still pointing her face toward the sun, Kay closed her eyes.

"Kay, what do you think of my suggestion?"

"I heard you, Anna. I'm thinking." Kay was thinking—thinking hard trying to find a reason why she shouldn't go diving again with Matt.

"I have to haul traps with Dad tomorrow. You've got time to decide. We couldn't dive again until Friday."

Kay's need for an excuse to not go diving ended when Anna chimed in. "Matt, you told Kay's mom and dad you do artifact diving, and Kay's mom knows she's a professional diver—"

"Certified." Kay tilted her head at Anna. "I'm certified."

"That's perfect," Matt said. "We *are* diving for artifacts. Do you think your mom will approve?"

"Not that she doesn't trust you, Matt, but I'm not sure she'll go for it."

"But it's the truth. Gold coins are artifacts," he said.

"This is exciting," Anna said. "Finding treasure. We're kind of like pirates or something."

"Yeah, buccaneers, arrrggghhh." Matt held up a bottle of water. "Let's drink a toast to the crew of the pirate ship *Maria*."

Anna touched her bottle to Matt's. "Arrrggghhh."

Kay didn't share their excitement, but the pressure to join in was too much. She forced a smile, raised her bottle. "Arrrggghhh. To the crew of the *Maria*."

CHAPTER TWENTY-FOUR

"That was delicious, Matt," Kay's mom said. "Thanks for bringing—and cooking—the lobster."

"You can thank Kay and Anna, too. I put them to work."

"Did you go swimming, too?"

Matt shot a glance at Kay. "Yes…yes, I did. It was warm today."

Kay tilted her head toward Matt and set up for the discussion about the diving. "When are you lobster fishing again?"

"My dad and I are going tomorrow to finish hauling the traps we didn't do today. The day after I thought I would do some diving for artifacts. I found an area that may be good for using my metal detector."

Her mom asked, "An underwater metal detector?"

"Yes, ma'am. It works great. Ask—"

Kay cleared her throat. Her eyes bugged at his near mistake.

Matt winced and shot a quick glance at Kay. "I've found some interesting things, especially around piers and boat ramps."

"That sounds interesting," Kay's mom said. "How deep do you dive?"

"No more than thirty or forty feet. That way I can stay down a longer time."

"Kay, Jim, and I did some scuba diving in the Cayman Islands. I loved the visibility."

"The visibility here in these waters is not bad most of the time. Nothing like the Caribbean, I'm sure. I'd like to go diving there some day."

Kay stood behind her mom and made a rolling motion with her hand for Matt to get to the point.

Matt gave a slight nod. "My dives are so shallow that you can pop to the surface in a matter of seconds if you need to. But I use a compass and a GPS, and I've never had any problems."

"What have you found?"

"Boat equipment and some personal items and sometimes coins."

Kay coughed. "Excuse me. I need to get some water." She went to the kitchen overlooking the living room. With her mom's back to her but still in Matt's line of sight, Kay shook her head with wide swings. She mouthed the words, "No gold."

He again nodded at Kay. "These were coins that must've fallen out of somebody's pocket—maybe a crew member on a lobster boat." He raised his hands and grinned. "Or maybe someone was making a wish."

Kay walked back into the room.

"I was planning on going diving Friday," Matt said. "Kay told me she's certified, and I thought maybe she could dive with me."

Kay's mom leaned forward in the chair. "Kay? Diving? I'm not sure I feel comfortable with this. She's made quite a few dives, but always with her dad."

"I understand. I thought maybe—"

"We won't be going deep. Right, Matt?" Kay couldn't believe she was trying to convince her mother to let her do something she wasn't certain she wanted to do.

"That's right. And I've made more than a hundred dives."

Bobbie glanced at Matt and turned to Kay. "Are you sure you want to do this?"

"Yeah, I'm sure. It'll be…an adventure."

"Then, I suppose it's OK. What have you got planned for Friday?"

"I don't have anything planned and Anna doesn't either, do you?"

"Nope. I'll go with them. Maybe I'll do a one-minute swim. The water's so cold I think I would turn into a block of ice if I stayed in longer."

"If that's what you want to do, Kay. Please be careful."

"I'll be careful. Don't worry."

"We'll meet at the dock at noon on Friday," Matt said. "We'll have a great time."

Kay gave a weak smile. "Great. Yeah, a great time." Her voice trailed off. "I can't wait."

CHAPTER TWENTY-FIVE

Kay played with her hair, tucking it behind her ears. "He said noon so we could catch the slack high tide. It's 12:17."

Anna checked her watch. "He'll be here. Relax."

Kay hoped Matt wouldn't show, but she knew that wouldn't happen. She gazed in the direction of the lighthouse and the area where they would be diving.

"He's coming," Anna said.

Kay kept her lighthouse vigil.

"Did you hear me?"

Kay huffed. "Yes, I did, Anna."

The *Maria* eased next to the dock. Matt tossed the lines to the girls. "Sorry I'm late. I had to go to the marina and gas up the boat."

"Giving harbor tours, Hubbard?"

Kay and Anna whipped around at the sound of a man's voice behind them.

"Hi, Mr. Tripley," Matt said. "Nope. Taking some friends for a ride."

"You should try lobster fishing some day." Tripley smirked, stepped backed from the edge of the dock, and walked away. Without turning around, he said, "Oh, that's right, your dad does try it now and then. You tell your dad I said hello."

Kay handed Matt her backpack. "Who was that guy?"

"His name is Monte Tripley and, yes, he's a jerk. He threatened my dad at a town meeting. Said my dad should leave town for what he did."

Kay asked, "What did he do?"

Matt reached out for Anna's bag, and the two girls climbed in the boat.

"Let's get going." Matt maneuvered away from the dock. He twisted around and said to Kay, "That man on the dock—Mr. Tripley—he and my dad used to be friends. When the sardine cannery here in town closed, a lot of people lost their jobs. It was a bad situation. Some folks worked there for more than fifty years."

Kay held onto the rail by the controls. "Why is he mad at your dad?"

"Some people around here wanted a lobster-processing plant to take over the cannery. My dad and Mr. Tripley had different opinions on what to do. My dad and I also thought Mr. Tripley was mad because, when Dad lost his job, he got a lobster-fishing license. Mr. Tripley knew my family sold supplies to fishermen years ago and that we were not old-time lobstermen."

"Is the man jealous?"

"That's what my dad thinks. But I don't know why he should be jealous. Mr. Tripley had some financial problems for a while. But he seems to be doing well."

Kay squinted. "What do you mean?"

"We can't figure it out. He went from almost being bankrupt to rebuilding his boat with two new engines and adding a room on his house."

Within twenty minutes, the two divers sat on the rail, suited up.

Kay's heart beat faster. She adjusted her mask strap three times.

Matt touched her arm. "Are you OK?"

"I think so," she said, but her trembling hands and a rapidly beating heart said otherwise.

"We'll swim to the spot I saved on my GPS." Matt motioned to Anna. "Would you please hand me the camera in my bag?"

Anna rummaged through the gear bag. "Why do you need the camera to look for gold?"

"I want to take a photo to document what we find. I may need to prove this someday. Here we go, Kay." He fell back into the water with a loud slap. Kay followed.

The two swam to the anchor line. With swooshes of air, the divers slipped beneath the surface.

Touching the sandy bottom, Matt checked his compass, GPS, and the settings on his detector. He pointed in a direction and swam off, swinging the detector in quick side-to-side motions. Five minutes passed. He stopped his search and gave his dive buddy the OK sign. She returned it.

Matt eyed his compass and GPS and started a new search area. Traveling a hundred feet, he laid the detector on the bottom and probed with his knife. Kay held on to his jacket and pulled herself close to the dig. Through a cloud of silt, she saw two gold coins pinched between Matt's fingers. She held out her hand. He laid them one at a time in her palm, took the regulator from his mouth, and showed his teeth in a huge grin.

With better visibility than the first dive and finding more gold coins, Kay's confidence rose. She swam ahead and pointed to an area she thought Matt should search with the detector. The squeal of the device sent the two digging through the sand. Kay raked away small rocks along with the sand. Three coins appeared. She plucked them out of the remaining silt and handed them to Matt. They gave each other a high five.

Matt tucked the coins in his pocket and swung the detector. He stayed on a course that took them next to a lobster trap. A blue and green camouflaged container floated inside.

The divers looked at each other and shrugged. Matt made a sweep around the trap. The detector squealed. He gestured to Kay to look in that spot while he continued to scan.

Within a minute, Kay had dug out five coins. With the sound of engines above, she reared her head. Waves tumbled on the surface.

Matt stopped in the middle of a sweep with the detector.

The engine noise increased. The hull of a boat hovered overhead.

The divers backed away from the dig area and dropped to their knees. Matt continued his gaze upward until Kay grabbed his arm and pointed. The trap slid ten feet, lurched off the bottom, and headed up. Kay reached for her pressure gauge—plenty of air left in her tank. She let go of the gauge, sat on the sandy seafloor, and stared up at the surface.

CHAPTER TWENTY-SIX

"**W**hat to do?" Kay scribbled on the slate attached to Matt's jacket.

Matt wrote, "Wait."

Ten minutes passed.

With a muted slapping sound, the trap hit the water and headed toward the bottom. It moved first in one direction and then another, like a flat sheet of paper gliding to the floor. Kay and Matt sat motionless. The trap settled into a path and came to rest less than twenty feet away.

The engines started. Kay leaned her head back. The hull disappeared, and the engine noise faded. She looked down and followed Matt to the trap where the mysterious container floated inside.

Matt pulled the camera out of his pocket.

Kay motioned that she wanted to take the container out of the trap.

Matt held up his hand to stop.

Kay motioned again.

Matt shrugged and nodded. He opened the trap, took out the container, and handed it to Kay.

She rotated it all around to get a better look. What was this thing?

Matt signaled to hold it out in front of her. He held up the camera, moved in for a close-up shot, and clicked the shutter.

Kay fell back, drew her fins up beneath her to regain balance, and lost her grip on the container. She rolled over, struggling to reposition herself. The box floated up. She kicked hard to go after it. Matt

reached out and grabbed her right fin, stopping her ascent. She aimed her mask down at him. He shook his head and waved his index finger from side to side.

Kay settled to the bottom and tilted her head back, staring at the mysterious container bobbing on the surface.

CHAPTER TWENTY-SEVEN

"**W**hat is this?" Anna craned her neck, surveying the object from all sides.

Kay shrugged. "I have no idea. It was in a lobster trap. Somebody pulled the trap and put it back with the container still inside."

"I saw the boat when I was snorkeling. The name on it looked like 'ruff read.' I couldn't see it that well. I think they saw me in the water. Some man was pointing over here."

Matt took the binoculars. "No sign of any boat in the area."

Kay picked up the container. "This thing is weird. Why would somebody put this in a lobster trap?"

"Weird or not, we need to put it back before somebody finds out it's gone," Matt said.

Anna swiped her fingers across the container. "How did you get it?"

"I wanted to look at it so I took it out," Kay said. "While Matt was taking pictures of it, I let it get away."

Anna touched the container with her foot. "Could we open it and see what's inside?"

"I'm curious, too," Kay said.

Matt stood over the container, staring down at it for ten seconds. "OK, let's take a look." Kneeling down, he flicked open the spring-loaded latches, working his way around all four sides. He lifted the top and placed it beside the container.

"What is that?" Kay peered over his shoulder.

Matt removed the plastic-wrapped package and placed it on the deck. "I'm not sure, but I have an idea."

Anna moved closer and punched the white block with her finger. "It feels soft and hard at the same time—like a bag of flour."

Kay touched it and stepped back. "Are these some illegal drugs?"

Matt said nothing. His eyes wide, he focused on the package.

"What are we going to do with this?" Anna asked. "Should we tell the police?"

Matt swallowed hard. "I don't know. I don't think we need to go to the police. Let's put it back and forget about it."

Kay reached into her backpack and pulled out her phone. She tapped the camera icon. "Hold the package up, Anna. That's it. Turn it around. Hold up the container, and let me get a few shots of that."

"Why do you need photos?" Anna asked.

Kay checked the settings on the camera and snapped another photo. "I don't know. This thing is so weird."

"It's weird and I want to get rid of it," Matt said.

Kay turned her phone for another shot.

"That's enough photos." Matt took the plastic-wrapped package from Anna, dropped it into the container, and closed the cover.

"I almost forgot." Matt rolled his dive gear over to reach his jacket pocket and retrieved the coins. He handed them to Anna.

"You found more?" Anna laid the coins on the deck one at a time, counting. "One, two, three…that's ten, plus the one you found the other day—eleven. How much are they worth?"

"If they're an ounce each, that's eleven ounces," Matt said, lifting his dive jacket and tank. "I'd say fifteen thousand." He turned to Kay. "Let's get our gear on and put this thing back in the trap."

"Can't we pull the trap instead of diving again?" Kay asked.

"Someone could be watching us with binoculars. You can get in trouble if you pull another person's trap."

Kay took a deep breath. "If that's what we have to do."

CHAPTER TWENTY-EIGHT

"**Y**ou *look* tired," Anna said. "Let's ask Matt if he'll give us a ride to the house. It's only a short distance."

"I don't know. Matt plays it straight. And what if my mom sees us drive up with you and me inside and the bikes in the back?"

"He can drop us off before we get to the house. Let's ask him."

Anna walked her bike from the rear of the truck to the driver's window. Kay followed a few feet behind.

"Do you think you could give Kay and me a ride to the house, we—"

"What?" Matt raised his head and jerked it to the left. "A ride? Sorry, no. I've got to go." He started the truck, snatched the gear lever, and accelerated out of the parking lot, bouncing hard over the dip near the street.

Anna put her hands on her hips. "What's the matter with him?"

"I'm not sure," Kay said. "Something happened after he got in his truck."

CHAPTER TWENTY-NINE

Kay sat on the edge of the bed and dried her hair with the towel. "That shower felt so good. It warmed me up after that dive—both dives." She let the towel fall from her head. "What are you doing?"

"Trying to find my phone. It's vibrating." Anna hit the speaker icon. "Hi, Matt."

Kay recalled his coolness toward her and Anna when he left the parking lot. "I'm here, too."

"I need to apologize for leaving the way I did this afternoon. It was rude. I found a note in the truck. That's what upset me. I didn't know what to say."

Kay folded her arms. "What kind of note?"

"It said to stay away from the area near the lighthouse. I'm glad we put the container back."

Anna held up the phone and gave Kay a puzzled look. "You think the note is about the container?"

"That's my guess. It didn't say anything about the trap or poaching."

Kay asked, "What are you going to do?"

"I don't know. I don't want to go to the local police. I'll have to explain too much and my dad'll find out."

Kay winced. "And my mom will find out, too." She glanced at Anna. "I know someone who's not from around here and who'll help us. We can trust this person."

"When will you contact him?"

"I'll send an email as soon as we hang up. And he's a she."

"The FBI agent you told me about?"

"That's the one."

"Let me know what she says as soon as you hear from her."

Kay reached for her laptop. She typed for ten minutes.

Anna sat with her back to the headboard and read.

Kay closed her laptop and placed it on the nightstand.

"That was a long e-mail," Anna said, looking up from her book.

"I had a lot to say."

"To Matt?"

"No. We talked only a few minutes ago. Why would I send him an e-mail?"

"I don't know. I thought that—"

"That Matt and I have a thing going?" Kay heard her own words spilling out. "I'm sorry, Anna. This situation with the container and the note is stressing me out. I can't believe I pushed Matt to take the thing out of the trap. That was stupid."

"It's done, Kay. Let's think about what we're going to do. What did you say to Terri?"

"I told her we were diving for artifacts and found the container. I sent her the pictures, too."

"Do you think she'll e-mail you back? Maybe she's had enough of us this summer with the thing at the park."

"She told us to call her anytime if we had a problem or wanted to talk. I guess we bonded with her."

"I agree, and I believe she also felt responsible in some way for you almost falling off the Washington Crossing Bridge. Maybe she'll try and make up for that and help us."

"I hope so." Hanging by her hands seventy feet above the Delaware River flashed through Kay's mind. She shook her head to get rid of the thought. But another one popped in her head—the note Matt found in his truck. Kay needed Terri to respond—and soon.

CHAPTER THIRTY

"Thank, you Terri. We need you." Kay read the agent's e-mail. "'Hi, Kay. I'm coming up to Maine to check out what you, Anna, and your friend found. I'll be working out of the Bangor office. I'll be there tomorrow. I found a few places to stay, but I'm not sure about them. I'd like something close to your location. Any suggestions? Also, I have to ask based on our previous interactions, do your parents know what you found? Let me know.'"

Kay walked to the porch and stood next to her mom's chair. "I got an e-mail from Terri Keenan and—"

"The FBI agent? The one we met in New Jersey?"

"Yes. She's coming to do some work for the FBI office in Bangor." Kay rocked back and forth on her heels and toes. "I was wondering if she could stay with us. She could sleep in the room downstairs on the futon."

"How did she know we were in Maine?"

"I e-mailed her. She had asked us to stay in touch."

"It's fine with me," her mom said. "But you'd think she'd had enough of us with all the intrigue back in Jersey."

Kay shrugged. "I guess not. I'll let her know she can stay with us." She headed for the bedroom and her computer. Intrigue in New Jersey? Now it's in Prospect Harbor.

CHAPTER THIRTY-ONE

"It's the FBI!" Kay opened the door, her voice echoing through the foyer.

"Very funny, Kay. You made my arrival sound like a raid." Terri laughed, gave Kay a hug, and reached around the teen to shake hands with Kay's mom. "Thanks for inviting me. Staying here with friends will make my work in Bangor more enjoyable."

Anna came into the foyer.

Terri hugged her.

"Show our guest downstairs to her room," Bobbie said.

Kay led the way.

Terri placed her hand on Kay's shoulder. "Thanks for working it out with your mom for me to stay here. I'm glad to see you both."

Kay glanced up at the stairs and listened for her mom. "What do you think we should do about the package we found?"

Terri laid her jacket across a chair. "Let's discuss this tomorrow away from your mom. I have some information and some ideas."

• • •

Terri sat in a chaise on the porch. "Thanks for dinner and for the company. I've been eating a lot of meals alone."

Bobbie set her coffee mug on the side table. "Traveling a lot?"

"Some. But I've been busy with work—long days. We're a bit short-handed in my division."

"What're your plans while you're here?"

Kay's eyes widened. She had no idea what Terri planned to do with the information Kay had given her.

The FBI agent winked at Kay and then at Anna. "I thought maybe the girls and you could give me a tour of the area tomorrow morning. The bureau owes me some time off."

Anna swiped her phone screen. "I texted Matt last night, and he wants to take us for a boat tour of the harbor." She whispered to Kay, "I told him about Terri."

"Did you want to go, too, Mom?" Kay was being polite. Her mom was prone to motion sickness, and she was sure her mom would decline. Kay and Matt had some things to talk about with Terri, and having her mom along would make that impossible.

Bobbie rose and picked up her mug. "No, I need to do some reading. I'm in the middle of a real page-turner. Besides, for the boat ride I'd have to take some seasick pills. Motion sickness used to never bother me."

Terri followed her into the kitchen. "In that case, let's all go out to dinner tomorrow night—my treat."

"That would be nice," Bobbie said. "We haven't been out to eat since Jim was here."

"Perfect." Terri stuck her head back out into the porch, gave a thumbs-up to Kay and Anna. "Dinner tomorrow night."

"Thanks, Terri," Kay said.

The agent walked back to the kitchen.

Kay drew her legs up in the chaise and wrapped her arms around her knees.

Anna shifted in the chair. "What are you thinking?"

"This was to be a quiet and peaceful vacation, but…"

"But what?"

"I promised no excitement or crazy stuff, and I just invited the FBI here." Kay extended her legs and leaned back. "Nope, not a peaceful vacation at all."

CHAPTER THIRTY-TWO

"You must be Matt." The FBI agent climbed down the ladder and handed the teenager her backpack. "I've heard a lot about you from Kay and Anna."

Kay rolled her eyes at Terri and tossed her head back.

Anna's mouth fell open.

Terri smiled at the girls and shook Matt's hand.

"I'm pleased to meet you," he said. "Let's get underway." He backed away from the dock. "These two know the drill. There're life vests in the box aft—the one covered by the cushion."

Kay caught Matt looking at her, grinned, and said, "Terri, you're going to get a lot of that nautical talk while you're aboard the *Maria*."

"The *Maria?*"

Matt pointed over the side.

Terri leaned over and read the name. "Pretty name. Who—"

"Matt, where're we going first?" Anna asked, putting her hand on Terri's arm.

Matt twisted the key. The engines rumbled. "You guys tell me." He grinned. "I'm the chauffer today."

Kay leaned in toward Terri. "It's named for his mom. She died two years ago."

Terri nodded and moved next to Matt. "In that case, skipper, could we go toward the lighthouse and the area where you were diving?"

With one hand on the dual throttles and one on the wheel, Matt guided the boat through the anchorage.

Terri hung on to the handrail by Matt. "Tell me what's been going on. I understand that you and Kay made an interesting discovery."

Approaching the lighthouse, Matt slowed. "That's true, and this is the area where we were searching for—"

"Searching for artifacts." Kay slipped between Matt and Terri. "Matt's found some interesting things diving around old piers and such."

"Yeah, that's right, we were looking for artifacts," Matt said. "We found this lobster trap with the weird-looking container inside."

"Kay sent me some photos. She said you brought up the container and found what you thought might be drugs."

"Yeah, it looked like it could be drugs. We put it back." Matt spun the wheel. "There's the buoy for the trap."

Terri leaned on the rail. "What do you think's going on?"

Matt maneuvered the boat and adjusted the throttles.

Kay jumped in. "I'm not sure. Like I told you in the e-mail, Matt got this note telling us to stay away from the trap near the lighthouse. I think that whoever has something to do with the package in the trap saw Matt's boat and is familiar with his truck."

Anna pulled her wide-brimmed hat down lower to block the sun. "I was snorkeling while Kay and Matt were diving. The sun glare was terrible. I saw something written on the back of the boat. All I could see were the words 'ruff read."

"I did some research, and there is a boat named the *Ruff 'n' Ready*," Terri said. "Its address is Corea. How far is that from here, Matt?"

"Not far."

"Could we cruise over there?"

"Sure. What are you looking for?"

"I don't know. Maybe we'll see something that will help us in the investigation."

Matt shoved the controls forward. The *Maria* skimmed the water, heading out of Prospect Harbor and north to Corea.

Twenty minutes later, Terri surveyed the anchorage. "There are quite a few boats in here."

"You can't haul traps on Sunday, so a lot of the boats went out yesterday. My dad and I fished, but we didn't get many lobsters."

"Thanks for taking me out today," Terri said.

Matt maneuvered at idle speed between the anchored boats. "I'm glad to do it. I got Kay and Anna involved in this mess. I feel responsible for them."

The girls sat on the bench above the storage box. Terri glanced at the two girls. "I know what you mean. I feel I have an obligation to them myself."

"I understand," Matt said. "Kay and her mom and dad told me about the letter and the bridge incident."

Anna tapped Terri on the arm. "Let me use the binoculars. I think I see the boat." She pointed with her left arm and held the glasses to her eyes. "Yes, that's the one."

Terri asked Matt, "Can you take us far enough back so I can read the name on the stern—but not too close?"

Matt circled the anchorage, keeping several boats between the *Maria* and the *Ruff 'n' Ready*.

"There's a dinghy coming from the dock," he said.

Terri spun around. "Let's move back among the other boats in case that's the owner."

Kay and Anna stood on either side of the helm next to Matt and Terri. The dinghy picked its way among the anchored lobster boats.

"They're heading for the *Ruff 'n' Ready*," Kay said. "What do we do?"

"Let's keep a good distance and follow," Terri said. "I want to see where they're headed."

The only sound aboard the *Maria* for the next few minutes was the hum of the idling twin engines.

Matt checked his position and spun the wheel. "She's getting underway."

Terri handed the binoculars to Kay. "When you can't see the name on the stern, let Matt know, and we can start following. That should be far enough back."

Kay put the strap around her neck. "What are you going to do?"

"I need to send a text to my office." Terri swiped the phone screen and typed.

Three minutes later, Kay said, "I can't read the name."

Pushing the throttles ahead, Matt steered toward the *Ruff 'n' Ready*. "Here we go."

Anna grabbed the handrail to steady herself. "Do you think he's going for the trap with the package?"

"We'll know in a few minutes if he turns into Prospect Harbor," Terri said.

The twenty-eight-foot *Maria* bounced into the choppy water, sending an occasional sprinkling of water over the top.

Anna wiped the spray from her face. "Look over there."

Kay pivoted and brought the binoculars up to her eyes. "That's a yacht." She swung back to follow the lobster boat. "The *Ruff 'n' Ready* is turning toward it."

"I think he's going to meet it," Matt said. "He's slowing, and the yacht doesn't seem to be moving."

Anna moved near Terri, who sat on the bench staring at her phone. "Did you get some information?"

"That I did. Kay, let me have the binoculars, please." Terri stepped into the shade of the top and stood next to Matt. "Hold it here. Looks like the *Ruff 'n' Ready's* coming alongside that boat."

A wave rocked the *Maria*. Kay widened her stance and grabbed the handrail. "What are they doing?"

"Based on information I received, he's not selling lobsters. The crew on the yacht is *giving* something *to him*."

Anna's eyes bugged. "Drugs?"

"That would be my guess," Terri said.

Kay asked, "What do we do?"

The FBI agent lowered the binoculars and let them hang around her neck. "We wait."

CHAPTER THIRTY-THREE

"The *Ruff 'n' Ready* is pulling away from the yacht." Matt put the engines into gear. "She's on a heading that'll put her into Prospect Harbor."

Kay stood close to Terri. "Do you think he's going to the trap?"

"Looks like that's his intention. Let's pull back around the point. We can't see them, but they can't see us either. If they're going to the trap, they'll be looking around to see if any boat is near."

The foursome waited for the crew of the *Ruff 'n' Ready* to do whatever it was they were going to do with the trap.

Twenty-five minutes later, Matt steered around the point and into the harbor. Kay took another turn with the binoculars. "They're gone."

"Anna, wake up." Kay held her friend's arm to keep her from falling off the bench.

"What? What is it?" Anna rubbed her eyes and stood by the rail. "Where're they going?"

Kay stared out into the open water. "What do we do?"

Terri reached into her backpack, pulled out a small black box, and opened it. "I thought we could plant a bug—a GPS tracking device—on the package in the container. But let's make sure the *Ruff 'n' Ready* is well away from the area."

"If someone sees us they could think we're lobster poaching," Matt said.

"If they do, I'll flash my FBI badge."

"That should take care of it," he said.

• • •

Thirty minutes later, Matt tossed the buoy for the trap over the side of the boat.

"Thanks. Great job," Terri said. "But I would suggest—let me rephrase that. You *must* stay away from this area until the investigation ends."

Kay and Anna nodded.

Matt kept his attention forward, steering the boat toward the dock.

Kay walked up beside, Matt. "Are you OK? I mean with not diving here?"

"What? Yeah, sure."

The *Maria* headed toward the dock. Kay moved back to the bench seat. She fixed her gaze toward the waters offshore of the Prospect Harbor lighthouse. Matt didn't sound sincere. But Terri was here. Surely he would listen to the FBI.

CHAPTER THIRTY-FOUR

"**H**ow was work in Bangor?" Kay asked, opening the door for Terri.

"Two days in the office there was enough. It was interesting, but it's more fun being here."

"Hi, Terri," Bobbie said. "Dinner in a few minutes."

"Thanks. Let me change into some jeans." Terri went down the stairs, motioning to the two girls. She laid her computer and bag on the futon. "Close the door. I have something to show you." Opening her computer on the nightstand, the agent typed on the keyboard and waited.

"That looks like the view of a map on the Internet," Anna said.

"Correct. But these images came from a special government surveillance satellite which can read a car license plate from space."

Kay got on her knees and leaned in toward the screen. "I get it. The satellite followed the package with the tracking device and whoever was carrying it."

Anna stepped back and glanced at Terri. "They must've followed the boat we saw at the yacht."

"They followed *a* boat, but not the *Ruff 'n' Ready*."

Kay stood. "But I thought—"

"We all thought it would be the one we saw in Corea," Terri said. "But I questioned that idea even before I saw the satellite photos. It turns out that a boat picks up the package from a larger craft traveling up and down the US coast."

"The *Ruff 'n' Ready*?" Kay asked.

"Yes, and puts the package in the trap. Then another one gets the package. We're still trying to find out how the whole operation works."

Anna sat on the bed. "What happens next?"

"The FBI's working with the DEA, the Drug Enforcement Administration. We've made them aware of what we know, and they're taking over the investigation."

Kay pointed at the computer screen. "You said the satellite could see a license plate from way up high. So what's the boat's name that makes the pickup?"

"We couldn't get the name on the stern. Cars are stable platforms and go in two directions. And they stop often. Unfortunately, boats move in many directions at once. And there are hundreds of boats that look alike from above. So we don't know yet who's making the pickups from the trap and what the next step is."

Anna asked, "How do you know it's not the *Ruff 'n' Ready*?"

"At the time of these photos, the *Ruff 'n' Ready* stayed anchored in Corea harbor. The DEA's had eyes on the boat and the crew since we followed it."

Kay stood, her head tilted toward the screen. "When will they catch these guys and put them in jail?"

"It could take a few days, a few weeks—maybe several months. The DEA agents want to make sure they have a solid case. Plus, this may be part of a larger operation up and down the coast. The feds want to catch *all* the bad guys involved. So, please stay away from that area near the lighthouse."

"Dinner," Bobbie said, standing at the top of the stairs.

"You two go ahead," Terri said. "I need to wash up."

Halfway up the stairs and a step below Kay, Anna whispered, "Did you see Matt's face when Terri told us to stay away from the area near the trap?"

Kay stopped and faced Anna. "Yes, and it wasn't a happy one."

"Do you think he'll listen to Terri?"

"I can't tell what he'll do." Kay did have an idea what Matt would do—an idea that made her heart race.

CHAPTER THIRTY-FIVE

"**D**uty calls—boring duty, that is, back in DC." Terri grabbed Anna's left hand and Kay's right. "You two stay out of trouble." She furrowed her brow and then chuckled. "I don't want to see your faces on any FBI wanted posters."

Anna laughed.

Trouble? Kay had a sinking feeling that staying out of trouble wasn't going to be that easy.

"I'll make sure of that," Bobbie said. She held up her cell phone. "Let me get a photo of you three. Stand closer. Kay, will you smile, please?"

Terri reached inside the rental car and grabbed her phone. "Would you take a shot for me? This will go in my favorite-people album."

Terri drove out onto the street. Bobbie and the girls waved.

Walking to the house, Anna squeezed the phone from her jeans pocket. "It's Matt."

"I'll ask." Anna covered the phone. "Mrs. Telfair, can Kay and I meet Matt at the deli?"

"Of course," Bobbie put on a fake frown. "Leave me here all alone."

"We don't have to go, Mom," Kay said. "We can stay—"

"I'm kidding. Go. Have fun. The vacation won't last forever, and you won't see Matt after this week." She cleared her throat. "Or for a while. I'm sure you'll stay in touch. I'm going in the house. Let me know when you leave."

"I was enjoying our vacation up here so much, I didn't think about not seeing Matt after we left," Anna said.

"I thought about it...a little. We live in New Jersey, five hundred miles away. The chances are we won't see him after the summer."

"Unless we come back to Prospect Harbor," Anna said.

"Maybe." Kay shook her head. "But I doubt it."

CHAPTER THIRTY-SIX

"**H**i, ladies. Apologies for being a little late."

Anna gave a hand salute. "No excuse, Cap'n Hubbard. The crew's been here waiting." She grinned. "I thought maybe you'd fix us some lobster rolls. Instead you invite us to the deli?"

"They make decent ones here, but lunch isn't what's on my mind—although I am hungry."

Kay alternated her gaze between Anna and Matt. "Please tell us. If it's not food, what is it?"

Matt looked around the room and leaned in. "I want to dive for the gold. If I wait till they catch the druggies, it could be the middle of winter, and then I can't dive until almost next summer. Plus, I won't have my trusty dive buddy."

Kay and Anna stared at each other. Five seconds passed.

"What is it? What's wrong?" Matt turned his head toward Kay, then to Anna, and back to Kay.

Kay placed her hands together and leaned on the table. "Matt, you heard what Terri suggested—"

"*Told* us," Anna said.

"Excuse me, *told* us. She said to stay away from the area near the trap with the container."

"I heard," Matt said. "But why stay away now? We were in the area and put the tracker on the package a few days ago. But, we'll stay away from that trap...if we can...although we did find some coins close to it."

Kay tucked her hair behind her ears. "The Drug Enforcement Administration's taking over for the FBI."

Matt shrugged. "Maybe they'll catch the druggies in a few days and there'll be no problem."

"Terri said it could be weeks or months." Kay pushed herself back in the chair. "Can't it wait—the gold, I mean? Why the hurry?"

"There're two reasons. First, my dad got laid off yesterday from the company in Bangor. It was only part-time. He's got a job in Portsmouth. It's temporary for only six months. But it's full-time and pays better."

"I don't understand," Kay said. "Your dad will be making more money. Why do you have to go after the gold?"

"He has to live down in Portsmouth during the week, and that cuts into his pay. And we still owe a ton on my mom's medical bills. Plus, my truck is dying, and Dad's car needs some work."

"Can't he commute every day?"

"It's more than two hundred miles one way, Anna."

"That answers that question," Kay said. "But don't you have the lobster business?"

"Dad'll only be here weekends, and we may not be able to pull enough traps to make it worthwhile. If we can find enough of that gold, maybe he can find another job closer to home. The job might pay less, but he'll be home every night, and he won't have the extra living expenses."

"But if you could make it till next summer financially, the DEA will probably have caught the drug dealers," Kay said. "Then you could dive for the gold."

"That'll be too late, which brings me to my second reason for going after the gold now. They're going to dredge the channel in the harbor before winter and dump the material around the point at the lighthouse. It will bury whatever gold is there."

"Can't they dump it some other place?" Kay asked.

"The navy and the coast guard want the stuff dumped there to protect the shoreline. My dad said the federal government is paying for the dredging so it doesn't cost the town anything."

Kay sat back.

Anna asked, "What's your plan to get the gold?"

Matt hesitated, lowered his gaze, and gave Kay a pleading look.

"What? Me? You want me to dive with you—again? What if one of those lobster boats comes for the container while we're down there?"

"We'll get ready before we get to the dive site. That way we won't have to be in the area too long. Anna will stay with the boat and keep the engines running in case another boat comes close. She can cruise around and come back and get us."

"Me? I don't know how to run a boat."

"It's easy. Like driving a car."

"I don't know how to drive a car either."

"I can't trust anybody else. And I can't tell my dad—not yet. Not till I've found more of the gold."

"You figured you had fifteen thousand in coins," Kay said.

"Yeah, that was my estimate. But I did some research, and it depends on the historic value of the coins or the purity. Could be a lot less or a little more. I also found out that the government can take a lot for taxes—almost half."

"Taxes?" Kay asked. "But *you* found the gold. It was laying there on the bottom."

"My dad says the government's going to always get its share," he said. "That's why it's so tough to have a small business like lobster fishing. Anyway, what we have is not enough to get us out of this money mess. What d'ya say?"

"I say we do it," Anna said.

"Again, Anna—*we*? Are you going to put on the dry suit and go in that cold water?"

Anna smirked. "Kay, you know what I mean. Matt can teach me how to drive the boat. Won't you, Matt?"

"Of course. It's easy."

Kay sat back in the chair and stared at the ceiling. How did she get herself into these situations? She sighed. "The thought of diving again in that cold water makes me hungry. Let's get a sandwich or something."

Matt held up both hands for high fives. "To the crew of the *Maria*."

"To the crew," Anna said, slapping Matt's left hand.

He kept his right hand up, waiting for Kay.

Anna glared at her friend. "Well?"

Kay hesitated, raised her hand, and sighed. Instead of a slap at Matt's palm, she touched it, and said in a low voice, "To the crew."

CHAPTER THIRTY-SEVEN

"**M**att wants to go diving Wednesday," Kay said, the computer resting on her lap.

"What are you telling him?" Anna wrapped the towel around her wet hair and sat on the bed with her comb.

Pecking out a reply on the keyboard, Kay glanced at Anna. "I'm telling him we'll go, like I promised."

Anna fought the tangles in her hair. "You've been getting a lot of e-mails and phone calls from him. I think that proves he likes you."

Kay fluffed the pillows on her bed and adjusted the laptop's screen. "You get calls and messages, too."

"I *did.*"

"You remember when we first met him, he gave *you* his cell number, and he only texted or called you, not me. And what if I do get calls and texts? We're talking about diving or what we're *all* doing while we're here."

Anna crawled under the covers, plucked the bookmark from the end of her book, and spread the pages. "I still think he likes you."

Kay stopped typing. "He likes both of us. You know that."

"I think he likes you more than me."

"That's ridiculous. Why do you say that?"

"You guys have bonded with the diving and all. You're his dive *buddy.*"

"Do you want to go diving with him?"

"You know I can't. That was a dumb thing to say."

"I agree. It's as dumb as you saying he likes me more than you. He's a friend to both of us. Besides, we won't see him again after this week."

"He could come down to New Jersey, or you could make a trip up to Maine."

"Anna, that's…" Kay peered over the top of the computer. "First of all, he doesn't like me more than you. And second, until I get my license and a car, my mom and dad are my transportation. Matt's out of our lives in five days."

"Whatever you say."

"Anna, it's not what I say. Matt likes us both. Drop it, please. This conversation is making me uncomfortable."

Anna shrugged and nestled deeper into the bed, cradling her book.

Kay typed. "Hi, Matt. Sorry I wasn't so thrilled about diving again when we were at the deli. On our first dives, the cold water and diving with somebody other than my dad made me nervous. But I am worried because of the drug thing and Terri saying we should stay away from the trap. I appreciate your friendship, and I understand your situation with your dad and the money. I want you to know that I'm behind you 100 percent. See you Wednesday."

She hit send and pushed herself back into the pillows.

A minute later, an e-mail popped up. "Thanks. I appreciate that. BTW, I like you very much. I'm glad we got to spend some time together this summer. I hope we can stay in touch after you go home."

Kay's heart beat faster. She hit reply. Her fingers lingered over the keyboard. She peeked over the top of the screen.

Anna flipped a page in her book.

Kay did like Matt, but Anna was her best friend. She knew the chances of seeing Matt again after the summer were slim. She needed to keep the relationship with Matt as only friends—nothing more. She typed. "You're a great friend, Matt. I'm sure we'll stay in touch after I leave Maine. Best, Kay."

CHAPTER THIRTY-EIGHT

"**A**re you and Anna getting along? She didn't want to come grocery shopping with us. She seemed annoyed when you asked her. And I didn't hear much talking in your room last night."

"Maybe she's not feeling well, and maybe we're talked out. We've been sharing the room for almost four weeks."

Bobbie pulled the cart to one side of the aisle and put her arm over her daughter's shoulder. "Don't let little things come between you. None of us are perfect, and you sometimes have to overlook things in a relationship. Best friends are something to cherish."

"You're right," Kay said. "I'll talk to her when we get back to the house."

Bobbie hugged her daughter. "Sometimes your mom does know something. Let's finish the shopping and go home." Bobbie checked her list. "We need some chips and cookies. I think they were in that area near where we came in."

"I'll get some." Kay moved down one aisle and up another. "Not much to choose from. Maybe I'll—"

"You and your friends should stay away from the trap near the lighthouse."

Kay jerked her head around, her body following in a swirl. "What?"

"You should stay away—"

Kay scurried to the end of the aisle. She glanced back at the man who wore a brown T-shirt, camouflage hunting pants, and boots. He stared at her with piercing eyes, turned, and walked toward the checkout.

Kay flitted from aisle to aisle, looking for her mom.

Bobbie rounded a corner, almost running into her daughter. She smiled. "Did you panic when you couldn't find me? You used to do that when you were a toddler."

The words wouldn't come out. Kay struggled to breathe.

Her mom's smile faded. She put her arm around her trembling daughter. "What's the matter? You look as if you've seen a ghost."

Kay scanned the area around her and forced a weak smile. "I guess I did have one of those childhood panic attacks, thinking you had left me. I know it sounds silly." It did sound silly, but what else could she say? Kay couldn't tell her mom about the drug container, the gold, Terri's warning, and now this. Who was this man, and how did he know she was diving near the lighthouse?

"Let's get you home. I can come back later and get the rest of the things on my list."

Her hands quivering, Kay gripped the handle of the shopping cart. "I'll be fine. We're almost done, aren't we?"

"Are you sure?"

"Yes, I'm fine."

Ten minutes later, the two approached the checkout.

Kay leaned into the cart and placed items on the conveyor. She raised her head and gazed out through the large window in the front of the store. The man in the brown shirt and hunting pants sat in his pickup, talking on a cell phone.

Her mom stood at the card reader near the bagger. "Kay, the cashier's caught up."

"What? Oh. Sorry." Kay reached down and plucked the items from the cart. Placing the last one on the conveyor belt, she stole a look out the window. The man in the pickup dropped his cell phone on the seat and drove off.

Kay's mom swiped her credit card and chatted with the cashier. Kay slid her phone from her jeans and texted. "Matt, we have to talk."

CHAPTER THIRTY-NINE

"**A**nna," Kay said in a loud whisper and motioned to her friend. Anna lowered her book and peeked over the top. "What do you want?"

Kay gritted her teeth and pursed her lips. "Come here."

Anna rose from the sofa and followed Kay into the bedroom.

"Thanks for helping me shop and for bringing in the groceries," Kay's mom said.

Nudging Anna into the bedroom, Kay yelled back, "You're welcome."

Anna jerked her arm from Kay's grip. "Stop pulling on me."

Kay eased the door shut. "This man in the store told me to stay away from the trap near the lighthouse."

"Somebody who worked in the store?"

Kay growled and raised her hands, fingers spread. "No. Why would a store...never mind. This guy was shopping, and he told me to stay away from the trap."

"How did he know you were diving near the lighthouse?"

"That's the point, Anna." Kay leaned her head back. "No one ever saw *me*. Do you think they saw you when you were snorkeling? Maybe they thought you were me."

"If they did see me, they wouldn't know me because I had the mask on."

"I've got to call Matt."

Kay swiped the phone screen and hit speaker. Matt answered. In a rush of words, she described the incident at the store.

"This is weird," Matt said. "The big question is how did he know *you* were diving in that spot?"

"I guess this means we aren't going to dive for the gold," Kay said. No response.

"Matt?"

"I'm here."

"Are we still going to dive for the gold?"

"I am. You're not."

"Wait a minute. Terri said we should stay away from that area, and this stranger tells me to do the same. Don't you think this is dangerous?"

"Like I told you, if I'm suited up and ready to go when I get to the site, I can be in the water and out in less than forty minutes."

Kay gritted her teeth and grimaced.

Anna pried the phone from Kay's hand, shook her head at her friend, and asked, "Who's going to help you anchor?"

"I can do that by myself."

"That's going to take some time, dropping the anchor and pulling it in."

"I'll be fast. Don't worry."

"Who's going to be your dive buddy?" Kay asked.

"I won't have one this time."

Kay shook her head and clenched her fists. "You know the rule, Matt."

"I'll break the rule this time. I'll be fine."

"We won't let you do this by yourself," Anna said.

Kay lowered her head and squinted at Anna.

Anna whispered, "Yes, *we*."

Kay leaned in toward the phone. "When are you planning on going?"

"Tomorrow morning. Slack tide is around eleven."

"We'll meet you at the dock at ten," Kay said. "How's that?"

"Are you sure you want to do this?" Matt asked.

"Yes, *we're* sure," Anna said. "See you at ten."

"I need to make sure my mom doesn't mind."

"Do you think she won't let you dive?" Matt asked.

"I'm sure she won't mind as long as I'm with you." Kay said. She looked at Anna and gave her friend a fist bump. "I mean *we're* with you."

CHAPTER FORTY

"I've never seen fog so thick." Anna took off her sunglasses. "I don't need these."

Matt reached over the windshield and wiped off the moisture. "This is not heavy fog for this area. We've got one-hundred-foot visibility. There're times when you can't see twenty feet."

Matt guided the boat away from the dock, through the anchorage, and out into the open harbor. "Keep an eye out for boats."

Cruising toward the lighthouse, the ripples in the water slapped against the hull of the *Maria*. Being out on the water usually calmed Kay. She would fall asleep on her dad's boat within the first few minutes of leaving the dock. But Kay was not calm on this boat trip.

• • •

"Took us almost twenty minutes to get our suits on and get our gear ready," Matt said. "Now we can be in the water in five."

Kay forced a smile so Matt wouldn't see she was a nervous wreck, but she couldn't hide the fear in her eyes.

"Don't worry," Matt said. "We'll be fast. The GPS will put us on the spot where I want to start searching." He stepped in front of the wheel and put the engines in gear. "Here we go."

Anna moved over to Kay, sitting on the bench seat, and grasped Kay's right hand.

Kay forced a smile for her friend. "I'll... *we'll* be fine."

Matt touched the GPS screen. "We're almost on the spot. Fog's still a little heavy, but that also means it'll be hard to spot my boat. Should be lifting soon." He showed Anna how to steer and use the throttles and gearshift. "If somebody comes around, move away at a slow speed so they don't think you're leaving because of them."

"I can handle it," Anna said. "You two be careful."

"Look for us to surface thirty or forty minutes after we go in. We'll be near the shore away from most of the boat traffic. You can come get us if we're too far away. I'm not bringing a dive flag. I'll signal you if I want you to come for us." He chuckled. "We may have so much gold we can't swim."

Kay put her hands together, as if praying, and touched her chin with her fingertips. Gold or no gold, she wanted to get this over with as fast as possible.

As Matt predicted, within five minutes of arriving at the GPS coordinates, the two were in the water.

Holding on to Matt's arm, Kay descended. Filtered by the fog, the limited sunlight made the visibility much worse than on the other dives.

On the bottom, Kay leaned back but couldn't see the surface or the hull of the *Maria*.

The divers stood face to face, each giving the other the OK signal.

Matt adjusted the detector and tapped the headphones. He touched Kay on the arm and glided across the sandy bottom.

In a few seconds, only the tips of Matt's fins were visible. Kay's heart raced. She adjusted her buoyancy, lifted off the sand, and kicked hard to catch up with her dive buddy twenty feet ahead. The same thought recycled in her mind. Be calm. Don't panic.

CHAPTER FORTY-ONE

Matt wrapped his arms around himself to ask Kay if she was cold. She shook her head.

Arching her head back, Kay gazed at the surface. What would she and Matt find on this dive? Was Anna all right? All this started because she *had* to tell Matt about the letter. Stretching her body out to position her fins for swimming, she twisted, looking for Matt. Where was he? Her heart pounded. She jerked her head around and saw a cloud of murky water and swam toward it. Like fading from one scene to another in a movie, she saw the tips of his fins and then his legs, disappearing and reappearing. Kay swam up beside him. They exchanged OK signs and moved forward.

Twenty feet farther, the detector sounded. Matt broke the crusty sand surface with his knife and probed with his fingers. Holding his free hand straight up, he showed Kay two gold coins.

In the next fifty feet, they found three more coins. Examining the last ones they found, Kay dropped them in her pocket and pressed it shut.

The sea floor grew brighter.

"Fog lift," Matt wrote on the slate and showed it to Kay.

Kay gave the OK sign and skimmed across the bottom behind him.

Matt made wider swings with the detector and swam faster. He dropped the device and probed with his knife.

Kay waved the silt away from Matt's digging. The rectangular end of an object protruded up from the hard sand. With a cloud of silt shrouding her, she raised her head and backed away from the site.

Suspended above their dig, Kay waited. The water around her cleared, and more light from the lifting fog penetrated the cold water. Settling back to the bottom, she saw the lobster trap with the container twenty-five feet away. She tapped Matt on the arm and pointed toward it.

He shook his head and motioned to his dive buddy to help him uncover the buried object.

Kay stared at the trap. Matt tugged on her arm and pointed again toward the area where he was digging. The two divers pulled out handfuls of sand and small rocks. Murky water enveloped them and reduced visibility to a few feet. They dug more sand from around the greenish-brown, brick-shaped object.

Matt scraped the end with his knife. Kay stared wide-eyed at the discovery, but the sound of engines drew her attention away from the find and toward the surface.

Matt continued to poke at the hard-packed sand with his knife.

Kay patted his head and thrust her other arm up in several fast motions. He reared his head back, gazing up at the hull of a boat. The hull bottom was not the *Maria*'s. Wide-eyed, the two divers stared at the lobster trap. It slid a few feet, stirring up the sand, and rose with a jerky motion a few feet at a time. The divers sat, gazing at the trap. In less than a minute, it broke the surface.

Kay grabbed the slate and wrote. "What to do?"

Matt scribbled. "Stay–gone soon."

Kay checked her pressure gauge and showed it to Matt—four hundred pounds. Matt checked his gauge and held up ten fingers and then five. He pointed to her gauge and waggled his hand. Maybe fifteen minutes of air.

Kay's heart rate increased along with her breathing. She stared at the gauge. The needle moved lower with each breath. Ten minutes passed. She felt a chill. She tugged at Matt's left fin, grabbed herself, and shook from side to side.

He waved his hand down to stay put.

Kay started a slow recline until she lay on the sand, staring up at the surface. Matt returned to the object still buried in the hard-packed sand.

Hearing the muffled drone of more engines, Kay pulled herself up, flailing with her fins. Two hulls now floated side by side above her. She whirled around at the sound of a splash. The lobster trap descended with no buoy attached. The trap spiraled and twisted toward the teens.

Kay poked Matt, and the two swam ten feet away and stopped, watching the trap come to rest on top of their digging spot. Kay slid her hand down the line attached to her air gauge. The needle pointed to 150 pounds. That was below the amount of air to have when surfacing. Showing it to Matt, he held up five fingers.

Could she make it five more minutes? She mustn't panic. Matt was with her. She might have to surface straight up near the boats above them.

They waited. One minute. Two minutes. Three minutes.

Matt raised his arm to view his wrist computer. He bumped Kay with the other arm, pointed at her, and then pointed at himself. He extended his arm up. Time to surface.

Bubbles from her regulator gurgled around Kay's mask. She arched her head back, extended a hand up, and stared at the boat hulls on the surface. Adding air to her buoyancy jacket and drysuit, she rose off the bottom. Her heart beat faster. Who was up there? What was going to happen to her and Matt when they reached the surface?

CHAPTER FORTY-TWO

Kay sucked the last of the air from her tank, broke the surface, and yanked the regulator from her mouth, gasping. "I'm out."

"We're up," Matt said. "That's what counts."

Kay felt the sun warming the black hood on her head. She pulled her mask down around her neck and grabbed Matt's arm. She shook her hand toward the two boats twenty feet away. "Are they going to pick us up or—" She dipped below the surface, took in a mouthful of seawater, and coughed.

Still wearing his mask, Matt took out his snorkel, pointed at it, and motioned to Kay. She didn't respond. "Kay, put on your mask and use your snorkel."

A voice echoed from above. "Are you guys all right?"

Kay raised her head. Her mask fogged, all was a blur. She lifted the mask above her nose and let go of her bite on the snorkel. "Matt, it's the man from the store. He's the one who told me to stay away from the lobster trap." She put the tube back in her mouth, taking rapid short breaths.

Matt held on to her arm. "It's the coast guard. We're going to be OK. Look." Matt pointed at the boat with the red stripe and Coast Guard symbol down the side.

The man in the brown shirt and hunting pants waved at the divers to come aboard the Coast Guard craft tied to the lobster boat.

Matt stuck his thumb in the air. The two put their heads down and kicked toward the ladder at the stern.

Matt

floated in the water.
Tremblin   e deck, and glanced
back. "Hu

"I'm   d fished the two sets
of gear ou   an dressed in a blue
jumpsuit ;   next to Kay.

A won   ed over to the teens
and stuck   r Carmen Cordera,
United Sta

Kay's b

"Get tl   aid. The two divers
peeled off

Matt w   ...ay's shoulders.

The man who confronted Kay at the store stood at the rail of the Coast Guard boat, talking with the two crewmen in the lobster boat. The crewmen held rifles and stood on either side of two handcuffed men. The man walked over to the shivering divers. "I'm Agent Patrick Moller. I'm with the DEA." He frowned at Kay. "Kay, it looks as if you didn't heed my advice. I assume this is your friend, Matt."

Kay grabbed Matt's hand. "How do you know our names?"

"Agent Keenan sent me a photo of herself with you and a friend. She also told me you and your friend here found the container with the drugs."

"Terri Keenan?" Kay asked.

"Yes, Terri. She told me that she also advised you to stay away from this area."

"That's my fault," Matt said.

"This could have been dangerous for you," the DEA agent said. "I'm glad you're safe, but what were you doing down there?"

Kay glanced at the boat tied to the Coast Guard craft.

"We were diving for artifacts," Matt said. "I thought there might be some items of value near the lighthouse."

"Find anything?"

"Not much," Matt said, wincing and catching a glimpse of Kay.

She motioned with her head toward the lobster boat. "Isn't the man in the overalls the one who harassed you on the dock?"

Matt jumped up. "You're right. That's Monte Tripley."

Moller jerked his head toward the handcuffed man. "You know him?"

"I sure do. Now I know how he was able to fix up his boat and do all that work on his house."

Moller pointed at Tripley. "It turns out he's the only guy that knows how the whole drug-smuggling operation works."

"Maybe he was the one who left me the note," Matt said. "He knows my truck."

Moller folded his arms. "You got a note?"

"Yeah. It said not to dive near the lighthouse."

"If you still have it, we'll need it as evidence."

"I think I—"

Kay grabbed Matt and spun him around to face her. "Anna."

"I forgot about Anna." He stepped in front of Chief Cordera. "Can you take us to my boat? My friend must be a nervous wreck watching all this." He shuffled to the rail. "There it is. Over there."

Moller climbed over the rail into the lobster boat. "Chief, I'll stay with your crew."

Approaching the *Maria*, Kay made a megaphone with her cupped hands. "Anna, stay there. We'll come to you."

Bumping the *Maria*, Matt leaped aboard, tossed some fenders over the side, and hugged Anna. "I'm sorry. I was so focused on getting us out of the water, I forgot."

Near tears, Anna pulled back. "I was worried…and scared."

Kay climbed aboard and grabbed Anna. "We're fine." Anna started to shake. "Anna, we're OK." Kay squeezed Anna's hand and put her arm over her shoulder.

"Come over and tie up next to us," Chief Cordera said. "I need to talk to you and get some information for my report."

Report? Were they going to tell her mom?

CHAPTER FORTY-THREE

"I'm going to record your statements," Chief Cordera said. "I'll write my report from that."

Matt shrugged, sitting on a bench on the back of the Coast Guard boat with Kay and Anna. "We don't know much. We were diving for old stuff."

Kay stared at the handcuffed men and kept her arm over Anna's shoulders.

Agent Moller stood with the chief to his right and the teens on his left. "We don't have to question them. I have a report on these people from the FBI and how they found the drugs in the trap. I can share that with you. In fact, these two divers helped solve this case."

The chief put the recorder in her pocket. "How'd they do that?"

"They contacted the FBI when they found the drugs and then helped the agent place a GPS tracking device on one of the packages."

Matt jumped in. "I'm glad we could help. I have a great crew on my boat." He reached around Kay, patted Anna on the shoulder, and gave each a high five.

Anna punched Kay with her finger. "I drove the *Maria* while you and Matt were down in the water. That makes me a first mate or something."

Kay shook her head and shrugged. "Whatever makes you happy. I'm glad this is over with. If Matt says you can be the first mate, then you're the first mate."

"You're both first mates," Matt said.

Kay asked the DEA Agent, "What did you find out in the investigation? I'm curious. All we saw was this boat—the *Ruff 'n' Ready*—get a package from the yacht and put it in the trap."

"We've been watching this operation and others like it for some time," the agent said. "It looks as if the drug dealers ship their stuff by yachts from countries in South America and other places. One lobster boat picks up the package and drops it in a trap." The agent pointed to the one tied to the Coast Guard craft. "Another one picks up the package and delivers it to a storage unit. Someone then retrieves the package from the storage unit and delivers it to the distribution point."

"Sounds complicated," Kay said.

"It is—*was*—complicated. That's why it took us so long to nab these guys. None of the parties knew the others in the chain. When you guys discovered the trap and called in your friend from the FBI, we got a break."

"What happened to the trap?" Kay pointed over the side. "We saw it coming down. There was no buoy attached."

"The crew saw us approaching," Moller said. "They were taking the package out of the trap, and they panicked. One of the crew cut the buoy off and threw the trap over the side."

"Excuse me," Anna said. "May I have some water?"

Chief Cordera pointed at one of her crew, who reached in a cooler and handed a bottle to each teen. "It's way past chow. I'll bet you kids are hungry. We've got some sandwiches."

"Thanks, but I have some lunch in a cooler," Matt said.

The DEA agent put his hand on Matt's shoulder. "Why don't you kids shove off? I have your names and addresses, and I'll be in touch if we need you for statements."

Kay, Anna, and Matt jumped up at the same time as if they'd practiced the move. The agent and the chief shook hands with the two girls who hopped on board the *Maria*. Matt stood with the DEA agent and the chief for a minute and then climbed aboard his boat.

Agent Moller leaned against the rail and pushed the *Maria* away from the Coast Guard boat. "Good luck, guys. Thanks for your help."

Matt pushed the throttles ahead and spun the wheel.

Kay collapsed on the bench behind Matt.

Anna sat next to her. "Did you find any more gold?"

"We got five more coins," Matt said.

Kay asked, "What was that brick thing we were digging around when the boats showed up?"

"I'm not sure," Matt said. "I didn't get a chance to get a close look. Could've been a gold bar or maybe an old brick."

Anna moved toward the rail. "If it was a gold bar, that could be worth a lot?"

"A gold bar weighs four hundred ounces today," Matt said. "It would be worth a half million dollars. But I don't know if I can find the spot where we were digging. My GPS will get me to the general area, but I could've used the trap as a place to start searching again. Agent Moller told me the coast guard is going to send divers to get the container and the trap."

"I think I'm going to be sick." Anna sat next to the rail and hung her head over the side.

Kay knelt beside her and gave her a bottle of water. "Too much excitement?"

Anna wiped the water from her chin. "I think so."

Matt leaned back, holding the wheel with one hand. "I'll get you girls back to the dock and give you a ride home in my truck."

Anna held her stomach, took another swig of water, and sat upright. "That's illegal, isn't it?"

"If I get stopped, I'll flash these." He handed two cards to Kay and two to Anna. "Agent Moller and the chief gave them to me. They said to call if we had any problems explaining to our parents or anyone what's been going on."

Kay asked, "Are you going to tell your dad?"

"Nope. Well, not any time soon."

"Me neither," Anna said, glancing at Kay. "I'm not telling my parents."

Kay stepped back. "You think I'm telling? With my reputation this summer? Not unless I have to. No way."

CHAPTER FORTY-FOUR

Bobbie stood at the top of the stairs. "Everything all right?"

"I was tired from the dive," Kay said. "I begged Matt to give us a ride home."

"I drove slow, Mrs. Telfair. And it was only from the dock down the street."

Bobbie waved and stepped back into the house.

"I guess I should say good-bye," Matt said, unloading the girls' bikes from the truck. "My dad wants me to go to Portsmouth with him for the next few days and look for a place to stay. And since we'll be so far south, we're going to visit my aunt—my dad's sister and her family—in Rhode Island. I know I won't be back before you leave."

"I was hoping you and your dad could have dinner with us Friday night," Kay said.

"I'm sorry. That would've been a nice way to end your visit—for the both of you...and me."

Anna stepped between Matt and Kay. "Are you going after the gold again?"

"I don't know." He smiled at Kay. "I won't have my dive buddy to help me and my first mate to drive the boat."

"Do you have enough gold to help out with expenses?" Anna asked.

"It'll help a little. But it's not near enough. We'll make it somehow."

"I'm sure it'll all work out. Don't you think so, Kay?"

Only half listening, Kay ran through her mind the events of the last four weeks in Prospect Harbor. She was going home in three days and would probably never see Matt again.

"Kay?"

"What? Yeah, I'm sure everything will work out."

Anna held out her hand to Matt. "I'm glad we met. Thanks for some great times."

He took her hand and drew her close, as he had at the end of their first cruise aboard the *Maria*. But this time, after the hug, he kissed her on the cheek.

Anna blushed and gave Matt a peck on the cheek. "No air kisses today."

He laughed. "No air kisses, First Mate Anna. The real thing."

Kay took in a deep breath and moved toward Matt. She extended her trembling hand. "I had a great time—above and below the water. Well, mostly above the water."

"Me, too." He gave her a hug, and Kay returned it, holding him tighter. After a few seconds, she pulled back from the embrace.

Matt drew her close again, giving her a kiss on the cheek.

Kay blushed, gave him a quick kiss on the lips, and ran up the stairs. She waved from the top step and closed the door. Peeking out the open window in the living room, she sat and listened.

"You know, she likes you," Anna said. "Do you like her?"

"I...well...I...I like both of you."

"I like you, too. But I think you like Kay in a special way."

He put his hand on Anna's shoulder. "Thanks for being great friends. Tell Kay for me, will you?"

"Of course."

Kay's dive buddy fumbled with his keys and climbed in the truck. He drove out onto Main Street, waving his hand out the window.

Anna waved. "See ya."

Kay slid away from the window. With tears streaming down her cheeks, she whispered, "Good-bye, Matt."

CHAPTER FORTY-FIVE

"How was school?" Kay's mom asked.

Kay dropped her backpack in a kitchen chair. "It was good."

Her mom dried her hands and moved away from the sink. "You seem down these past few days. Is everything OK at school?"

"Maybe I'm a bit burned out from the summer, and I'm having to get used to a new school." She popped open a diet soda and shoved her hand into a box of cheese crackers.

Her mom sat next to her at the kitchen table. "How's your relationship with Anna? You two didn't talk much on the drive back from Maine. I hope you're still friends. She hasn't been over here in the four weeks since we've been home, and you haven't been to her house."

"I think we saw enough of each other all summer. I still like her. We had lunch together with some other girls today."

Pouring some of Kay's soda into her own glass, her mom said, "But you don't seem to be as close as you were when we first got to Maine."

"You know how teenage girls are."

"I do know how they are. I remember being a teenager. Did something happen?"

"I think she was jealous of me and Matt because we were dive buddies. It's silly."

"Perhaps you could come up with a reason to call her. You were both very close this summer. Didn't you say she was your best friend?"

"She still is...I think. I want her to be my friend. But I don't know if she wants to be friends with me."

"Maybe you could find a reason to give her a call. Her birthday's next week, isn't it?"

"I suppose I could."

"You both shared a lot of great—let me change that to *interesting*—adventures here and in Maine this summer. I do hope you'll stay friends—close friends. Speaking of friends, have you heard from Matt Hubbard?"

"I've only gotten one text from him since we came home. And that was to say hi."

"That's all he said, hi?"

"He told me that school had started and he missed summer. He did ask how I was doing."

Bobbie jumped up from her chair. "Some mail came for you today. It has a Prospect Harbor postmark."

Kay held the brown envelope in both hands, staring at it. Taking the scissors from her mom, she cut open the end and pulled a sheet of paper halfway out of the envelope. "It's a letter from Matt."

"That's nice," her mom said, walking away with a big grin.

Kay carried the envelope and her backpack to her room. She sat on the bed and took out the one-page letter with a newspaper clipping stapled to the back. Unfolding the clipping, Kay read in a low voice, "'*Local Teenager Helps Nab Drug Operation.* September 18. In a ceremony at the FBI office in Bangor, the DEA, the FBI, and the US Coast Guard recognized sixteen-year-old Prospect Harbor resident Matthew Hubbard for his help in an investigation into a drug-smuggling operation. Hubbard, a scuba diver since age 13, discovered a...'"

Kay scanned the rest. Her heart beat faster. "Thank you, Matt. You didn't tell them that Anna and I were part of this drama."

She detached the clipping and read the letter. Matt recounted the bike rides, scuba diving, Kay's birthday party, and dinners at the rental house. "Hmmm. He didn't mention the gold." Kay closed her door, sat back again on the bed, and read aloud the last sentences. "'I enjoyed meeting your mom and dad. I'm glad you got to meet my dad. I'll always remember the times we had together in Maine, and that includes Anna. But I miss you especially. I hope we can see each other

again some day. When you see Anna, tell her I said hi. Your friend always, Matt.'" A single tear rolled down her left cheek.

Kay lay back on the bed, the envelope tucked under her back. She pulled it from beneath her and ran her hand deep inside. "This is a photo of Matt, and that's his dad. But that isn't Matt's truck."

She flipped the photo over and read the message. "'My new truck, Dad's new car, college tuition covered, and no more medical bills.'"

Kay grabbed her cell phone and tapped in a number. The phone rang once, twice, three times. The ringing stopped. A voice answered.

"He did it, Anna. Matt got the gold!"

The End

About the Author

Sonny Barber developed an interest in American history at an early age, reading and collecting newspapers, magazines and other materials on historic US and world events. He's coupled that interest with his fiction writing to create a modern-day "mystery history" series for preteens and older. Sonny graduated from Georgia State University with a degree in journalism. His work as a writer, editor and photographer has taken him across the United States and to many other countries. He and his wife live in South Florida. They have two daughters, who provided some of the inspiration for the teenaged characters in his books.

J
Barber, Sonny
Gold hush

JUL   2015

Made in the USA
Charleston, SC
04 February 2015

CHANGE IS LIKE A SLINKY TEAM

ACQUIRING EDITOR:
Mark Tobey

COPY EDITOR:
Jim Vincent

BACK COVER COPY:
Julie-Allyson Ieron, Joy Media

COVER DESIGN:
Paetzold Associates

INTERIOR DESIGN:
Ragont Design

PRINTING AND BINDING:
Dickinson Press Inc.

The typeface for the text of this book is
AGaramond

NORTHFIELD
PUBLISHING

We hope you enjoyed this product from Northfield Publishing. Our goal at Northfield is to provide high-quality, thought-provoking and practical books and products that connect truth to the real needs and challenges of people like you living in our rapidly changing world. For more information on other books and products written and produced from a biblical perspective write to:

Northfield Publishing
215 West Locust Street
Chicago, IL 60610